PROCEDURAL HANDBOOK FOR INSTITUTES OF CONSECRATED LIFE AND SOCIETIES OF APOSTOLIC LIFE

Edited by

DONNA MILLER, JD, JCL
EILEEN JARAMILLO, DMIN, JCL

CANON LAW SOCIETY OF AMERICA

ISBN: 978-1-932208-60-3
Flex cover edition

Unless otherwise noted, all canons quoted are from the *Code of Canon Law, Latin-English Edition* (Washington, DC: Canon Law Society of America, 2020) and the *Code of Canons of the Eastern Churches, Latin-English Edition* (Washington, DC: Canon Law Society of America, 2001).

Printed in the United States of America.

Canon Law Society of America
415 Michigan Avenue NE, Suite 101
Washington, DC 20017-4502

Revised 2021

Hard cover edition: 928-1-932208-59-7
Previous ISBN: 0-943616-89-1

Contents

INTRODUCTION

In 2001 the *Canon Law Society of America* published the *Procedural Handbook for Institutes of Consecrated Life and Societies of Apostolic Life*. The editors of that original edition were Sister Catherine Darcy, RSM; Reverend Michael Joyce, CM; Reverend Robert Kaslyn, SJ; and Sister Margaret Sullivan, CSJ. The publication which they oversaw was a tremendous resource for those who work for and with institutes of consecrated life and societies of apostolic life.

Fifteen years after publication, the CLSA found that its supply of the handbook was depleted and, since portions of the book had become outdated, decided not to print additional copies. Yet, because there continued to be a great need for such a resource, the Board of Governors commissioned new editors to work on the revision process in 2020. The editors of this revised edition acknowledge that this introduction includes text taken from the original introduction along with new material.

In the canons pertaining to institutes of consecrated life and societies of apostolic life, the Code of Canon Law recognizes the need to balance fidelity to the traditions of a specific institute or society with an openness to today's world and its needs. The code achieves this balance through norms which apply to all institutes and societies and through the principle of subsidiarity, expressed primarily by the phrase "according to proper law." In other words, the code explicitly recognizes both the need to establish norms common to all institutes of consecrated life and societies of apostolic life as well as the need to provide for a certain freedom of action. This freedom allows institutes and societies—with the inspiration of the Holy Spirit and under the guidance of legitimate ecclesiastical authority—to adapt themselves to the particular circumstances of different cultures and countries as well as to new apostolic needs.

This combination of norms common to all institutes and societies—as well as specific norms and policies of a particular institute or society—can create difficulties for those persons entrusted with elected or appointed leadership. They must be aware not only of the requirements of the code but also those requirements expressed in their own proper law. Therefore, this handbook is offered as a helpful tool to work with the law. It might also be useful to those individuals appointed by a bishop as a vicar or delegate for institutes and societies. Additionally, we hope that canonists will find the materials beneficial in their ministries.

This handbook also reflects a wide variation through its authors and contributors. These men and women are not only members of institutes or societies; they have also devoted themselves to the study and practice of the law. Each chapter in the original handbook was written by one author, at times in combination with contributions by other individuals. In this revised edition, the newly commissioned editors initially contacted each of the original authors who were available and invited the person to revise the chapter. When an individual chose not to revise the chapter or was deceased, the editors selected other competent canonists and made suggestions about the content. This procedure is noted at the beginning of each chapter. As a result, each chapter reflects the experience and concerns of experienced canonists in both the original handbook and in this revised edition. When appropriate, each chapter also notes the differences between religious institutes and secular institutes as well as the distinctiveness of societies of apostolic life. The last two chapters of the handbook specifically present procedures unique to secular institutes and societies of apostolic life. These two communal forms are included in the handbook because secular institutes are a unique manner of living consecrated life and societies often proximate religious institutes.

This handy resource also addresses a variety of issues; the specific issue determines the content and outline of the chapter. For example, chapter four on "Admission of Candidates" includes examples of documents necessary to the admission process. Chapter three, "Institute-Wide Policies," is more general, suggesting topics suitable for policies as well as specific items that should be included. Therefore, the subject matter and the contributors determined the content of a chapter. At times, the handbook may appear more like a commentary than a book on procedures. Such elements have been included to give some background for readers not versed in the law.

We realize that with a text of this type, individuals interested in a specific topic—for example, planning a general chapter or formulating a new policy on admissions—may not read the entire text. Rather, they will turn to the chapter which deals with their concerns. Consequently, each chapter stands on its own, with references as necessary to other chapters. Readers, however, are encouraged to read the first half of chapter one, "Governance in General," which serves as a general introduction to terminology, types of law, and the types of texts used by institutes and societies to express their own norms, policies, and practices.

Another point needs to be made. Given the complex issues addressed by the law on institutes and societies as well as given the necessity of ensuring the protection of rights (both of the institute or society itself and of its members), those in leadership are encouraged to seek the advice of a competent canonist. If an institute or society does not have access to a canonist, referrals may be obtained from the diocesan chancery (through the Office of the Judicial Vicar or the Office of Canonical Affairs). The Administrative Office of the Canon Law Society of America may also be of assistance in this regard.

The editors also take this opportunity to express a word of gratitude to a number of people. Once the handbook was in its revised form, it was given to a committee for a formal examination of its contents with the possibility of making any necessary changes. Consisting of Sister Sharon Euart, RSM, Reverend Paul Golden, CM, and Sister Marlene Weisenbeck, FSPA, this peer review committee made invaluable contributions to the final product. Additionally, the editors appreciate the work of the original editors and contributors, the cooperation of the Board of Governors, and the support of the Publications Advisory Board (PAB) in the production of the work. Without the effort of all these people, this revision would never have become a finished product.

Editors

Donna Miller, JD, JCL

Eileen Jaramillo, DMin, JCL

August 2021

ABBREVIATIONS

AA	Vatican II, decree *Apostolicam actuositatem*, November 18, 1965: *AAS* 58 (1966) 837-864.
AAS	*Acta Apostolic Sedes*, Rome, 1909-.
AG	Vatican II, decree *Ad gentes*, December 7, 1965: *AAS* 58 (1966) 947-990.
c.	Canon
cc.	Canons
CCEO	*Code of Canons of the Eastern Churches: New English Translation* (Washington, DC: CLSA, 2001).
CD	Vatican II, decree *Christus Dominus*, October 28, 1965: *AAS* 58 (1966) 673-696.
CIC	*Code of Canon Law: Latin English Translation, New English Translation* (Washington, DC: CLSA, 2020).
CICLSAL	Congregation for Institutes of Consecrated Life and Societies of Apostolic Life
CLD	*Canon Law Digest*, 14 vols. and Index, Washington, DC: CLSA, 1934-2009.
CO	Congregation for Institutes of Consecrated Life and Societies of Apostolic Life, instruction *Cor orans*, April 1, 2018: *AAS* 110 (2018) 814-864.
ES	Paul VI, apostolic letter, *Ecclesiae sanctae*, August 6, 1966: *AAS* 58 (1966) 757-787.
LG	Vatican II, dogmatic constitution *Lumen gentium*, November 21, 1964: *AAS* 57 (1965) 702-712.
MR	Sacred Congregation for Bishops and Sacred Congregation for Religious and Secular Institutes, decree *Mutuae relationes*, May 14, 1978: *AAS* 70 (1978) 473-506.
PB	John Paul II, apostolic constitution *Pastor bonus,* June 28, 1988: *AAS* 80 (1998) 841-912.
PC	Vatican II, decree *Perfectae caritatis*, October 28, 1965: *AAS* 58 (1966) 702-712.
RD	John Paul II, apostolic exhortation *Redemptionis Donum*, March 25, 1984: *AAS* 88 (1996) 377-486.
RI	Religious Institute
USCCB	United States Conference of Catholic Bishops
VC	John Paull II, apostolic exhortation *Vita consecrata*, March 25, 1996: *AAS* 88 (1996) 377-486

CHAPTER 1

GOVERNANCE IN GENERAL

Nancy Bauer, OSB[1]

Introduction

Institutes of consecrated life are of two kinds: religious and secular. Similar to these are societies of apostolic life (c. 731 §1). Canonically, governance in an institute or society is carried out by superiors or moderators,[2] with the assistance of their councils, and by chapters. It is exercised according to the norms of universal church law and the proper law of each institute. The role of governance is to foster the patrimony or charism of the institute which, according to the Code of Canon Law, consists of the mind and designs of the founder(s) regarding the nature, purpose, spirit, and character of the institute plus its sound traditions (c. 578).

This chapter on procedures for governance in general will address the following:

- Foundational principles of governance
- Types of law governing institutes
- Structures of governance within institutes
- Record keeping, including archives
- The relationship between a canonical and civil entity

---

1 This chapter was written by Father Robert J. Kaslyn, SJ, for the 2001 edition of the *Procedural Handbook.* Father Kaslyn acknowledged the following contributors to the chapter: Sisters Nancy Reynolds, SP, Sally Tolles, DHS, Esther Redmann, OSU, and Dominica Brennan, OP. Father Kaslyn died on March 13, 2019. Sister Nancy Bauer, OSB, revised this chapter of the *Procedural Handbook.* The revision includes text taken directly from the original version along with new text.

2 The Code of Canon Law, for the most part, uses the term "superiors" in relation to religious institutes and "moderators" in relation to secular institutes and societies of apostolic life. Hereafter, in this chapter, the term "superiors" will be used to include moderators unless otherwise indicated. Likewise, the term "institute" will be used as a general term to include religious institutes, secular institutes, and societies of apostolic life, unless the context indicates otherwise.

- The role of a commissary
- Governance of a federation of monasteries of nuns

Foundational Principles of Governance

Every member of an institute of consecrated life or society of apostolic life is responsible in some way for the effective governance of the institute or society. It can be said that governance in institutes and societies is more collaborative than in any other entity within the Church. As far back as the sixth century, St. Benedict in his Rule for Monasteries required the abbot to seek the advice of all the members of the community, including and especially the youngest, before making major decisions and to seek the advice of a smaller group of members before making less important decisions. Today, canon law recognizes institutes and societies as collegial bodies which means that the members participate in decision-making (c. 115 §2).

Nonetheless, canon law recognizes that specific persons, whether as individuals or as groups, must take the lead in governing an institute. Because the state of consecrated life pertains to the life and holiness of the Church (cc. 207 §2; 574 §1), the exercise of governance in institutes of consecrated life is both spiritual and administrative and requires concern for the individual members and the common good of the community as a whole. Canon 618 of the Code of Canon Law expresses the manner in which superiors of religious institutes exercise the office of governing. First of all, superiors receive their power from God through the ministry of the Church and exercise it in a spirit of service. Although they have the authority to make decisions, they foster voluntary obedience by treating the members with reverence and by listening to them. Canon 619 beautifully expresses the pastoral role of superiors. Their primary function is to "strive to build a community of brothers or sisters in Christ, in which God is sought and loved before all things." They are to provide for the spiritual needs of the members and have a particular concern for the vulnerable—the sick, the fainthearted, and the restless. While this chapter focuses on the mundane canonical "how" of governing, those who govern must always keep in mind the lofty "why."

Types of Church Law Governing Institutes

Universal and Proper Law

Governance within an institute is exercised in accord with the norms of universal law and proper law. The universal law regarding institutes is found primarily in the Code of Canon Law, but also in other ecclesiastical documents, such as apostolic letters, apostolic constitutions, and general decrees.[3] Proper law is a form of particular law. Particular law that is territorial applies to people in a specific geographic territory, such as within the boundaries of a diocese. Particular law that is personal or proper is applicable to a specific group of people, such as the members of an institute, and it follows them wherever they go. In other words, proper law of an institute is observed by the members whether they are residing in a house of the institute, assigned to a ministry that requires them to live elsewhere, or traveling. Proper law is unique to each institute in order to preserve the specific charism of each and, in that way, protects the great diversity of institutes given by the Holy Spirit to the Church and world.

The proper law of an institute consists of its constitutions or fundamental code, plus norms in other codes. The proper law may include: (1) constitutions; (2) a secondary book complementary to the constitutions giving them greater specificity; (3) general directories or handbooks; and (4) regional or provincial statutes or policies. The Code of Canon Law often gives a general principle regarding an aspect of consecrated life and indicates that its concrete application is to be addressed either in the constitutions or in the proper law of each institute. The constitutions are approved by the general chapter of the institute and also require approval of ecclesiastical authority—the diocesan bishop for an institute of diocesan right and the Holy See for institutes of pontifical right. Revisions in the constitutions also require approval by ecclesiastical authority. For that reason, they should contain "only those juridic elements that are most basic to the institute,"[4] that is, those that are expected to perdure. "Those things likely to change with places, times, or circumstances, or which are clearly secondary or purely technical" are not included in the constitutions but in other types of codes which do not require approval of ecclesiastical authority.[5]

Constitutions

Constitutions combine both spiritual and juridic elements of the institute (c. 587 §3), reflecting first of all the original inspiration of the founder(s). The

---

3 *Perfectae caritatis*, the Second Vatican Council's "Decree on the Up-to-date Renewal of Religious Life" is an example of universal law for institutes. More recently (2016), Pope Francis issued the apostolic constitution *Vultum Dei quaerere* which contains revised papal legislation for monasteries of contemplative nuns around the world.

4 Robert J. Kaslyn, "Procedures for Governance in General," in *Procedural Handbook for Institutes of Consecrated Life and Societies of Apostolic Life* (Washington, DC: CLSA 2001) 8.

5 Ibid.

Code of Canon Law, in canon 587 §1, prescribes that fundamental norms regarding the following must be addressed in constitutions.

Governance of the Institute

The constitutions define the general governmental structure of the institute. More specifically, the constitutions of a religious institute must include the following:

- the length of time a religious must be in perpetual profession in order to be appointed or elected validly as a major superior (c. 623);
- matters related to the canonical election of the supreme moderator which is carried out by the general chapter (c. 625 §1);
- the manner in which other superiors are selected, that is, whether they are elected or appointed (c. 625 §3);
- the composition of the council at each level of the institute, the manner of operating, and the qualifications for the role of councilor (c. 627 §1);
- the composition of the general chapter and the extent of its power (c. 631 §2).

For secular institutes, the constitutions prescribe the manner of governance, the term of office of moderators, and the manner in which they are designated (c. 717 §1). The constitutions also determine the governance of a society of apostolic life (c. 734). However, the canons on superiors, councils, and chapters of religious institutes (cc. 617-633) apply to societies, with necessary adaptations (c. 734).

The Discipline of Members

All members must observe faithfully the patrimony of their institute (c. 578). Patrimony is understood as fidelity to everything that the founder or foundress intended. This includes the nature, purpose, character and wholesome traditions of the institute that has been approved by competent ecclesiastical authority. The constitutions define the major aspects of the life of the members including, for religious institutes and societies of apostolic life, the observance of common life. For secular institutes, the constitutions determine the manner in which members "lead their lives in the ordinary conditions of the world . . . whether alone, or in their own families, or in a group living as brothers or sisters (c. 714)." Causes for *ipso facto,* mandatory, and discretionary dismissal from a religious institute are covered, for the most part, in the canons (cc. 694-696). The constitutions of a secular institute are to determine causes for discretionary dismissal (c. 729). The constitutions of a society of apostolic life govern the departure and dismissal of a member who is not yet definitively incorporated (c. 742).

Incorporation and Formation of Members

Within the parameters of universal law, the constitutions identify the stages of initial formation and the purpose and length of each stage. The Code of Canon Law addresses two stages of initial formation for religious: the novitiate and the period of temporary profession. Requirements for a pre-novitiate period, such as a postulancy or aspirancy, are determined by the constitutions of each institute.[6] Regarding the novitiate, the constitutions determine whether one or several periods of apostolic activity outside the community of the novitiate can be added to the required twelve months spent within the community of the novitiate (c. 648 §2). For secular institutes, the constitutions define the manner and length of the period of initial probation as long as it is no less than two years (c. 722 §3) and the length of first incorporation as long as it is no less than five years (c. 723 §2). For societies of apostolic life, the proper law, which could be the constitutions or another document, determines the admission, probation, incorporation, and formation of members (c. 735 §1), although some canons on admission to the novitiate of a religious institute also apply to admission to societies (c. 735 §2).[7]

The Proper Object of the Vows or Sacred Bonds

Members of religious institutes profess the evangelical counsels by public vows (c. 607 §2),[8] while members of secular institutes profess the same counsels by other forms of sacred bonds established in the constitutions (c. 712).[9] The constitutions of each religious or secular institute define the obligations that arise with profession of the evangelical counsels (cc. 598 §1; 712), although the

---

6 The stages and length of initial formation for monasteries of contemplative nuns differs from that prescribed in the canons of the Code of Canon Law for other religious. See Pope Francis's 2016 apostolic constitution *Vultum Dei quaerere* and the 2018 instruction *Cor orans* issued by the Congregation for Institutes of Consecrated Life and Societies of Apostolic Life.

7 Canons 642-645 on admission to the novitiate of a religious institute apply to societies of apostolic life. Canon 643 prescribes requirements for valid admission to the novitiate which, by canon 735 §2, apply to valid admission to a society.

8 A vow is "a deliberate and free promise made to God about a possible and better good" which "must be fulfilled by reason of the virtue of religion" (c. 1191 §1). A public vow is one that is accepted by a legitimate superior in the name of the Church (c. 1192 §1).

9 The Code of Canon Law does not define the term "sacred bonds." Sacred bonds could be, for example, oaths or promises or other forms of commitment defined in the constitutions of the secular institute.

evangelical counsel of chastity obliges all to the triad of chastity, perfect continence, and celibacy. The obligations that arise with profession of poverty varies, even among religious institutes and especially between religious and secular institutes. In some religious institutes, members are required to renounce ownership of personal possessions while in others they may own personal possessions but may not administer them or use the revenue that accrues from them without permission (c. 668 §2). Members of secular institutes are usually self-supporting. The evangelical counsel of obedience requires submission to legitimate superiors whose scope of authority is prescribed in the constitutions (c. 601).

Members of societies of apostolic life do not profess religious vows (c. 731), although, in some, they assume the evangelical counsels by a bond defined in the constitutions (c. 731 §2). Nonetheless, members are obligated by chastity, perfect continence, and celibacy and are subject to their moderators according to the norms of the constitutions regarding the internal life and discipline of the society (c. 738 §1). Members may acquire, possess, administer, and dispose of personal possessions, although the proper law may impose some limits on this capacity (c. 741 §2).

In addition to the above, the constitutions of each institute must address the following.

Providing for Needs of the Members

A religious institute is obligated to "supply the members with all those things which are necessary to achieve the purpose of their vocation" (c. 670). Such needs are spiritual and material, including the ability to participate in the prayer life of the community, the sacramental and liturgical life of the Church, and an annual retreat (cc. 663-664); basic human needs such as food, shelter, clothing, and health care; ongoing formation; and education and training to carry out assigned works of the apostolate. The constitutions of a society of apostolic life address the society's "concern for leading the members to the purpose of their proper vocation" (c. 737).

Permission for Publication

The norms of the constitutions of a religious institute should designate the competent superior to give permission to members to publish writings dealing with questions of religion or morals (c. 832). However, such a provision might be included in the secondary book because the Congregation for Institutes of Consecrated Life and Societies of Apostolic Life does not list it as being required in the constitutions.

Finances

The constitutions of a religious institute contain some provisions for the manner of administration of temporal goods of the institute, including any exclusions or restrictions on the power of the institute, provinces, or houses to acquire, possess, administer, and alienate temporal goods (c. 634 §1). Unless other provision is made, religious institutes are governed by the prescripts of Book V of the Code of Canon Law on temporal goods (c. 635 §1).

Other Codes of Proper Law

In addition to its fundamental code, institutes often have a secondary, complementary book prepared by the general chapter which provides further specification to the broad matters addressed in the constitutions. The proper law of institutes also consists of other directories or handbooks to bring even greater specificity to the norms of the constitutions and complementary book. Canonically, the following are left to the proper law of a religious institute:[10]

Governance

- specification of the duties and powers of superiors (c. 617);
- delineation of the manner in which the supreme moderator exercises power over the provinces, houses, and members of the institute (c. 622);
- determination of the number of years in perpetual profession required prior to election or appointment as a (non-major) superior (c. 623);
- provision for terms of office for superiors other than the supreme moderator (c. 624 §2);
- reasons for removal from office or transfer of superiors (c. 624 §3);
- norms to be observed by superiors in the conferral of offices and by members during elections (c. 626);
- determination of the cases, besides those prescribed in universal law, in which superiors require the consent or counsel of their councils for validity of acts (c. 627 §2);
- designation of superiors to conduct, and frequency of, visitations (c. 628 §1);
- absences of superiors from their respective houses (c. 629);
- provisions for suitable confessors (c. 630 §2);

---

10 When the canons specify that a matter is left to the proper law, it can be addressed in the constitutions, a secondary book, or other directories or handbooks.

- specifications of the rights and obligations of the institutes and their members, such as:
    - the manner of celebrating the liturgy of the hours (c. 663 §3);
    - the manner of observing cloister (c. 667 §1);
    - the designation of the superior competent to give permission to change dispositions of patrimonial goods (c. 668 §2);
- any exceptions to the provision that those things accruing to the religious by pension, subsidy, or insurance are acquired for the institute (c. 668 §3); any provisions for the renunciation of goods after perpetual profession (c. 668 §4);
- provisions for goods acquired by members after an act of renunciation (c. 668 §5);
- norms regarding the habit of the institute (c. 669 §1);
- requirements for a transfer from one autonomous monastery to another (c. 684 §3);
- a determination of time and manner of probation in the receiving institute in cases of transfers of professed members (c. 684 §4);
- an elaboration of serious causes for dismissal of the perpetually professed member beyond those specified in universal law (c. 696 §1);
- a statement of causes for dismissal of temporarily professed members (c. 696 §2).

Chapters and Other Gatherings

- determination of the order to be observed in the general chapter, especially for elections and other business (c. 631 §2);
- arrangements for individuals, provinces, and communities to freely send ideas and suggestions to the general chapter (c. 631 §3);
- plans for other chapters or gatherings within the institute, their nature, authority, composition, manner of proceeding, and frequency (c. 632);
- regulations governing the operations of those non-chapter bodies providing membership participation and consultation (c. 611 §1).

Formation

- designation of major superiors capable of admitting candidates to the novitiate (c. 641);
- impediments to admission to the novitiate beyond those specified in universal law (c. 643 §2);

- specification of testimony to be gathered regarding the requisite suitability of candidates and their freedom from impediments (c. 645 §3);
- program of formation for novices (c. 650 §1);
- provision for an extension of the period of the canonical novitiate for up to six months (c. 653 §2);
- definition of the period of temporary profession, within the norms specified in universal law (c. 655);
- delineation of the reasons for and length of time of any extension of temporary profession, in such a way that the entire time of temporary profession does not exceed nine years (c. 657 §2);
- norms establishing conditions for perpetual profession beyond those established by universal law (c. 658);
- definition of the program of continuing formation for all members of the institute (c. 659 §2).

Finances

- provisions for the goods of suppressed houses (c. 616 §1);
- norms governing the use and administration of goods so that the poverty appropriate to the institute is fostered (c. 635 §2);
- provisions for the appointment of finance officers at each organizational level within the institute (c. 636 §1);
- delineation of the manner in which finance officers and other administrators are to render an account of their administration to competent authority (c. 636 §2);
- designation of the boundaries of ordinary administration and of the requirements for valid acts of extraordinary administration (c. 638 §1);
- designation of officials, in addition to superiors, who validly incur expenses and perform juridic acts of ordinary administration (c. 638 §2);
- provision to reflect faithfully the content of canons 1291 through 1294 on alienation of temporal goods and any transaction which could worsen the patrimonial condition of the institute (c. 1295).

Provincial or Regional Statutes or Policies

In the case of larger widespread institutes, there may be norms or policies in the form of provincial or regional policy manuals or statutes. These are normally prepared and given preliminary approval at the level where they will be binding. The constitutions, complementary books, or directories should specify how pertinent local statutes or policies are to be developed and approved. Local statutes or policies specify, among other things, the content of the constitutions, complementary book, and directories, adapting their content to the local mission, culture, and needs of the institute.

Matters Left to Proper Law of Secular Institutes

In addition to matters which must be addressed in the constitutions, the following matters are left to the proper law of secular institutes:

- how members are to participate actively in the life of the institute (c. 716 §1);
- administration of temporal goods (c. 718);
- obligations of the institute, especially financial ones, towards members who carry on work for it (c. 718);
- designation of spiritual exercises (c. 719 §1).

Matters Left to Proper Law of Societies of Apostolic Life

The following are left to the proper law of a society of apostolic life:

- admission, probation, incorporation, and formation of members (c. 735 §1);
- the manner of probation and formation, especially doctrinal, spiritual, and apostolic, adapted to the purpose and character of the society, in such a way that the members are suitably prepared for the mission and life of the society (c. 735 §2);
- observance of common life and absences from common life (c. 740);
- administration of temporal goods of the society (c. 741 §1);
- norms regarding acquisition, administration, possession, and disposing of temporal goods of members (c. 741 §2).

Structures of Governance within Institutes

Major Superiors

The Code of Canon Law identifies three forms of governance within an institute: superiors, councils, and chapters. Superiors are to fulfill their function and exercise their power in accord with universal and proper law (c. 617). They have personal authority which means they have the competence to "decide and prescribe what must be done (c. 618)." The scope of their authority should be defined in proper law, especially when the institute is a large congregation with various levels of superiors. Members must know to whom they are bound regarding the essential aspects of their consecrated life.

Major superiors are those who govern an entire institute, a province of an institute or part equivalent to a province, or an autonomous house, as well as their vicars (c. 620). An abbot primate and superior of a monastic congregation are described in the Code of Canon Law as comparable to major superiors, but they do not have all the power which universal law grants to major superiors (c. 620). The supreme moderator holds power over all the provinces, houses, and members of an institute, in accord with proper law (c. 622). The supreme moderator is designated by canonical election carried out by the general chapter (c. 625 §1). Other superiors are elected or appointed, according to the norm of the constitutions (c. 625 §3). They are to have terms that are defined in proper law unless the constitutions determine otherwise for the supreme moderator and superiors of autonomous houses (cc. 624 §§1-2). It is common for monasteries to elect major superiors for life, or until a specific age, such as 75.

For secular institutes, the constitutions prescribe the term of office of moderators and the manner in which they are designated (c. 717 §1). The supreme moderator must be a member who is incorporated definitively (c. 717 §2). The constitutions of societies of apostolic life determine the governance of the society, although the canons on religious superiors apply to moderators.

Major superiors of clerical religious institutes of pontifical right and of clerical societies of apostolic life of pontifical right are personal ordinaries (c. 134 §1). As such, they can grant dimissorial letters on behalf of the members of their institute or society (c. 1019 §1) and they can grant to any presbyter the faculty to hear confessions of the members "and of others living day and night in the house" (c. 969 §2).

Councils

Major superiors must each have a council "whose assistance they must use in carrying out their function" (c. 627 §1). How a council is constituted, the qualifications and number of members,[11] and frequency of meetings are addressed in the constitutions. "It is important to note the distinct roles of superior and council, i.e., the superior *has* a council and is not part of it."[12] Universal and proper law require the superior to seek the consent or the counsel (advice) of the council to carry out specific acts validly (cc. 627 §2; 127). In

11 The supreme moderator must have a council of at least four members to proceed with dismissal of a member from the institute (c. 699).

12 Rosemary Smith, "The Governance of Institutes," in *New Commentary on the Code of Canon Law*, ed. John P. Beal, et al. (New York/Mahwah, NJ: Paulist Press, 2000) 788.

these cases, the superior does not vote with the council, even to break a tie.[13] When a superior requires the consent of council, the superior may not act without that consent. However, the superior can choose not to act even after having secured the consent. When the superior requires the advice of council, the superior must seek and consider the advice, but is not required to act in accord with that advice, even if it is unanimous. If the superior refrains from acting, it must be based on a very serious reason (c. 127 §2, 2°). It might be confidential and known only to the superior.

Cases Requiring Consent

Major superiors must have the consent of their councils for:

- the validity of alienation or other business transactions which could potentially adversely affect the patrimonial condition of a religious institute (c. 638 §3); by canon 741 §1, this applies to societies of apostolic life;[14]
- the erection, transfer, or suppression of a novitiate of a religious institute (c. 647 §1);
- allowing an individual candidate to make the novitiate in a house other than the designated canonical novitiate (c. 647 §2);
- permitting a member to live outside a house of a religious institute for a longer period of time; this period may not exceed one year "except for the purpose of caring for ill health, of studies, or of exercising an apostolate in the name of the institute" (c. 665 §1);
- permitting a perpetually professed member of a religious institute to transfer to another religious institute (c. 684 §1). In this case, the consent of two councils is required: that of the community in which the member is perpetually professed as well as of the community to which the individual is seeking to transfer. The same applies to transfer from one secular institute to another (c. 730) and from one society to another (c. 744 §1);
- permitting a member to transfer from one autonomous monastery to another of the same institute, federation, or confederation (c. 684 §3).

---

13 In 1985, the Holy See issued an authentic interpretation on this matter. See Smith, 788, note 33.

14 For religious institutes and societies of apostolic life, alienation of property which exceeds an amount set by the Holy See requires permission of the Holy See. At the time of publication, the amounts for the United States are based on the number of Catholics in the (arch)diocese in which the property is located. At time of publication, the limit is $5,705,000 in (arch)dioceses with less than 500,000 Catholics and $11,408,000 in (arch)dioceses with more than 500,000 Catholics.

In this case, consent of both major superiors and of the chapter of the receiving monastery is required;

- the granting for up to three years of an indult of exclaustration to a religious in perpetual vows (c. 686 §1); the granting of an indult of living outside a society of apostolic life to a definitively incorporated member of the society (c. 745). Two further qualifications should also be noted: if the member is a cleric, consent must first be obtained from the ordinary of the place where the cleric must reside (cc. 686 §1; 745); and to extend the indult for more than three years or to grant an indult for more than three years requires consent of the Holy See if an institute of pontifical right or of the diocesan bishop if of diocesan right (c. 686 §1);
- the petitioning of the diocesan bishop for a religious institute of diocesan right or of the Holy See if of pontifical right for imposed exclaustration on a member of the institute (c. 686 §3);
- the granting of an indult to leave a religious institute for a member in temporary profession (c. 688 §2);
- readmission without the requirement of repeating the novitiate of a member who left the institute after the novitiate or after profession (c. 690 §1). The superior of an autonomous monastery enjoys the same favor (c. 690 §2);
- the immediate expulsion from the religious house of a member in the case of serious exterior scandal or very grave imminent harm to the institute (c. 703). If there is danger in delay, then even the local superior with the consent of the council can expel the member.

Cases Requiring Consultation

Major superiors are to seek consultation from their councils for:

- admission to temporary profession in a religious institute (c. 656, 3°); this may be either a consenting vote or consultative, depending upon the proper law. For secular institutes, canon 720 allows the constitutions to determine the roles of major moderators with their councils regarding admission and incorporation of members. For societies of apostolic life, proper law determines admission, probation, incorporation, and formation of members (c. 735 §1);
- exclusion of an individual from a further profession in a religious institute after the expiration of temporary profession (c. 689 §1);
- issuing a declaration of *ipso facto* dismissal of a religious who has notoriously defected from the Catholic faith, attempted marriage, or has been illegitimately absent for twelve months (c. 694). The same applies to societies (c. 746). The council of a secular institute declares

ipso facto dismissal of a member for defection from the faith or attempted marriage (c. 729);

- beginning a process of dismissal of a member from a religious institute (c. 697, 1°). Similar provisions are applied to secular institutes by canon 729 and to societies of apostolic life by canon 746.

Supreme Moderator and Council Act Collegially

The Code of Canon Law identifies one situation in which a superior and council proceed collegially. In the case of potential dismissal of a member from an institute or society, the supreme moderator votes with the council, which must consist of four members (cc. 699 §1; 729; 746). The supreme moderator must act in accord with the will of the majority, even if he or she votes contrary to the majority.

Convoking the Council

Canon 127 §1 addresses how the superior seeks the consent or counsel of the council:

> When it is established by law that in order to place certain acts the superior needs the consent or counsel of some college or group of persons, the college or group must be convoked according to the norm of can. 166 unless, when it concerns seeking counsel only, particular or proper law provides otherwise. For such acts to be valid, however, it is required that the consent of an absolute majority of those present is obtained or that the counsel of all is sought.

Canon 166 presumes the physical presence of the members of the council at a meeting convened by the superior. During the COVID-19 pandemic, the Congregation for Institutes of Consecrated Life and Societies of Apostolic Life received requests from superiors to hold council meetings virtually through the various means of telecommunications. Pope Francis granted to the congregation the "extraordinary faculty" of dispensing in individual cases from the requirement of personal presence.[15] In a July 1, 2020, letter to supreme moderators, the Congregation for Institutes of Consecrated Life and Societies of Apostolic Life noted that superiors must submit a request to the congregation to use telecommunications for formal council meetings. If the request is granted, the following must be observed:

- minutes of the meeting are drawn up as customary;

---

15 CICLSAL, Letter to General Moderators, July 1, 2020, Prot. N.Sp.R.2452/20.

- in the use of connection systems, confidentiality must be ensured; secrecy, when required, must be ensured;
- the identity of the participants must be verified;
- the possibility of intervening in real time during the deliberations must be verified.

The congregation emphasized that use of telecommunications for council meetings is "not the ordinary solution for the governance of an Institute or of Province" and that, once the pandemic is resolved, "*habitual* recourse to telecommunications would render meaningless the service of authority which, in consecrated life, calls for personally and responsibly maintaining a network of relationship through correct and effective communication in order to safeguard and promote communication in the Institute."[16]

Chapters

Chapters can be held at various levels of an institute—general, provincial, or local. Monasteries have regular monastic chapters throughout the year to attend to spiritual and temporal matters. However, it is the general chapter that holds supreme authority in the institute while it is in session (c. 631 §1). Representing the entire institute, the general chapter has the following functions: elects the supreme moderator; treats the most important affairs of the institute; protects the patrimony of the institute and promotes suitable renewal in accord with the patrimony; and issues norms binding on all (c. 631 §1). The general chapter drafts and approves the constitutions and revisions in the constitutions, which must then be approved by ecclesiastical authority. Affairs handled by the general chapter include, for example, questions related to the proper apostolate of the institute, changes in the composition of provinces and other parts of the institute, financial matters, formation, and future planning.

The composition of the general chapter and the extent of its power are defined in the constitutions, while other proper law addresses the details on how the chapter will proceed, especially in what pertains to elections and the manner of handling other matters (c. 631 §2). The general chapter is a collegial body in which each participant has equal voice and vote.[17]

Following are matters to be considered in preparing and celebrating a general chapter.

---

16 Ibid.
17 Smith, 794.

How Convoked

- Applying canon 166 to religious institutes, the supreme moderator convokes the general chapter.
- Proper law should determine how preparation for the chapter should occur.
- On July 1, 2020, CICLSAL issued a letter saying that general and provincial chapters cannot be held by means of telecommunications, nor the combination of partial physical presence and partial presence through telecommunications, but only by means of physical presence. However, on May 31, 2021, CICLSAL issued further guidance providing an exceptional basis—from May 31, 2021, through December 31, 2022—that an institute or society may petition CICLSAL to use computerized and telematic means as an alternative to personal presence provided that the provisions in its letter are met.[18]

Officials of the Chapter

- Unless otherwise determined by proper law, the supreme moderator is the presiding officer of the chapter.
- Tellers (c. 173):
    - Prior to any election in a chapter, at least two tellers are to be designated; these tellers must be members of the group.
    - The tellers gather the ballots, determine in the presence of the presiding officer that the number of votes cast equals the number of electors (otherwise the election is invalid), read the ballots and announce the votes each person received.
    - A secretary appointed by the presiding officer records accurately the acts of the election and preserves them.

Participation

- Canon 633 §1 states that the general chapter should have as its purpose the concern and participation of all members for the good of the entire institute.
- Canon 631 §3 states that provinces, communities, and any member may submit proposals, suggestions, or desires to the chapter. Chapter preparation should provide for feedback from membership. Proper law may determine the proper procedure.

---

18 See CICLSAL, Letter to General Moderators, July 1, 2020; and see CICLSAL Letter to Moderators and Supreme Moderators, May 31, 2021, Prot. N.Sp.R. 2452/20.

Membership

- There should be a balance of *ex officio* and elected delegates, in accord with proper law. Delegates may be elected at large, i.e., by the entire institute, or by a subgroup, such as a province, house, or age group.[19] The membership must represent the institute as a whole (c. 631 §1).
- Praxis of the Apostolic See regarding a *chapter of the whole:*

  Some institutes have requested to have a chapter of the whole in which all members of the institute participate, especially in the election of the supreme moderator. The Holy See has permitted this when the institute has fewer than 100 members. Some larger institutes have received favorable responses if they have submitted a well-developed plan which provides for a truly whole-member chapter, that is, one which will actually involve nearly all members. Key criteria include geographic proximity, impact on ministry and on financial resources, tradition of chapters in the particular institute, numbers of members who would be disenfranchised if they can neither come in person nor vote for a delegate, and conduciveness of numbers for good decision making. In general, the Apostolic See requires that chapter members be perpetually professed, but indults have been granted as exceptions (see *CLD* 10, 102-105).

Procedures for Election

- Convening of electors (cc. 166-167):
  - All must be convoked.
  - The notice of convocation is valid if directed to domicile, quasi-domicile, or actual residence of each elector.
  - If any elector is overlooked and not present, the election is valid. However, if the one overlooked can provide proof of the right to vote, the election must be rescinded by competent authority, provided recourse is made within three days of the notice of election.
  - If more than one-third of the electors is overlooked, the election is invalid by the law itself, unless all those overlooked were actually present.
  - Voting by mail and proxy votes are not permitted unless provided for in proper law.
  - If an elector is present in the place of election but cannot be present at the election due to illness, his or her written vote is collected by the tellers.

---

19 Smith, 795.

- Eligibility to vote (cc. 169; 171)
    - No one can vote who is not a member of the general chapter.
    - An elector must be capable of placing a human act. Questions concerning a person's mental capacity must be addressed before the election. Medical personnel should be called on to help assess the person's mental capacity so that the determination regarding ability to vote is based on objective criteria.
    - Members with active voice may vote; those with passive voice may be elected. Exclaustrated members lack active and passive voice (c. 687).
    - A person who has defected notoriously from the communion of the Church is not qualified to vote.
    - A person who is under a penalty of excommunication imposed through a judicial sentence or declared through a decree is not qualified to vote.
    - If an ineligible person votes, that person's vote is null, but the election is valid unless it is evident that, without that vote subtracted, the one elected did not receive the required number of votes.
- Requirements in the voting itself (c. 172)
    - A vote must be **free,** that is, the elector cannot be coerced directly or indirectly by grave fear or fraud to vote for a certain person.
    - The vote must be **secret**.
    - The vote must be **certain**, that is, for a specific individual.
    - The vote must be **absolute**, without conditions attached.
    - The vote must be **determinate**, that is, clearly stated without ambiguity.
- The one elected
    - To be elected, a majority of those convoked must be present, unless proper law provides otherwise (c. 119, 1°).
    - The person must receive an absolute majority of those present (one over half). Abstentions are considered part of the total vote unless proper law determines otherwise. After two inconclusive ballots, the choice is limited to the two individuals who have received the most votes or, if a tie exists among several members, the two persons senior in age stand for election in the following ballots. After three inconclusive ballots, the one senior in age is considered elected (c. 119, 1°).

- The one elected must be informed of the election (if not present) and has eight days to accept or decline (c. 177).
- If the office does not require confirmation, the one elected acquires the office by acceptance of the election (c. 178). If the election requires confirmation, the person elected must personally or through another seek confirmation from the competent authority within eight days of the election (c. 179 §1). Confirmation must be given in writing (c. 179 §3).
- Canon 174 allows for compromise (if provided in proper law), that is, to transfer the right of election to a qualified individual or individuals; the electors must unanimously agree and express their consent in writing.
- Canon 153 §2 allows for an election within six months prior to that office becoming vacant. The one elected acquires the office only when the office does in fact become vacant.

Other Matters Decided by the General Chapter

Canon 119, 2° addresses votes for deciding matters other than elections. The general rule requires an absolute majority of those present (who are a majority of those who must be convoked) but does not limit the number of ballots. The canon also provides for the possibility of the presiding officer to break a tie vote.

Record Keeping in General and Archives in Particular

It is important that an institute, at its various levels, maintain documentation of policies and various actions undertaken by superiors and members. Proper record keeping provides consistency through changes in leadership and can assist in ensuring proper and consistent implementation of policies.

Minutes should be kept of council meetings. They should:

- give the date and place of the meeting;
- name persons present;
- record decisions taken;
- Note whether a vote was consultative or consenting;
- Note whether a vote was secret;
- Note how many votes were positive, negative, abstentions;
- be signed by the secretary;
- be approved by the council.

When a decision is made in council and must be communicated to another person, either to give information or to have action taken, a written act is made. Acts should be:

- assigned a protocol number, e.g. 23/98 (act 23 of 1998);
- dated, with the place given;
- signed by the superior and the secretary;
- imprinted with the official seal;
- copied, and copies should be kept in the appropriate file.

Files

Records should be grouped for filing in such a way as to

- reflect the institute's organization;
- reflect how responsibility is exercised;
- serve as a basis for all files.

Archives

Archives serve to gather, preserve, and make accessible valuable records relevant to the institute or local community. They serve administrative needs of governance and provide a basis for research, including historical research. Just as importantly, they help maintain the identity of the institute, which is not only a historical entity, but a living organism continually developing.

Each institute should develop its own record groups with the appropriate series of topics in each group. Each institute should also be aware of issues of confidentiality—under civil law and canon law—and of access, and they should develop policies and procedures accordingly.

For practical help, recourse can be had to:

- The Society of American Archivists https://www2.archivists.org.
- Association of Catholic Diocesan Archivists http://diocesanarchivists.org/.
- Archivists of Congregations of Women Religious https://archivistsacwr.org/.

The following is an indication of the kinds of things that should be preserved in archives.

OFFICIAL DOCUMENTATION

- Governance
  - Constitutions, Rule
  - Directory, policies, procedures
- History
  - Institute
  - Provinces
  - Biographies
  - Annals (duplicates)
- Formation/Education
- Foundations
- Ministries/Institutions
- Membership listings
- Minutes of chapters
- Minutes of council meetings
- Official documents:
  - Acts
  - Finances
  - Property and buildings
- Correspondence: Holy See congregations, local ordinaries, provincials, etc.

GENERAL MATERIALS

- Books and articles published by members
- Commemorative booklets
- Community newsletters
- Community studies: ministry, government, finance, etc.
- Financial and photographic records of buildings, changes in use, etc.
- Journal articles relevant to community or members
- Orders of liturgical ceremonies
- Photographs
- Prepared publicity

INDIVIDUAL RELIGIOUS MATERIALS

- Artifacts of artistic value (e.g., statues, paintings, sacred vessels, furniture, books), or
- Artifacts of significance in the history of the institute or house

Secret Archives

Applying canons 489 and 490 to consecrated life, the manifest need exists to protect the confidentiality of all members, including former members. As canon 489 suggests for the diocesan curia, an institute should therefore make provision for "a secret archive or at least in the common archive there is to be a safe or cabinet, completely closed and locked, which cannot be removed; in it documents to be kept secret are to be protected most securely."

In analogy with canon 490, proper law should designate the major superior as the sole individual with the key to this archive. Proper law should already have provision in case of the sudden death of the major superior; the person upon whom leadership devolves in such a situation might be allowed access, under specific conditions. Finally, proper law should clearly define the limited access to the secret archive; such a policy properly enforced will encourage the freedom of individuals in discussing personal matters with the major superior and with medical personnel, including psychiatrists or psychologists.

The institute should have a clear policy on the location of specific types of documents; the secret archive should not include all documentation. The secret archive might include:

- results of psychological testing, received either before admission or afterwards;
- results of medical testing, again, received either before admission or afterwards;
- for a clerical institute or one with clerics as members:
    - records of dispensations from impediments and irregularities to orders or to the exercise of orders;
    - documents concerning loss of the clerical state through invalidity, penalty, or dispensation (see cc. 290-293);
- decree of dismissal from the institute (see c. 700);
- documentation of penal investigations concerning present or former members; also, documentation if penalties were imposed.

Given the complex legal situation in the United States concerning access to archives, the major superior should consult a civil lawyer in establishing policies concerning the secret archive, especially policies regarding retention and destruction of records. It cannot be presumed that secret archives are protected from civil laws regarding discovery and evidence. Furthermore, destruction of files regarding criminal behavior on the part of a member could create problems in civil procedures.

The Relationship between a Canonical and Civil Entity

Religious institutes and their provinces and houses, secular institutes, and societies of apostolic life and, unless the constitutions determine otherwise, the parts and houses of societies, are public juridic persons under canon law (cc. 634 §1; 718; 741 §1). As such, they act in the name of the Church (c. 116 §1) and their temporal goods are ecclesiastical goods (*bona ecclesiastica*). Administration of the temporal goods of institutes and societies are subject to proper law and universal law, especially Book V of the Code of Canon Law on "The Temporal Goods of the Church." Unless proper law provides otherwise, superiors are the administrators of the temporal goods of institutes and societies (c. 1279 §1), although they usually require the advice or consent of their councils to place major acts of administration regarding those goods. The Code of Canon Law explicitly requires each religious institute and province and each society to have a finance officer who is distinct from the superior (cc. 636 §1; 741 §1) and each public juridic person is to have a finance council (c. 1280).

Because canon law requires the use of civil legal structures to hold title to property and to protect church assets, institutes and societies and their major parts are incorporated under state statutes as nonprofit civil corporations. Thus, certain actions under specific conditions (for example, the alienation of property) are governed both by canon and civil law. Both canonical and civil legal advice should be sought. The following table, initially compiled by Cecilia Meighan, RSM, JD, and edited for this update, is a useful reference table.[20]

---

[20] See Cecilia Meighan, RSM, "Conducting the Affairs of the Religious Institute in Council and Conducting the Business of the Corporation within its Corporate Structure," at https://1qszqk2yh2vo7yv012x55d7i-wpengine.netdna-ssl.com/wp-content/uploads/2019/01/VII-GeneralInfoforCouncilsandConductingtheAffairs.pdf.

CONDUCTING THE AFFAIRS OF THE RELIGIOUS INSTITUTE IN COUNCIL AND CONDUCTING THE BUSINESS OF THE CORPORATION WITHIN ITS CORPORATE STRUCTURE

Cecilia Meighan, RSM, JD

	RELIGIOUS INSTITUTE (RI)	CORPORATION (CIVIL)
I. LEGAL STATUS	Collegial public juridic person recognized by competent ecclesiastical authority whose members take vows as required by the Constitutions of the Institute (Canon 573-746)	Civil or religious not-for-profit corporation incorporated under appropriate state statute; person under civil law. [Canon Law requires use of civil law structures to protect church assets and to hold title to property.]
II. GOVERNING DOCUMENTS (Define duties and authority)	Constitutions and Directory **Constitutions** • Nature, end, and spirit of RI • Governance of RI • Admission of candidates and formation of members • Obligations and rights of RI and members • Apostolate of RI • Separation of members from RI • Approved by RI and CICLSAL or diocesan bishop **Directory, Policies, Procedures** • Norms by which RI is governed • Directory, which needs approval of chapter • Policies and procedures need approval of council	Articles (Charter) And Bylaws (Code of Regulations) **Articles** • General and specific purposes • Indemnification of directors and officers • 501(c)(3) requirements • Dissolution clause **Bylaws** • Specific responsibilities of Board of Directors • Procedures for valid corporate acts • Committee structure • Designation of officers • Methods for amending foundational documents

	RELIGIOUS INSTITUTE (RI)	CORPORATION (CIVIL)
III. GENERAL PURPOSES	• Profess evangelical counsels • Live a common life • Share assets • Undertake certain works of charity • Follow the same set of directives (rule)	• Further and promote charitable, religious, educational purposes [purpose must meet 501(c)(3) requirements of Internal Revenue Code] • Support the works of public charity of RI • Receive and administer funds for religious and charitable purposes
IV. SPECIFIC PURPOSES	Carry out the particular purpose(s) of the RI according to Constitutions, Directory and canon law	Carry out business and administer property and assets of RI according to the Articles, Bylaws, and corporate law
V. GOVERNING BODY	Major Superior and Council; chapter when in session (elected by membership according to Constitutions)	Board of Directors (self-perpetuating)
VI. FORMALITIES	Council Meetings • Separate agenda • Separate minutes • Annual reports • Periodic meetings • Financial reports	Board of Director Meetings • Separate agenda • Separate minutes • Annual reports • Annual and regular meetings • Proper notices • Election of officers • Annual budget/audit financial statements • Corporate seal

	RELIGIOUS INSTITUTE (RI)	CORPORATION (CIVIL)
VII. RESPONSIBILITIES OF GOVERNING BODY	• Administrator of ecclesiastical goods (Book II, Part III, Section I, Title II, Chapter II, Art. 3 and Book V of the *CIC*) Perform acts of ordinary and extraordinary administration - alienation (transfer of property) • Obtain permissions of competent authority > Generalate level - receive requests for approval from provinces; request necessary approvals from CICLSAL > Province level - approve and make requests to generalate • Attend to issues/matters as determined by Constitutions and/or Directory • Preserve official records of a non-current nature in Congregation archives • File reports as requested by appropriate canonical authority	• Receive gifts, bequests, grants in name of RI and in accordance with applicable canons • Make contracts • Sue and be sued • Receive state or federal grants • Approve merger or dissolution of corporation • Hold property • Purchase or lease real and personal property • Sell, convey, dispose of real and personal property • Receive, take title to, and use proceeds of stocks, bonds, etc. • Keep corporate files, correct, and complete books and records of accounts, transactions, and minutes of the proceedings of the Board of Directors and its committees • Preserve official records of a non-current nature in administrative archives • File reports with state/federal governments • Hire, fire employees and administer personnel policies consonant with local, state, and federal laws, such as the: > Civil rights laws (re: disability, age, sex, gender, race, nationality, marital status, military service, etc.) > Immigration laws > Family and medical leave laws > Health insurance laws > Fair labor standards and wage laws > Tax laws

	RELIGIOUS INSTITUTE (RI)	CORPORATION (CIVIL)
VIII. MINUTES	**Council Minutes** Should reflect actions taken on: Canonical Issues • Admission of candidates • Admission to novitiate • Admission to vows • Exclaustration • Transfer • Readmission • Dismissal • Dispensation • Permissions for alienation Personnel Issues • Education • Sabbatical leave • Placement Sponsored Apostolates • Canonical approvals • Membership responsibilities • Board of Directors Reports • Committees • Task forces • Planning Patrimony of the Institute • Purchasing • Alienating	**Board of Directors Minutes** • Should note quorum present • Should follow requirements of state law re notice (date, time, place of meeting) or waiver of notice • Should note minutes of previous meeting reviewed, approved, signed by secretary or president of board • Should note passage of corporate resolutions required by banks, state or federal requirements, e.g. open bank accounts, change authorized signatures on accounts • Should note passage of all corporate resolutions • Other corporate matters > Taxes > Budget > Property sale, purchase, improvement > Leases > Loans > Amendment of articles or bylaws > Approval of merger or dissolution
IX. CANONICAL REQUIREMENTS WITH CIVIL LAW IMPLICATIONS	• Patrimony • Cession of administration of property • Wills	• Taxes • Power of attorney • Wills must meet requirements of state last will and testament statutes

	RELIGIOUS INSTITUTE (RI)	CORPORATION (CIVIL)
X. DOCUMENTS	• Personnel files > Wills > Cession instruments > Health records • Archives > Council meeting minutes • Personnel files of dispensed and deceased members	• Property files > Deeds > Appraisals > Surveys > Mortgages > Leases • Financial files > Audits > Budgets > Reports • Contracts

The Role of a Commissary[21]

The Code of Canon Law, promulgated in 1983, did not envision the reality that was on the horizon for many institutes in the United States and elsewhere—the sharp decline in the number of new members with the consequent demographic shift to much smaller and much older memberships. While the code provides for options such as mergers and unions of institutes (c. 582), even these options are rarely practical in today's circumstances. It makes no sense to merge a small non-viable institute into a slightly larger non-viable institute or to unite three aging institutes into one larger aging institute. Furthermore, members wish to fulfill their vocations within the charism and communities to which they were called and to which they devoted their lives. Recognizing these realities, canonists are assisting institutes in "coming to completion" rather than undergo suppressions and mergers. An institute that is coming to completion is one that has decided to discontinue receiving new members but to continue its existence until all of the remaining members have entered eternal life.

One of the first indications that an institute needs to consider the option of coming to completion is the lack of members able and willing to assume leadership roles, especially the office of supreme moderator. In these cases, the institute may request to suspend ordinary governance and have a "commissary" appointed to act as canonical superior. An institute of pontifical right makes the request to the Holy See and an institute of diocesan right to the diocesan bishop. The request can include a recommendation of a person to be named as

21 Information on commissaries is taken primarily from handouts and workshops presented by the Resource Center for Religious Institutes (https://www.trcri.org) and the writings of Amy Hereford, CSJ, many of which are available at www.ahereford.org.

commissary. The commissary need not be a member of the same religious order or family but can be a secular cleric or a member of a different institute located in the same region as the community that is coming to completion and therefore shares the same culture and ecclesial experience. The petition to suspend governance and have a commissary appointed should include the following:[22]

- Petition from Community
    - Request for Commissary
    - Reasoning
    - Brief History Leading to Petition
    - Consultation and Votes of Community
    - Nomination of Commissary
    - Indication of Financial Security
    - Conclusion
    - Signed by Canonical leader
- Appendices – tables and lists communicate the information more concisely
    - History of Community from foundation to present (1-2 pages)
    - Sisters, ages, living arrangements and ministry (1 page)
    - Timeline of Meetings / Decision with Community and Commissary (1-2 pages)
    - Council Minutes of Community Resolution for the petition (1 page)
    - USCCB-NRRO Retirement Needs Analysis Report
- Letters of Support
    - Commissary (the one nominated) (1-2 pages)
    - Commissary's Community (1 page)
    - Bishop (1-2 pages)

The role of the commissary is defined in the decree of appointment. It may be as extensive as including all the rights and obligations of the supreme moderator and his or her council. It certainly includes being attentive to the

---

22 See Amy Hereford, "Religious Institutes Coming to Completion and Their Legacy," available at http://www.ahereford.org/canonlaw/doku.php?id=rcri.legacy (accessed on March 1, 2021).

needs of the members, both spiritual and material, and fostering their ongoing community life.[23]

The following "Q&A" on commissaries for religious institutes, prepared by the Resource Center for Religious Institutes, provides more information on the appointment and role of a commissary.[24]

25 Q&A's

COMMISSARY FOR RELIGIOUS INSTITUTES

---

1. What is a Commissary?

A Commissary is a person appointed to act as the canonical superior of another institute.

2. Who appoints a Commissary?

Church authority, either the Holy See for pontifical institutes or the Diocesan Bishop for diocesan institutes, appoints a Commissary. This is sometimes referred to as a "Pontifical Commissary" or "Episcopal Commissary."

3. Is a Commissary a new canonical figure?

Historically, a Commissary has been used in many different situations in which, for various reasons, the religious institute is unable to carry out the functions of its general government.

4. Under what circumstances is a Commissary being used today?

Today, it is used to assist an institute which is unable to elect a full general government (superior general and council) from its members, but which wants to continue living according to its own history, identity, and legacy.

5. Who can be appointed a Commissary for a religious institute?

Generally, a Commissary for a women's institute is a woman religious with a similar experience of living religious life. However, clerics can also be appointed to serve in this role. There have been some situations in which a Diocesan Bishop has served in this role. Currently a lay person cannot be appointed a Commissary for a religious institute.

---

23 During the process when the necessity of a commissary is being contemplated, it is extremely important to enter into dialogue with a civil attorney who is competent to help with the simultaneous restructuring of civil entities and documents, especially articles of incorporation, bylaws, and boards of directors, all of which will almost certainly be affected by the change in the canonical governance structure to a commissary. Failure to pursue the necessary changes can impact the tax-exempt status and corporate standing of the institute or society's civil corporate entity.

24 Sharon Euart, RSM, "25 Q&A's: Commissary for Religious Institutes" (Silver Spring, MD: Resource Center for Religious Institutes, updated in 2019). Used with permission, with slight modifications.

6. Can the institute hire a Commissary without approval by the Holy See or Diocesan Bishop?

The institute may recommend a person to be appointed as Commissary; however, the appointment of the Commissary must come from competent church authority, the Holy See or the Diocesan Bishop.

7. Does the institute have any role in the selection of the Commissary?

The institute is encouraged to recommend a suitable person that is known to the institute as the candidate for appointment as Commissary for the institute.

8. How is the Commissary's appointment communicated?

The Commissary receives a letter of appointment from the Holy See or the Diocesan Bishop describing the role, the effective date of the appointment, and the extent of the authority attached to the office.

9. Is the Diocesan Bishop required to consult the superior general or provincial of the individual to be appointed Commissary for a diocesan institute?

Consultation by the Diocesan Bishop with the superior general or provincial of the sister to be appointed, though not required, is appropriate in the spirit of *Mutuae relationes*. It is also the responsibility of the individual being asked to serve as Commissary to consult her/his superior general or provincial prior to accepting the appointment.

10. What is the scope of the Commissary's authority?

As a rule, the Commissary is given the canonical authority of the superior general for governance of the institute according to universal law, the constitutions of the institute she/he is serving, and the letter of appointment. If the governance structures of the institute are too complicated or burdensome, dispensations from the Constitutions from Rome or from the Diocesan Bishop may be granted.

11. May a Province petition for a Commissary?

Currently most petitions for a Commissary come from a superior general for an institute. Generally, a superior general would provide for the canonical governance of a province when the province is unable to provide for its own governance. In cases where this is not possible, a superior general may petition the Diocesan Bishop (where the Province Motherhouse is located) or the Holy See for a Commissary for a province. The petition should include approval from the superior general for the request as well as an indication that there is no institute-wide member available to serve in the role of provincial superior.

12. Does the Commissary have to be in a leadership position in another religious institute?

It is not necessary for a Commissary to be in a leadership position in another institute. Leadership experience is an advantage but not a requirement.

13. Is the appointment for a term?

Usually, there is not a specified term for the Commissary. The decree may indicate *ad nutum Sanctae Sedis* (at the pleasure of the Holy See). If the religious appointed is in leadership in her/his own institute, that term does not define her/his time as Commissary. It is the person who is appointed, not the one holding the office in another institute. The person who is appointed as Commissary remains in that role after completing her/his term of office in her/his own institute; the role does not pass to her/his successor in her/his own institute.

14. Should the appointment be given in a decree or a letter?

The appointment can be made either way by the Holy See or the Diocesan Bishop.

15. What happens if the Commissary becomes unable or unwilling to continue?

If the Commissary can no longer continue in this role, she/he can resign and offer to assist the community in seeking a new person to recommend for appointment as a Commissary.

16. Does the Commissary need a "council?"

The Commissary, as with every major superior, must have and use a council (c. 627). If possible, all or at least some of the council members (sometimes called consultors) should be members of the institute she/he is serving. The Commissary can, however, ask assistance from members of her/his own institute.

17. How many councilors are needed?

When the institute is small, a general council can be composed of three members in addition to the superior. In some cases, a council of two members has been permitted by the Holy See.

18. What is the role of the councilor?

The role of councilor is not necessarily a full-time role, but the councilors provide the "collective wisdom" needed for important decisions.

19. Do the councilors need to be members of a religious institute?

The councilors should also be religious. Different arrangements can be made for the work of the treasurer. Such arrangements may have been made before the request for a Commissary.

20. Are the Councilors appointed or elected?

In most circumstances the councilors will be appointed by the Commissary, following consultation with members of the institute being assisted. If they are from the Commissary's own institute, they need approval of their superior if the Commissary is not that superior.

21. How does an institute prepare for a Commissary?

A guided communal discernment among the members should precede a decision to seek or request a Commissary.

22. What questions should members consider in discerning timeliness for a Commissary?

Is there a need for a Commissary? Are there capable members in the institute for leadership positions but who may be reluctant to assume the responsibility? What important decisions have we made, or do we have yet to make regarding ministries, property, vocations, care of members, etc.? Should we address these issues before or after seeking help with governance?

23. What qualities and experience should be looked for in a person to recommend as a Commissary?

The members might consider a person who would be familiar with the institute's spirituality and mission, the institute's local culture or missionary outreach.

24. What factors should the institute consider regarding the readiness of the members for a Commissary?

Is the institute able to accept a Commissary with councilors to assist her/him with their knowledge of the institute? Are the members ready and willing to accept a religious of another institute to govern the institute with the canonical authority of the superior general/president and to collaborate with her/him?

25. What is the procedure for requesting a Commissary?

The procedure for requesting a Commissary includes:

- In prayerful discernment assess the canonical governance needs of the institute
- Determine the appropriate canonical governance structure for the immediate future and assess the need for assistance.
- If the institute determines it needs assistance, look at the alternatives that fit the situation, e.g., additional council member(s), Commissary plus councilors.
- If the institute wishes to request a Commissary, the superior general/president prepares a petition to the Holy See, if a pontifical institute, or the Diocesan Bishop, if a diocesan institute.
- Identify, with the members of the institute, a person(s) familiar with the institute, its traditions and spirituality as well as its local circumstances
- Consult the person(s) identified as capable of fulfilling the canonical responsibilities of Commissary regarding her/his interest and availability.
- If a pontifical institute, consult the Diocesan Bishop of the diocese in which the Motherhouse/headquarters is located for a favorable votum to accompany the petition. (This may not be required but can be helpful to the process.)

• Identify any civil law implications for the institute resulting from the appointment of a Commissary.

• Prepare a petition to the Holy See or the Diocesan Bishop for suspension of the institute's ordinary governance structure and the appointment of a Commissary with authority for the canonical governance of the institute including a description of the situation, the reasons leading to the petition, and a recommendation for a person to be appointed to the role.

Governance of a Federation of Monasteries of Nuns

In 2016, Pope Francis issued the apostolic constitution *Vultum Dei quaerere* with new papal norms for monasteries of contemplative nuns. In 2018, the Congregation for Institutes of Consecrated Life and Societies of Apostolic Life issued the instruction *Cor orans* on how to implement the new legislation. Monasteries of nuns, like all monasteries, value and protect their autonomy. Legal autonomy means each monastery is a public juridic person, elects its own superior who is a major superior, and admits and forms new members (*CO* 15). However, to prevent isolation, Pope Francis decreed that, while retaining their autonomy, every monastery of nuns must henceforth be joined to a federation, unless dispensed by the Holy See (*VDQ* Art. 9 §1). Most monasteries of monks and sisters are members of a monastic federation or congregation, with a president at the head. The scope of authority of the president in relation to the member monasteries is defined in the constitutions but is considerably less than that ascribed to the supreme moderator of a religious institute. The governance of a federation of monasteries of contemplative nuns is defined in *Cor orans*.

The Federal President

The president of the federation is elected for a six-year term by the federal assembly, which is comparable to a general chapter. She is not a major superior, but has the following functions: acts as co-visitator for canonical visitations of the member monasteries, along with the regular visitator, who is the diocesan bishop for monasteries entrusted to his special vigilance (c. 615) or the religious ordinary for monasteries juridically associated with a male institute (*CO* 111);

- visits a member monastery "whenever the need requires it," accompanied by one of the federation councilors as co-visitator and the financial administrator of the federation (*CO* 113);
- makes maternal or sisterly visits to a monastery with the agreement of that monastery's superior (*CO* 114);
- verifies during canonical visitation how *Vultum Dei quaerere* is observed (*CO* 116);

- watches over initial and ongoing formation in the monasteries and reports to the Holy See about the monastery's ability to provide suitable initial formation (*CO* 117);
- oversees the federation's program of formation for the formators of the monasteries and requires participation in the program (*CO* 118);
- provides formation for those called to authority in the monasteries and requires their participation (*CO* 119);
- reports to the Holy See when a monastery no longer possesses "real autonomy of life," that is, when it is no longer viable (*CO* 121);
- after consulting her council, communicates to the Holy See when the major superior of a member monastery denies consent to a nun who wishes to transfer to another monastery of the same institute (*CO* 122).

In addition to the above, a monastery that is being suppressed or needs assistance with revitalization can be entrusted to the federal president.

The Federal Council

The federal assembly elects four solemnly professed nuns for six-year terms to serve on the federal council (*CO* 123). *Cor orans* identifies the following situations in which the president consults or seeks the consent of the council:

- consults when writing a report to the major superior of a monastery following canonical visitation (*CO* 125);
- consults regarding times and places for formation courses for formators and those called to authority (*CO* 126);
- at the end of the six-year term, president and council collaborate in drafting a report to the Holy See on the state of the federation and member monasteries (*CO* 127);
- consults before sending a request to the Holy See for suppression of a monastery or affiliation of a struggling monastery with one that is thriving (*CO* 128);
- seeks consent before appointing or removing the federal formator (*CO* 129);
- seeks consent to grant an indult of exclaustration for a nun for a second or third year, after the major superior of the monastery granted the first year (*CO* 130);
- seeks consent to send a request to the Holy See for an extension of exclaustration beyond three years (*CO* 132).

The federal council also serves as the council of a monastery that is entrusted to the president.

The Federal Assembly

The federal assembly, like the general chapter of a religious institute, "is a sign of unity in charity, whose primary task is to protect the charismatic patrimony of the Institute among the federated monasteries and to promote an adequate renewal in harmony with it (*CO* 133)." An ordinary federal assembly is convened every six years and an intermediate federal assembly every three years to assess progress (*CO* 135-136). The president, with the consent of the federal council, can convoke an extraordinary assembly (*CO* 137). The federal assembly does the following (*CO* 141):

- receives the report of the federal president on the state of the federation and the individual monasteries;
- elects the federal president and council;
- elects the federal financial administrator;
- deals with issues of major importance;
- makes decisions and issues norms that all nuns are required to observe, after the definitive approval of the Holy See;
- develops the formation courses that each community is obliged to carry out;
- promotes the creation of new foundations;
- identifies a monastery as the place of initial common formation;
- establishes a formation plan for those called to authority and for formators.

Other federal offices include the federal financial administrator, federal secretary, and federal formator.

Cor orans also gives some prerogatives to the major superiors of monasteries of nuns that they did not have previously. In derogation of canon 667 §4, dispensation from cloister rests solely with the major superior, with no intervention from the diocesan bishop or religious ordinary (*CO* 174-175). The major superior, with consent of her council and after hearing the diocesan bishop or religious ordinary, can authorize a nun to be absent from the monastery for up to one year (*CO* 176). In derogation of canon 686 §2, the major superior, with the consent of her council and after hearing the diocesan bishop or religious ordinary, can grant an indult of exclaustration for up to one year (*CO* 177).

SIGNIFICANT SIMILARITIES AND DIFFERENCES

RELIGIOUS INSTITUTES	SECULAR INSTITUTES	SOCIETIES OF APOSTOLIC LIFE
1. Definition	1. Definition	1. Definition
A religious institute is a society in which members, according to proper law, pronounce public vows, either perpetual or temporary which are to be renewed, however, when the period of time has elapsed, and lead a life of brothers or sisters in common. (Canon 607 §2)	A secular institute is an institute of consecrated life in which the Christian faithful, living in the world, strive for the perfection of charity and seek to contribute to the sanctification of the world, especially from within. (Canon 710)	§1. Societies of apostolic life resemble institutes of consecrated life; their members, without religious vows, pursue the apostolic purpose proper to the society and, leading a life in common as brothers or sisters according to their proper manner of life, strive for the perfection of charity through the observance of the constitutions. §2. Among these are societies in which members assume the evangelical counsels by some bond defined in the constitutions. (Canon 731)
2. Proper Law	2. Proper Law	2. Proper Law
Constitutions and other norms (canon 587)	Constitutions and other norms (canon 587)	Constitutions and other norms (canons 587. 732)
3. Commitment	3. Commitment	3. Commitment
Profess the three evangelical counsels: poverty, chastity, obedience (canons 599-601)	Profess the three evangelical counsels: poverty, chastity, obedience (canons 599-601)	a. All members embrace celibacy (canons 277, 739) b. In some: members embrace the evangelical counsels (canon 731 §2) c. Personal property (canon 741 §2)
4. Bond	4. Bond	4. Bond
Public Vows (canons 607 §2, 1192 §§1-2)	Determined in the constitutions: private vows, oath, promise, other (canon 712, 1192, 1199-1201)	Determined in the constitutions: private vows, oath, promise, other (canons 731, 735, 1192, 1199-1201)
5. Community Living	5. Community Living	5. Community Living
Fraternal life in common (canons 602, 665, 668 §3, 670)	Fraternal life but not normally in common (canons 602, 714)	Fraternal life in common (canons 731, 740, 741 §2)

RELIGIOUS INSTITUTES	SECULAR INSTITUTES	SOCIETIES OF APOSTOLIC LIFE
6. Witness	6. Witness	6. Witness
Public witness to Christ and the Church and a certain separation from the world (canon 607 §3)	Living in the world like a leaven endeavoring to permeate everything with an evangelical spirit. (canons 710, 713)	Pursue the apostolic purpose proper to each institute (canon 731 §1)
7. Apostolate	7. Apostolate	7. Apostolate
Corporate apostolate in the name of the Church and of the institute (canons 673-675, 677, 678, 680-682)	Ordinarily members are engaged in their own professions or avocations in the world (canon 713)	Corporate apostolate proper to each one (canon 731)
8. Status	8. Status	8. Status
Clerics are incardinated in the institute (canon 266 §2)	a. Lay members retain their own status. b. Clerics normally incardinated in the diocese (canons 266 §3, 711, 713 §3, 715 §1)	Clerics are incardinated into the society unless constitutions say otherwise (canons 266 §2, 736, §1)
9. Admission	9. Admission	9. Admission
a. Celibate b. 17 years complete c. First profession: at least 18 d. Final profession: at least 21 (canons 643, 656, 658)	a. Celibate b. Majority age c. First commitment after 2 years d. Final commitment after 5 years (canons 97, 721-723)	a. Celibate b. 17 years complete c. First and final commitment: determined in proper law (canon 735 §2 with conditions also established for institutes)
10. Ordination	10. Ordination	10. Ordination
Studies universal and proper law (canon 659 §3) Pontifical clerical institute: major superior issues dimissorial letters (canon 1019)	Same as diocesan clergy (canon 1019 §2)	Studies same as diocesan clergy (canon 736 §2) Pontifical clerical society: major superior issues dimissorial letters (canon 1019)
11. Government	11. Government	11. Government
Superiors have religious authority according to universal law and constitutions (canon 596 §1) Clerical religious institutes: power of governance (canons 134, 596 §2)	Superiors have authority according to universal law and constitutions. (canon 596 §§1 and 3)	Superiors have authority according to universal law and constitutions. (canons 732, 596 §§1 and 3) Clerical societies: power of governance (canons 134, 596 §2, 732)

This chart was designed by Reverend Michael O'Reilly, OMI, for a course on consecrated life at St. Paul University, Ottawa, in 1990. With approval from Fr. O'Reilly, Eileen Jaramillo, DMin, JCL, has made changes and kept it updated. Used with permission.

CHAPTER TWO

NEW INSTITUTES, MERGERS AND SUPPRESSION

Sharon Holland, IHM[1]

Despite the existence of countless religious institutes, secular institutes and societies of apostolic life in the Church throughout the world, the Spirit continues to give new founding gifts. These must be submitted to the competent authority of the Church in order to assure their authenticity. There are four major steps in the procedure from the original inspiration of a founder to the final possible step of pontifical recognition: inspiration, association, diocesan erection and pontifical recognition.

The foundational canon is canon 579, which states: "Diocesan bishops, each in his own territory, can validly erect institutes of consecrated life by formal decree, provided that the previous permission of the Apostolic See has been given in writing."[2] This consultation was determined to be *ad validitatem* (for validity) by Pope Francis, effective June 1, 2016.

Canonists often speak of four "stages" in the development of a new institute or society: inspiration, association, diocesan institute status, and pontifical recognition.

Stage 1: Inspiration

Before any juridic action, the inspiration which has been received by a founder must be evaluated by the hierarchy. Conciliar and post conciliar documents are rich in teaching, which not only can help founders, but also can guide the bishops who have the responsibility of welcoming and distinguishing among charisms (*LG* 12b).

---

1 Marlene Weisenbeck, FSPA, and Rita-Mae Bissonnette, RSR, contributed to the writing of this chapter. Sharon Holland, IHM, was the original author and also revised this chapter.

2 The last phrase of the canon, requiring written permission, was added by Pope Francis in *Authenticum charismatis*, on November 1, 2020.

Criteria for Discernment

Mutuae relationes, number 51, helps explain contemporary procedural practices, offering criteria to bishops. What was written in 1978 regarding religious institutes can be applied also in evaluating certain other initiatives.

> In some regions there is noticeable a certain overabundance of initiatives to found new religious institutes. Those who are responsible for discerning the authenticity of each foundation should weigh with humility, of course, but also objectively, constantly, and seeking to foresee clearly the future possibilities—every indication of a credible presence of the Holy Spirit, both to receive His gifts "with thanksgiving and consolation" (*LG* 12) and also to avoid that "institutes may be imprudently brought into being which are useless or lacking in sufficient resources" (*PC* 19).[3]

Bishops are asked to have a great openness, but also wise prudence and strong realism. Not every good initiative or work of good will is destined to be the beginning of a new institute of consecrated life or society of apostolic life. Those who are asked to evaluate a possible new form of consecrated life, (c. 605) should study carefully articles 12 and 62 of the 1996 apostolic exhortation *Vita consecrata.* These articles treat, respectively, new forms of consecrated life and new forms of evangelical life.

At a time when many religious congregations, long established, find themselves struggling with diminishment issues, there is, in fact, also a certain phenomenon of new foundations and new forms of consecrated and of evangelical life. In an expression most uncharacteristic of canon law, the 1983 code recognized this future possibility in canon 605 (*CCEO* c. 571).

Already recognized were two forms of *institutes* of consecrated life—religious and secular—and two individual forms of consecrated life—consecrated virgins and hermits (the Eastern code and *Vita consecrata* also add consecrated widows). Similar to the institutes but distinct and very diverse among themselves are the societies of apostolic life.

Canon 605 has left before us a possibility which we do not know exactly how to recognize. The Church's most recent experience with this came in 1947 when secular institutes were formally recognized as a "new" and complete form of consecrated life, lived *in the world*, expressed in secular occupations and organized without the common life typical of religious. These consecrated

---

3 *MR* 51.

persons would be dedicated to a discreet leavening of the social fabric of a needy world.

Today we see, in many parts of the world, new growing religious institutes, but we also see new structures, which may or may not be new forms of consecrated life. New organizations today often are deliberately structured to represent a microcosm of the Church, with branches of celibate men and of celibate women, a branch of secular clerics and another of married couples. All share a common spirituality and mission; they want ecclesial recognition. Sometimes they ask explicitly to be recognized as a form of consecrated life. Bishops are faced with the discernment of which *Lumen gentium* and canon 605 speak.

Vita consecrata offers some help in this discernment, without claiming to do so definitively. One of the commissions announced in the apostolic exhortation is precisely for the purpose of determining criteria of authenticity to help with the discernment necessary in these cases (n. 62-e). However, three numbers are of particular usefulness for dealing with such questions in the interim: number 30, discussing the relationship between baptismal consecration and consecration through profession of the evangelical counsels; number 12, on new expressions of consecrated life, and number 62, on new forms of evangelical life.

Relationship to Baptismal Consecration

Article 30 of *Vita consecrata* responds to the synod's desire for a clearer expression of the relationship between baptismal consecration and consecration through profession of the evangelical counsels, which, Vatican II teaches, is rooted in the former (*PC* 5; *LG* 44). Historically, religious profession has been presented as a sort of second baptism. Vatican II presented profession as a special and fruitful deepening of baptismal consecration; a means of drawing deeper into union with Christ and of being more authentically configured to him (cfr. *RD* 7).

But this new consecration also differs from baptismal consecration of which, states the text, "it is not a necessary consequence" (*VC* 30). All of the baptized are called to the chastity proper to their state of life, to obedience to God and the Church and to a reasonable detachment from possessions. All are called to holiness, to the perfection of charity (*LG* 42). Baptism, however, does not ask for celibacy or perpetual virginity. It does not require renunciation of possessions or obedience to a superior in a form particular to the evangelical counsels. Here there necessarily enters the concept of distinct vocations. There is a fundamental equality of dignity through Baptism, and there are distinct vocational gifts. The life of the evangelical counsels is a particular following of Jesus' way, as proposed by him to his disciples and personally lived by Jesus (*VC* 31). Chastity for the sake of the Kingdom is called the "door" of consecrated life (*VC* 32). This also provides a key for reading article 12 on new expressions of *consecrated* life and article 62 on new forms of *evangelical* life.

The distinctions made in these articles can be very helpful to those who deal directly with persons who feel called to make new foundations. The importance of this early stage of discerning charism is critical. Sometimes founders or foundresses themselves do not adequately recognize the diverse options for approval within the Church.

Emerging Forms of Consecrated Life

In speaking of "new expressions of consecrated life," *Vita consecrata* 12 recognizes both new foundations of traditional types and the renewal of existing institutes. Then it moves to "new experiments which are seeking an identity of their own in the Church" and which are awaiting official recognition from the Holy See, in the sense of canon 605, which reserves that recognition to the Holy See.[4]

The underlying unity and the characteristic mark of all forms of consecrated life is the one call to follow Jesus—chaste, poor, and obedient—in the pursuit of perfect charity. This must mark new forms as well. What that means and does not mean is more fully drawn out in article 62 on new forms of evangelical life.

Emerging Forms of Evangelical Life

This article (*VC* 12) indicates some of the characteristics of new foundations emerging in the Church today, under the same action of the Holy Spirit. A first point of newness or originality is often that new communities are mixed: men and women; clergy and lay; married and celibate.

---

4 The *Annuario Pontificio*, in a section entitled "Altri Istituti di Vita Consecrata" (Italian translation: Other Institutes of Consecrated Life), lists seven (Rome: Libreria editrice Vaticana, 2019), 1642-1643. They are pontifical. They are not considered religious institutes, secular institutes or societies of apostolic life. Therefore, they fall under canon 605. They are frequently referred to as ecclesial families. For example, on April 15, 2000, the Verbum Dei Missionary Fraternity was established as an ecclesial family. It is a single structure, formed by two branches of consecrated celibates together with a branch of married couples (CICLSAL, Decree of Pontifical Approval of the Verbum Dei Missionary Fraternity, Prot. N. MA. 2-1/98). The two celibate branches profess public perpetual vows and the members of the married couples branch assume the evangelical counsels according to their married state by means of a perpetual promise.

While there are diverse forms of commitment to evangelical life, these new communities tend to be characterized by "an intense aspiration to community life, poverty and prayer" (*VC* 62). Both clerics and lay persons have a share in the governance of such groups and the apostolate focuses on the new evangelization.

The text turns next to the importance of discernment regarding these charisms. If they are to be recognized as consecrated life, as a matter of principle, they must be founded upon the essential theological and canonical elements proper to the consecrated life. Here, in the footnote, reference is made to the initial doctrinal-theological canon of each code (*CIC* c. 573; *CCEO* c. 410).

Bishops are also offered some specific criteria for use at the diocesan level. In studying new groups, they must examine:

- the witness of life and the orthodoxy of founders;
- the spirituality of founders;
- their ecclesial awareness in carrying out their mission;
- methods of formation;
- the manner of incorporation;
- the suitability of members who desire to receive holy orders.

Article 62 moves next to clarify a point which now occurs with increasing frequency, as new communities seek some form of ecclesial recognition: the question of married persons. Appreciation is expressed for the commitment of married persons, and for the *consecration* received through the sacrament of matrimony in the sense of *Gaudium et spes*, number 48. In some new organizations, conjugal chastity is confirmed by a vow. "However," the article continues, "by reason of the above-mentioned principle of discernment, these forms of commitment cannot be included in the specific category of the consecrated life" (*VC* 62).[5]

Characteristics of Authentic Charisms

The above text from *Mutuae relationes* number 51 first indicates motives which are insufficient for a new foundation: simple usefulness or suitability in a field of action or the life of someone who has experienced devotional phenomena. The same number 51 then lists characteristics of authentic charisms:

---

5 They are often referred to as new ecclesial movements.

a) its special origin from the Spirit, distinct, even though not separate, from special personal talents, which become apparent in the sphere of activity and organization;
b) a profound ardor of love to be conformed to Christ in order to give witness to some aspect of His mystery;
c) a constructive love of the Church, which absolutely shrinks from causing any discord in Her.[6]

In the same document, number 12, there is a further indication of a genuine charism, that is, its newness or "genuine originality." The document acknowledges openly: "In its surroundings it may appear troublesome and may even cause difficulties, since it is not always and immediately easy to recognize it as coming from the Spirit" (*MR* 12). The necessary discernment will be aided by the list of qualities and attitudes which ought to characterize founders and their followers:

> ...fidelity to the Lord; docility to His Spirit; intelligent attention to circumstances and an outlook cautiously directed to the signs of the times; the will to be part of the Church; the awareness of subordination to the sacred hierarchy; boldness of initiatives; constancy in the giving of self; humility in bearing with adversities.[7]

In a letter dated May 2, 2016, and addressed to the presidents of conferences of major superiors, the Congregation for Institutes of Consecrated Life and Societies of Apostolic Life requested contributions toward the revision of the 1978 document *Mutuae relationes*. In it, a newly enunciated principle—the "co-essentiality" of the hierarchical and charismatic gifts—was highlighted.[8]

Stage 2: Association (cc. 298-329)

As a *charismatic* gift to the Church, a new institute begins without formality. However, as a charismatic gift *to the Church*, the time comes for seeking a first juridic recognition from the Church.

In the past, a new institute at this stage was referred to as a *pious union*. In the code, this reality is called an "association of the faithful." From canon 579, this stage is not obvious, but the practice is not new. For a new institute, this is the time of growth, of clarification of its identity, and of proof of its stability and authenticity. It is the time for developing its statutes or constitutions.

---

6 *MR* 51.
7 *MR* 12.
8 When the revision of *Mutuae relationes* eventually is released by the Holy See, it hopefully will describe how the concept of "co-essentiality" is evidenced.

Role of Ecclesiastical Authority

The clearest reference to this stage is found in *Pastor bonus,* article 111, regarding the competence of the Congregation for Institutes of Consecrated Life and Societies of Apostolic Life. This in no way alters the responsibility of the diocesan bishop at this stage. Rather it indicates that such associations are a particular category, established with a view to a different future identity.

> Art. 111. Its competence also embraces the third orders and associations of the faithful which are erected with the intention that, after a period of preparation, they may eventually become institutes of consecrated life or societies of apostolic life.[9]

While the legislation regarding this stage is less specific, it is a critically important stage because it lays the foundation for the desired future. New groups seeking approval, and the bishops under whose guidance they are developing will find help in the above cited canons on associations. Some are of particular use in seeing the relationship to ecclesiastical authority.

Canon 299 §1: Associations will be purely private at first, a free initiative of individuals, established by private agreement among themselves. They may remain private unless established for purposes of teaching Christian doctrine or promoting public worship (c. 301 §1). If the name Catholic is to be used, however, there must be permission (c. 300). Obviously, an association seeking recognition as an institute of consecrated life will be working toward erection as a public association.

Canon 299 §2: The praise or recommendation of ecclesiastical authority will be of significant encouragement to a new association if and when the bishop feels that this is merited. Such recommendation does not change the status of the association from being private; however, it gives a note of assurance to prospective members. The group remains under canons 321-326.

Canon 299 §3: To be considered a "recognized" association in the Church, its statutes must be "reviewed" by the competent authority, i.e., the diocesan bishop (c. 312 §1, 3°).

Canon 305: Associations are subject to the vigilance of ecclesiastical authority, including the local ordinary of the diocese. The scope of this vigilance includes the integrity of faith and morals and ecclesiastical discipline. The

---

9 *PB* 111. A new document, *Praedicate evangelium*, is expected to be published by the Holy See to replace *Pastor bonus*. It will make changes to the Roman curia. Parts of this section of the chapter will then need to be compared to the provisions of that new document in case any competencies of the various dicasteries are modified.

bishop has the right of visitation according to law and statutes (cc. 396-398, especially 397). Associations are subject to the governing authority of the bishop according to the other canons on associations.

It is the diocesan bishop who may erect a public association in his own territory (cf. c. 312 §1, 3°). This is done with a formal decree (cf. cc. 48, 50-51), in which it should be explicitly stated that this association is destined to become a religious institute (or a secular institute or a society of apostolic life).

The same bishop, with the same decree, has the authority to approve the statutes of the new association (c. 314). The statutes of an association must recognize a stronger role for the bishop than will be the case later for a diocesan institute. For example, he retains a role in the designation of moderators as well as chaplains (c. 371). Nevertheless, the statutes (or constitutions) should be written, to the greatest extent possible, according to the doctrine and canons which regulate the form of life intended by the founder.

Spiritual Heritage of the Institute

In canon 578 of the common norms for all institutes of consecrated life, there is an exhortation to remain faithful to the spiritual heritage of the institute. In the case of a new foundation, this heritage is just being formulated. This is the time of establishing what is the nature, end, spirit, and character of the institute being formed.

While these four terms from the canon are given diverse explanations at times, their general intent can guide those preparing statutes and those charged with the responsibility of approving them.

- What is the juridic nature of the new foundation? Is it to be religious? secular? monastic? apostolic? clerical? lay? Obviously, these are not all mutually exclusive.
- What is the end or purpose which the founder wishes to accomplish? Why is a new foundation called for? To what needs does it respond?
- What is the spirituality of the new institute? What values of the Gospel urge the founder and his or her followers? What are the characteristics of the spirituality and how are they to be realized in the institute?
- What synthetic expression of the nature, end and spirit gives the institute its particular identity?

According to the determination of this comprehensive identity, the statutes can be developed, including the most suitable form of consecration in a life of the evangelical counsels (or other form of commitment in a society of apostolic life), the most appropriate form of community life in common (or other provisions in the case of secular institutes), the apostolate, norms for formation, initial structures of governance, and, in the case of clerical institutes, the provision for incardination at this early stage.

Stage 3: Diocesan Institute

Although a well-established association will appear very much like a diocesan institute or society, it does not yet enjoy that rightful autonomy of life, in particular of government, which is spoken of in canon 586. It is not yet juridically an institute of consecrated life or a society of apostolic life.

It is at this third step in the overall process that canon 579 formally comes into play. It is at this point that one must consider the full meaning of the phrase "provided that the previous permission of the Apostolic See has been given in writing." In the end, it will be the diocesan bishop who, by his decree, erects the new institute but first he requests the permission to proceed. That the requirements of the canon are for validity was added by Pope Francis, effective June 1, 2016. The requirement to obtain previous written permission of the Holy See was added by the apostolic letter *Authenticum charismatis* in November of 2020.[10]

The list of required documents given to bishops wishing to present an institute to the Holy See includes the following points:

- The names of the founder and of the first superior general, with a brief *curriculum vitae* of each. Obviously, the founder is the key person for understanding the new institute; from him or her comes the spiritual heritage to which future generations must remain faithful. Since it often happens that a bishop or priest begins an institute of women, it follows that the first superior general may well be a different, but also very important, figure in shaping the beginnings.
- An historical-juridical account of the institute from its beginnings, including a copy of the document by which the ecclesiastical authority first approved it. Reading this history, together with the material in the first point above, the Church can consider the petition in the light of the characteristics and criteria called for by ecclesial documents. The decree of erection of the association of the faithful indicates a critical step in the juridic history. It often happens that twenty or more years

10 Shortly after issuing *Authenticum charismatis*, Pope Francis similarly modified the *CCEO*, requiring eparchs to secure written permission before erecting autonomous monasteries and congregations. See Francis, apostolic letter *Ab initio*, effective December 8, 2020, modifying *CCEO* canons 435 §1 and 506 §1.

pass from this decree to the petition for written permission. This, too, highlights the importance of laying sound foundations.

- The constitutions and the directory of the institute, revised in accordance with the Code of Canon Law. If, in fact, the statutes of the association of the faithful are well done, with necessary revisions according to experience, and with increasing clarity around the identity of the new foundation, their preparation as constitutions for the new diocesan institute or society should not be difficult. If the members already are living with integrity the life intended by the founder, the changes needed will be, above all, in the area of government. Certain matters, once reserved to the bishop, will become the competence of the chapter and of the superiors. Further, the vows, or other sacred bonds, previously private, will become public or formally recognized by the Church.

  The proper law—constitutions and directory (by whatever title)—will be studied with care, according to what type of institute is envisioned. Observations will be sent to the diocesan bishop by the Holy See regarding recommended revisions to be made before the bishop may approve the proper law. Written permission may be given at that time, or the Holy See may request to review the changes before giving the written permission now required by canon 579.

- Where applicable, there is to be included a picture of the religious dress of both a professed member and of a novice.

- Up-to-date statistics of membership (year of birth and of temporary and perpetual profession), of houses (including the place and diocese where they are located), and of the works of the institute.

  It is important to note that for the erection of a new institute of diocesan right, at least forty members are needed, the majority of whom have made perpetual private vows (or other form of permanent commitment). Before erecting an institute of consecrated life or a society of apostolic life, the Church asks proof of stability, of the capacity to persevere and grow in the service of the People of God. It is not prudent to recommend to the faithful, through the formality of diocesan erection, an entity which does not offer this hope of vitality.

  Regarding statistics, however, two exceptions are to be noted:

  - For a secular institute, there is no listing of houses as for religious institutes, since there is no obligation to common life or corporate works.

  - For a new foundation dedicated to contemplation, approval is given to proceed with a smaller number.

- An account of the financial patrimony of the institute, including a declaration of debts. It is not necessary to send a detailed report, but one sufficient to indicate to what extent the institute enjoys financial autonomy and whether it has means for the support of its members and works.
- A statement regarding each of the following points:
  - any facts of an extraordinary nature with reference to the institute, such as visions, etc.
  - particular devotions or exercises of piety, specific to the institute, and
  - whether in the diocese of origin there exists already any other institute with the same name and purpose.
- Testimonial letters from the diocesan bishops of those dioceses in which the institute is represented. These letters are to be sent directly to the Holy See, giving the opinion of the bishops about the following: usefulness, stability, discipline of the institute; formation of members; government; administration of goods; liturgical and sacramental dimensions; a sense of being with the Church, particularly in regard to the observance of ecclesiastical discipline as expressed in the common law of the Church and in the diocesan directives.

Stage 4: Pontifical Recognition

The fourth stage, pontifical recognition, is an option but not an obligation. Nevertheless, if an institute has spread into diverse parts of the world, this recognition can reflect better its identity and facilitate its governance.

The documents and information to be sent to the Holy See are essentially the same as for the diocesan process, updated to the current situation. The number of members expected is about 100. It is the bishop of the principal house, at the request of the congregation, who sends the petition, and it is the Holy See which grants the decree.

Mergers and Unions

Various possible reconfigurations of institutes are frequently referred to simply as *mergers*. Nevertheless, the realities are diverse and consequently so also the procedures to be followed in effecting mergers (*fusiones* in the text of the canon) or unions.

A typical example of a merger is that of a small institute being completely absorbed into another larger institute. After the merger, only the larger institute exists as a distinct entity.

In the case of a union of institutes, two, four, or even fifteen institutes unite to create one new institute composed of all of them but not identical to any one of them.

Rationale

Before examining the procedures as such, it is useful to recall why such mergers or unions might take place. In *Perfectae caritatis* we read the concern of the Council Fathers for institutes (and monasteries) which seemed to offer no hope of development. The words are strong:

> Religious foundations and monasteries, however, may sometimes be clearly devoid of any real chance of survival. When this is the conviction of the Holy See and the opinion of the local ordinaries, the acceptance of more novices should be forbidden. Such establishments should, if possible, be amalgamated with some other religious body or monastery of similar character and outlook, one with a more promising future.[11]

Number 22 then speaks of unions between institutes "if their constitutions and customs are practically the same and a kindred spirit animates them . . . especially when of themselves they are excessively small."

Ecclesiae sanctae II then published more specific norms in 1966. In number 39 there is insistence on the importance of a suitable spiritual, psychological and juridical preparation. Number 40 notes the most important points to be taken into consideration: the good of the Church, the proper character of each institute and the freedom of each member. At the end of number 41, there is an important canonical principle to be observed before proceeding to a merger or union: every religious is to be heard and all is to be done in charity.

Mergers

Canon 582 reserves procedures for mergers and unions to the Holy See:

> Mergers *(fusiones)* and unions of institutes of consecrated life are reserved to the Apostolic See only; confederations and federations are also reserved to it.

Despite this reservation, the greatest part of the preparation takes place before a formal petition is submitted to the Holy See. Considerable time and

---

11 *PC* 21.

energy are needed for the spiritual and psychological, as well as juridic preparation.

A small institute must study its situation well—the lack of vocations, the age of members, the institute's economic state, and the difficulties in responding to apostolic commitments. All of the members need to participate in the discernment regarding a merger, and, having decided in favor of the idea, the superior general will most probably make contact with a number of institutes which have a similar purpose and spirituality.

The larger institute also needs to give careful consideration to the proposal and to its capacity to receive and integrate the members of the smaller institute. It may be the case that an eventual merger will affect one province in particular, in which case they should be involved in the discernment in a particular way.

Required Documentation from Institute Requesting Merger

The documents required eventually by the Holy See illustrate some of the kinds of information which will have been exchanged between the institutes beforehand.

The institute which is asking for the merger must present the following documentation.

- The petition of the superior general;
- A brief history of the institute;
- A list of the members: name, surname, date of birth, of temporary and of perpetual profession;
- A list of the houses, the dioceses in which they are located, and their ministry;
- The motives for requesting the merger; (Why with this institute? How will this merger serve the well-being of the Church?)
- The method used for voting and the result of the voting: in favor and against; (Such procedures may include various soundings of opinion, action in general chapter, and an individual referendum involving all members.)
- The intention of those who are opposed to the merger on the part of their institute.

Options for Individual Members

At this point a question often arises about what choices an individual who is opposed may have if his or her institute is deciding to merge with another institute. If those opposing a merger are few in number, their *No* will not prevent the process from going forward. However, such persons have every right to charity and to a clear explanation of their canonical possibilities.

They may, of course, remain and move with their institute into the new, even though this would not be their preferred solution. Another option is to request an indult of transfer to another institute, or they may ask for an indult of departure. These are hard choices which require charity and patience. It must be clear, however, that if the merger is effected through a decree of the Holy See, all members pass into the new in their present status of vows unless they have taken some other action.

Required Documentation from Receiving Institute

From the institute accepting the merger, less documentation is required. They must present a letter from the superior general, along with the consent of the general council. For this purpose, it is useful to submit an excerpt from the council minutes showing the formal act of readiness to accept the merger. The accepting institute should also present a brief history of the institute and the number of members.

Additional Requirements

Both institutes must present an account of the process through which they have prepared their members for the merger. Likewise, both must have ascribed to a preliminary agreement for the disposition of temporalities according to the norms of canon and civil law. This agreement should be signed by both superiors general.

It is the usual case that the temporal goods of the institute asking to merge go to the institute accepting it. However, it is always necessary to observe the intent of benefactors and to observe civil law in addition to canon law. It is necessary to have prudent advice regarding the manner and timing of changing civil titles of ownership and making necessary changes in civil documents of incorporation for the institute and for apostolic works separately incorporated civilly.

The final piece of documentation comes from the bishops concerned. The *nihil obstat* is asked of bishops where the requesting institute is located, especially if it is of diocesan right or is a pontifical institute represented in only a few dioceses.

Unions

As noted, the notion of a union is that of two or more institutes each relinquishing their distinct juridic identity to mutually form one new institute, with a name and proper law they will agree upon, and bringing together their respective temporal goods, observing canon and civil law. Its internal structure will vary depending on the number of institutes, of members and the geographic spread of the new institute.

As noted above, the Church has encouraged the union of institutes having almost the same constitutions, practices, and spirit. As is well known, there are many institutes which historically go back to the same founder and which are marked by the same spiritual heritage.

Spiritual and Psychological Preparation

It is often the case that before speaking of the union of institutes, there has been the formation of a federation in order to study together their common charism and to permit members to grow in mutual relationships. Federations frequently promote common projects not only of study but of apostolate; often formation resources have been shared. It is often from a federation-type structure that there emerges an informal organism which begins to coordinate efforts toward the spiritual and psychological preparation of members, prior to seeking juridic union.

Juridic Preparation

The eventual procedures and documents are analogous to those for merger. However, in this case, every institute is the institute which is asking for union and there is no receiving institute. Every institute must prepare and consult every religious. Each institute will study the matter in a general chapter, either ordinary or extraordinary.

While the code does not state the detail of these matters, it is the general practice that there must be a two-thirds vote in favor of union in the general chapter for an institute to continue to move forward toward a formal petition. After the chapters, there will be continuing preparations which, at a certain point must include anew a consultation with every member in order to know his or her intention in the face of an eventual union. In this case, it is the practice of the Holy See to consider a petition only if at least eighty percent of the members express themselves in favor of being a part of the new institute to be created by the union.

As the process continues, a union requires preparations not called for in the case of mergers. Since the result will be an entirely new institute, it will have to have a new name. Likewise, it will have to have its own proper law. Depending on the participating institutes there may be one text which can serve as a base for developing their new proper law. In some cases, a federation will already have moved to a common core text which can be the basis of development. Depending on the size and extension of the new institute, structures of governance will have to be decided upon. Provisional texts will often be reviewed in the individual general chapters of the participating institutes. Certain matters, such as the composition of the first general chapter of the new institute and certain points of governance, will have to be approved provisionally by the Holy See before the formal erection of the institute. Once it has been erected, some of the first acts of the new institute's general chapter will be the election of the general superior and council, and the approval of the constitutions to be submitted to the Holy See for formal approval.

As in the case of mergers, one of the documents presented with the petition for the union will be the preliminary financial agreements. Expert assistance is essential to make sure that not only canon law is properly observed but also the civil law of the places involved.

In cases of union, letters are asked from the bishops in whose dioceses the generalates are located. These are to be sent directly to the Holy See, expressing their opinion in the matter. It is useful if the bishop agrees to provide a copy to the requesting institute.

As in the case of mergers, every member, when the decree of establishment of the new institute goes into effect, becomes a member of the new institute, in the state he or she previously had in their original institute: perpetual vows, temporary vows, exclaustration, transfer. Anyone who has not taken positive steps to alter their status, moves into the new institute. Those who are definitely not in favor of the new have the same choices indicated for mergers. Obviously, these options also remain after the institute has been erected.

Coming to Completion and the Role of Commissaries[12]

Throughout history, hundreds of congregations, once flourishing, have ceased to exist. Reasons have been diverse. In today's complex society, institutes may find themselves diminishing in numbers, in finances, and in the ability to maintain life and ministry.

For many years, mergers and unions gave new life to declining institutes and their ministries. However, as Pope John Paul II noted that consecrated life will continue in the Church, but that "individual institutes have no claim to permanence" (*VC* 63). Other solutions have been sought more recently. In

12 Also see chapter one, The Role of the Commissary.

addition to the conferences of major superiors,[13] organizations such as the Resource Center for Religious Institutes (RCRI)[14] and the National Religious Retirement Office (NRRO)[15] have offered assistance to institutes in evaluating their resources, both personal and financial, for finding ways forward.

As institutes recognize that they can no longer continue as they are, they may already have moved to simplify governance structures and to employ persons with expertise to guide their finances. They may have made the difficult decision to no longer accept new members. They will have consulted both civil and canon lawyers. Essential will be their efforts to involve all members and to maintain clear and sensitive communication with all.

This sort of planning is sometimes called "coming to completion." This is not a process regulated by the code, although many of the steps will be guided by its principles. As the institute recognizes that it can no longer elect a general government from among its remaining members, their chapter may move to the difficult conclusion that they must request a commissary.

Although this figure of a "commissary" does not appear in the code, the practice of appointing religious commissaries has existed. In the variety of dictionary definitions, it usually carries the connotation of taking on a position of oversight, sometimes in the place of another.

The contemporary use for religious is a person, preferably a religious, appointed to serve in the position of superior general of a similar institute. When an institute determines to request such as appointment, it is best if they know someone to recommend.

The appointment of a commissary comes from the bishop or from the Holy See, depending on the status of the requesting institute (diocesan or pontifical). Most requesting institutes are of women religious, and preferably a woman religious is chosen to assist them. She will have a council, as must all superiors, to be used according to the canons (c. 627). The councilors may be from the requesting institute, or from the institute of the commissary. The constitutions of the institute requesting assistance are to be followed to the extent possible in governing.

---

13 In the United States, these include the Leadership Conference for Women Religious (www.lcwr.org); the Conference of Major Superiors of Women Religious (cmswr.org); and the Conference of Major Superiors of Men (www.cmsm.org).

14 See www.trcri.org.

15 See www.usccb.org/offices/national-religious-retirement-office.

Together with members of the institute, the Commissary will seek to plan for and to carry out all the necessary acts of closure when that time comes. Primary, of course, is the well-being of the remaining members, and provision for the final disposition of properties and financial assets, observing both civil and canon law.

By its nature as a collegial public juridic person (c. 120), the institute is perpetual unless legitimately suppressed. With a commissary in place, that formal act of suppression from the Holy See (c. 584) need not take place until the final member is deceased, then legally giving closure to the juridic person.

The process discussed here, with the Commissary leading an institute to completion, takes the place of much that is discussed below regarding suppression under other circumstances.

Suppression

The suppression of an institute of consecrated life or a society of apostolic life, whether diocesan or pontifical, is reserved to Holy See:

> Canon 584 The suppression of an institute pertains only to the Apostolic See; a decision regarding the temporal goods of the institute is also reserved to the Apostolic See.

The same is true of the only house of a religious institute (c. 616 §2) and of the suppression of an autonomous monastery of nuns.

> Canon 616 §4 To suppress an autonomous monastery of nuns belongs to the Apostolic See, with due regard for the prescripts of the constitutions concerning its goods.

Initiation of the Suppression Process

As has been seen, the Church prefers the merger or union of monasteries or institutes to their actual suppression. Should it be necessary however, the initiative may come from within the institute or monastery itself, or from external ecclesiastical authority. The criteria have been seen in *Perfectae caritatis* 21-22. If there is a grave crisis of government or if there is scandal there may be motive for suppression, even initiated against the wishes of the members. However, an institute able to govern itself and to provide for its members has the right to continue.

Juridic Steps

A first step toward suppression, whatever the source of the initiative, will be a formal visitation. For a diocesan institute, this will most probably be conducted by the diocesan bishop of the principal house, with the assistance of other appropriate persons. For a monastery this may be by the bishop or a member of the First Order if there exists this relationship. In the case of a pontifical institute, a visitator would be named by the Holy See.

A visitation will include meetings with the superior and council, with the community and with each individual. This should provide an overall indication of the situation and the disposition of each individual. A detailed report would then be sent to the Holy See, requesting the suppression, and explaining the reasons for it, noting the dispositions of the chapter and the individual religious, explaining how accommodation can be made for the religious who remain (in other monasteries of the same Order, with other religious congregations, in diocesan facilities for aged religious), and recommendations—taking the constitutions of monasteries into consideration—for the resolution of financial questions and the temporal goods which exist or which may be realized from the sale of properties. As in other similar matters, sound legal and financial advice will indicate how just and charitable provision can be made for the remaining members, establishing trust funds if necessary.

If, as has been seen, careful and lengthy preparation is needed in the case of mergers and unions, the same is surely equally true of suppressions.

The suppression of groups which are still public associations of the faithful, is regulated by canon 320.

Communication with the Holy See

The 1988 circular letter from the predecessor of the Congregation for Institutes of Consecrated Life and Societies of Apostolic Life providing criteria for the preparation of reports to be sent periodically to the Holy See from religious institutes and societies of apostolic life, was replaced in 2008. The current document draws upon the post-synodal apostolic exhortation, *Vita consecrata* (1996), for its criteria. The text also provides the option of sending the report given to the chapter of the institute, with any necessary additional information.

In 1988, there was a separate document addressed to secular institutes. The 2008 text is addressed to all institutes of consecrated life (not just religious) and to societies of apostolic life. This language reflects the organization of the code itself.

The text of the 2008 document, "Suggested Guidelines for the Preparation of Periodic Reports on the Status and Life of Institutes of Consecrated Life and Societies of Apostolic Life," follows.

CONGREGATION FOR INSTITUTES OF CONSECRATED LIFE AND SOCIETIES OF APOSTOLIC LIFE

SUGGESTED GUIDELINES FOR THE PREPARATION OF PERIODIC REPORTS

on the Status and Life of

Institutes of Consecrated Life and Societies of Apostolic Life

(cf. CIC can. 592 §1)

Attachment to Prot. n. SpR 640/2008

Prot. n. SpR 640/2008

The Holy See takes special interest in consecrated life "deeply rooted in the example and teaching of Christ the Lord, and a gift of God the Father to his Church through the Holy Spirit" (*Vita consecrata* 1). In particular, it expresses care for Institutes of Consecrated Life and Societies of Apostolic Life: their universal presence and the evangelical character of their witness are decisive elements for the mission of the Church and her call to communion and holiness (cf. *Vita consecrata* 9). For these reasons this Dicastery places great importance on the Report on the Status and Life of Institutes of Consecrated Life and Societies of Apostolic Life which Supreme Moderators are to send to this Congregation at the time of their General Chapters. In a clear manner these reports foster communion with the Holy See in conformity with can. 592 § 1 of the *Code of Canon Law*. In addition to supplying useful, factual information, an attentive reading of these reports enhances the theological, juridical and pastoral reflections of this Congregation for Institutes of Consecrated Life and Societies of Apostolic Life, thus helping to concretise the service which this Dicastery is called to offer to consecrated life in these times of social and cultural complexity.

To facilitate the preparation of this informative report, the Dicastery suggests a series of themes to be covered in order to ensure that the Report can serve the purpose for which it is sought. Supreme Moderators are asked either to follow the format of the enclosed brochure "Suggested Guidelines for the Preparation of Periodic Reports to the Holy See" when preparing the Document or to send the Report on the Status of the Institute presented to the Chapter with supplemental information regarding themes that might not be present in said Report. May the Lord abundantly bless you for your service of leadership in ecclesial communion. We send heartfelt greetings in the Lord to each member of your community as together you seek to live Gospel values in your search for God and His Kingdom.

Vatican, Pentecost 2008

Franc Card. Rodé, C.M.
Prefect

+ Gianfranco A. Gardin, OFM Conv.
Secretary

1. FOUNDATION, CHARISM AND MISSION OF THE INSTITUTE
(cf. *Vita consecrata* 36-37)

Provide a brief description of the identity of the Institute and of the aspects of the founding Charism which were most stressed in recent years.

2. A BRIEF AND SUMMARIZED STATISTICAL REPORT
(cf. *Vita consecrata* 40)

Members

- Number of perpetually professed members with age distribution.
- Number of temporarily professed members with age distribution.
- Number of *formandi* in each level of formation, divided by continent of origin.
- Distribution of members according to Continents.
- Number of departures and primary reasons.
- Houses/Regions/Provinces/Delegations/ Zones
- Number and divisions according to Continents.

3. CONSTITUTIONS, RULES, AND CUSTOMS OF THE INSTITUTE
(cf. *Vita consecrata* 36-37; 68)

- Date of the latest approved revision of the Constitutions?
- Are the Constitutions presently in need of revision?
- When was the *Ratio institutionis* last revised?
- What means are used in ongoing formation to assist members in their knowledge of and fidelity to the Constitution and Rules of the Institute?

4. THE PRIMACY OF THE SPIRIT
(cf. *Vita consecrata* 17-19; 35; 39; 88-90)

- What are some tangible signs of the members' desire to respond to the call to holiness through the *sequela Christi* and the living of Gospel values?
- Describe the members' commitment to Liturgy, the Word, and personal prayer as responses to the Spirit's promptings to be configured to Christ.

5. COMMUNION IN COMMUNITY
(cf. *Vita consecrata* 41-45; 69-71)

- Do the members manifest an appreciation of Consecrated life, lived as *signum fraternitatis*?
- Do they give witness to being communities rich in "joy and the Holy Spirit" (Acts 13,52)?
- How much emphasis is placed on *lectio divina*, faith-sharing and

community meetings, etc.?

- How much importance is placed upon "life lived in common" and the spiritual and human growth of individual members?
- How are elderly members cared for? What means are taken to form new leadership?
- How is authority exercised within the Institute at the various levels (Houses, Regions, Provinces, etc.) and what means are used to facilitate communication and relationships among the various levels?

6. MISSION AND MINISTRY
(cf. *Vita consecrata* 72-83; 96-99)

- How do members manifest their appreciation of Consecrated Life lived in the Church as *servitum caritatis*?
- In what ministries are members of the community currently involved and how do these ministries reflect the founding charism in the various Cultures where members serve?
- What programs of ongoing formation are offered to members in order to assure an updated and inculturated apostolic spirituality?
- In the light of internal demographic shifts, what measures are being employed by the Institute to respond to its mission in the Church?
- How is the Institute responding to new needs in the mission and the world?

7. VOCATION RECRUITMENT/FORMATION
(cf. *Vita consecrata* 63-71)

- When were the *Ratio formationis* and the *Ratio studiorum* last revised?
- What means are taken to recruit new members?
- What criteria are used in the selection and retention of new members?
- How are members formed in the Institute?
- Does the Institute form part of any Inter-Institute formation program?

8. RELATIONS IN THE CHURCH
(cf. *Vita consecrata* 45; 52-53)

- How are members formed in the spirituality of communion, in *sentire cum Ecclesia*, in insertion of communities into the Dioceses in which they serve, relationships with Bishops and Pastors?
- Does the Institute form part of any Federations or Unions of Institutes with similar charisms? (cf. can. 582)

- Is the Institute a member of the International and National Conferences of Superiors General?

9. FINANCIAL STATUS AND PROPERTIES
(cf. *Vita consecrata* 89-90)

- What is the status of the Institute's finances and properties?
- Is the community able to support its missions and members?
- What provisions are made for the sharing of goods within the Institute and for the medical and retirement care of the members?
- What initiatives does the Institute undertake to share its goods with the poor?

10. STATUS OF THE INSTITUTE
(cf. *Vita consecrata* 84-95)

- What are the major successes and challenges which the Institute has experienced in recent years?
- What are the major issues which the Institute must confront during the next administration?
- What are the short- and long-range plans for the future of the Institute?
- Other questions of particular interest.

Vatican, Pentecost 2008

CHAPTER 3

Policies in Institutes of Consecrated Life

Rosemary Smith, SC[1]

Institutes of consecrated life are human communities—living, social bodies—directed toward fostering in members lives of compassion, ministry and prayerful union with God. Laws and regulations within an institute of consecrated life should meet the human need for order while at the same time foster the life and spirit of the institute and free the members to live fully as children of God.

The constitution and directory, or secondary document, of each institute of consecrated life sets forth the skeletal framework of the institute. They articulate the character and purposes of the institute and describe the manner in which the evangelical counsels are observed according to the charism of the particular institute. These foundational documents bind all members. Changes to the constitution first require approval of the general chapter and then the approval of either the diocesan bishop for a diocesan institute or of the Congregation for Institutes of Consecrated Life and Societies of Apostolic Life (CICLSAL) for a pontifical institute. In addition to these foundational documents, both general and provincial chapters may enact particular law for the respective institute or province, and the leader of the institute or province may also issue directives within the limits of her/his authority.

Types of Policies

As guidance for members and leaders alike, institutes often find it helpful to develop additional policies to complement the institute's foundational documents and chapter enactments. The lowest level policy may simply be an informal, internal administrative guide to assist the superior or council member as she or he works with an individual member or a group on a matter of some

---

1 Margaret A. Stallmeyer, CDP, and Richard B. Williams, OP, contributed to the writing of the original version of this chapter. Rosemary Smith, SC, was the original author and also revised this chapter.

importance but one which is not an everyday occurrence. Such policies might resemble a checklist of questions to be asked or tasks to be done. Examples include a list of tasks to be completed when preparing for a major gathering of members, steps to be taken in deciding to take a congregational public stance, or a checklist for exploring a collaborative or co-sponsored undertaking with another institute. Informal policies such as these serve as guidance and bind only to the degree the superior finds them helpful.

Most institutes also find it beneficial to have in place other, often mundane policies regulating various aspects of community life. Having policies in place and accessible to all members can reinforce community values as well as forestall misunderstandings and obviate spur-of-the moment decision-making. Policies of this nature common to many institutes include those dealing with a range of financial matters, e.g., credit card use, checking accounts, member gifts, patrimony and cession of administration, and social screens for congregational investments. Other policies of this type concern areas of common life such as ministry changes, use of social media, healthcare power of attorney, sabbaticals, retreats, vacations and/or use of vacation homes, record retention, access to archives, travel, driving policies, cemeteries, gift acceptance, member income (especially from pensions), associates, expectations upon the death of a member in a local community, and fundraising.[2] These policies are best developed in consultation with members and experts in the respective field.

In a category by itself are policies dealing with member misconduct such as sexual abuse, financial malfeasance, substance abuse or other addictive behaviors. Emerging contemporary experience has raised awareness about the prevalence of these behaviors within all segments of society—including within institutes of consecrated life—the devasting harm caused by them, and the high costs of not attending to them. Such misconduct harms those who are victims, the perpetrating member, the institute and the Church itself. It is imperative that each institute have well-defined policies and procedures for 1) ongoing education of members, 2) safe environment expectations, and 3) handling of any allegations of misconduct of this nature. Policies should include clear definitions of:

- sexual abuse of minors,
- vulnerable adults,
- sexual harassment, and
- hostile work environments, etc.

---

2 Examples and fuller treatment of many of these areas can be found on the website of the Resource Center for Religious Institutes (www.trcri.org).

Policies should also include provisions for:

- the obligation to report such misconduct;
- how to address an allegation incriminating a current or former general superior;[3]
- the immediate reporting of any allegation of sexual abuse of a minor by a member to appropriate civil authorities; and
- the conducting of internal investigations or reviews of an allegation of sexual abuse by a member by an independent body of qualified individuals from diverse disciplines, e.g., law enforcement, social work, psychology, child development.

It is important that the institute's policies be followed assiduously as written; civil liability can increase when an institute's internal policy is not adhered to. Clerical religious institutes and societies of apostolic life are required by *Essential Norms* numbers 2 and 4 (particular law for the United States) to have a written policy and to establish a review board; lay religious institutes are strongly urged by church leaders, canon and civil lawyers to develop member misconduct policies and single institute or inter-community review boards. Some diocesan bishops in the United States are now requiring every institute of consecrated life to attest to the existence of a member misconduct policy and to an independent review board as a condition of ministering within the diocese.[4]

Developing Policies

Developing institute-wide or province-wide policies, when done with forethought and care, can be a rewarding undertaking. A small cross-section of members with pertinent expertise and broad experience collaborating with leadership to discuss an issue important to the institute and developing a policy for addressing it, can itself be educative and can build ownership. The commitment of necessary time and resources also conveys the importance of the matter being addressed.

---

3 See Francis, motu proprio *Vos estis lux mundi* 3 §§1, 3, May 7, 2019: *L'Osservatore Romano*, May 10, 2019.

4 As of May 2018, the Pontifical Council of the Laity, Family and Life began requiring all international associations of the faithful and lay movements seeking pontifical approval to have in place policies and procedures for the prevention, required reporting, and handling of sexual abuse by members or in their apostolates. Such associations and lay movements are also required to report and comply with civil law. A helpful resource from the Resource Center for Religious Institutes is a "Q&A for Review Boards for Lay Religious Institutes and Societies of Apostolic Life" at https://cdn.ymaws.com/www.trcri.org/resource/resmgr/2021updates/qa_for_review_boards_for_rel.pdf.

Institutes of consecrated life with multiple provinces may determine that some policies are best held at the institute level while other policies are more appropriately held at the province or regional level. Diverse cultures, financial and/or travel constraints, social milieux and different civil legal systems can influence which policies are best developed and administered at which level of governance. Since state laws vary, member insertion into different civil legal systems may necessitate a certain flexibility within some policies in order to conform with applicable civil laws and definitions. Examples of definitions which vary from state to state include the requirements for executing a valid power of attorney for health care and the definitions of sexual abuse and vulnerable persons.

Following are some general guidelines for developing policies for institutes of consecrated life:

- *Root the policy in the institute's charism and tie it to the institute's mission and purpose.* Institute policies which dovetail with community values can motivate members to strive for behaviors, conditions and processes which are life-giving for all.
- *Use clear, straightforward, unambiguous language.* All members should be able to understand what the policy is stating.
- *Define terms.* Never assume common understanding of technical terms, e.g., land trust, vulnerable person, power of attorney, etc. A simple glossary may be helpful as an addendum to the policy.
- *Be realistic.* Do not create expectations, e.g., time frame, type of response or action, which may not be able to be honored.
- *Write as for a public document.* The policy should be non-defensive, accurate and contemporary. Identify sources, authorities, and agencies, if applicable. Even if not intended, the document could become public.
- *Include a timeframe for regular review.* Regular review of the institute's policies helps assure they are current and useful.

Implementing Policies

Once a policy is finalized it must be made known to all whom it affects, namely, the members of the institute or of the province. The policy should be communicated in writing by the person with the authority to bind the members, together with notice about the date it takes effect.[5] Many institutes find it helpful

---

5 Canon 37 of the 1983 Code of Canon Law states that an administrative act which regards the external forum must be put in writing, and canon 7 states that a law is established when it is promulgated.

to publish for their members a manual, either online or in hard copy, in which the various administrative policies are compiled and readily accessible. For certain policies, circumstances may suggest circulation beyond the membership for the purpose of information. Examples where a wider audience might be applicable include policies on fund-raising, on access to the archives, or on compensation of members. Exceptions to policies may always be made by those in authority, i.e., the general superior for the institute or the provincial superior for the province or by others to whom the superior has delegated authority to grant exceptions.

Some form of education should precede or accompany a *new* policy. Education or socialization can deepen understanding about an issue, resolve questions and build ownership. Depending on the import of the policy, education can take the form of an in-service program, a written history and rationale, recommended readings, a sheet of frequently asked questions, or online resources such as an online conference, a prerecorded presentation, or a list of available resources. The amount and type of education depends upon the familiarity of the members with the matter of the policy, the urgency of the topic and the newness of the policy. For instance, if the policy is the result of chapter deliberation, education on the policy might revolve around some of the main points of chapter discussion. If the policy concerns a "hot-button" topic, the more opportunity the better for members to be able to ask questions and to wrestle with the issues and tensions prompting the institute or province to develop the policy.

The ordinary process for a policy to be changed would be to have the promulgating authority issue a revision, including the new effective date. Practically speaking, however, policy changes can sometimes be a result of informal custom, desuetude, or non-adherence. If this seems to be the fate of a policy on the books, the leadership should assess the extent and effects of non-compliance and decide on appropriate action—either reconsider the wisdom, value and timeliness of the policy, tweak the parts which seem to be problematic, or address those who are non-compliant.

The fundamental determinant for establishing, assessing, updating, or eliminating a policy should be: *Is the policy fostering the life of the community or is it a stumbling block?*

CHAPTER FOUR

ADMISSION OF CANDIDATES
CANONS 641-645

John Chrysostom Kozlowski, OP[1]

By completing the necessarily demanding admissions process, a candidate signals an earnest desire for the life of a religious institute or society of apostolic life. Admission, however, cannot be granted solely on the basis of a candidate's desire. The candidate's suitability must be demonstrated. A careful implementation of the few canons that regulate the admissions process (cc. 641-645) will promote a rigorous screening of candidates. This screening, in turn, will serve as a form of quality control to help ensure that only those whose suitability is demonstrated are admitted. Ultimately, a thorough vetting of candidates is in the best interests of both the religious institute/society and the candidate. To advance these interests, this chapter will briefly describe the canonical norms, explain how they can be implemented by an institute/society, and conclude with an appendix of various sample forms that an institute/society can modify to meet its own needs.

Canons 641-645

Canon 641

Canon 641, a canon that is only applicable to religious institutes, affirms that major superiors of such institutes, according to the norm of the proper law, have the right to admit candidates to the novitiate of their circumscriptions (e.g., provincial superiors for the province). The institute's proper law can determine whether the major superior must first receive the deliberative or consultative

---

1 The original author of this chapter, Rev. David M. Hynous, OP, died on March 24, 2016. In the original chapter, Rev. Hynous credited Sister Marianne Burkhard, OSB, Rev. James J. Conn, SJ, Rev. Bernard Johnson, OCSO (deceased), and Rev. Gary M. Luiz, CPPS, as contributors. The revising author, Rev. John Chrysostom Kozlowsli, OP, acknowledges Rev. Jacob Bertrand Janczyk, OP, and Tracey Sharp, SCRH, for their contributions, as well as Rev. Benedict Croell, OP, and Rev. Andrew Hofer, OP (authors of *A Living Sacrifice: Guidance for Men Discerning Religious Life* [Valdosta, GA: Vianney Vocations, 2019] 153-165), for their practical insights regarding the application process.

vote of his/her council or a specially designated vocation council before admitting a candidate.

Since canon 641 is not applicable to societies of apostolic life, this means that it is left to the proper law of societies to determine which superior is competent to admit candidates and whether he/she must first receive the deliberative or consultative vote of some council (see c. 735 §2). Further, a novitiate, strictly speaking, is not required for societies, although admission to a period of probation is required; thus, societies can call the probationary period a "novitiate" or use some other term (c. 735 §1). For the sake of continuity with religious institutes, this chapter will speak about admission to a society's novitiate, but that novitiate—like any probationary period in a society, regardless of its name—is not governed by canons 646-653. Rather, the society's proper law defines the nature and length of its probationary period.

Before being admitted to an institute/society, a candidate is to be suitably prepared for life in the same institute/society (cc. 597 §2 and 732). The current Code of Canon Law does not prescribe a formal pre-novitiate program known as postulancy, although this was required for many institutes under the discipline of the 1917 code. This means that the structure and length of the pre-novitiate preparations are left to each institute/society to establish in its proper law. That being said, for the period of preparation that takes place outside of a community of the institute/society the candidate should already be encouraged to deepen his/her routine of daily life in accordance with the prayer forms and spirituality of the proper law of the institute/society (e.g., attendance at weekday Mass insofar as possible, regular reception of the sacrament of reconciliation, praying morning prayer and evening prayer, personal prayer, etc.). This includes having a spiritual director and living in a manner that is befitting of someone who desires to one day profess the evangelical counsels.

As an exception, women's institutes entirely dedicated to contemplative life do not enjoy the same freedom to shape their pre-novitiate programs. Before a candidate can be admitted to the novitiate in these institutes, she must first observe a twelve-month aspirancy, during which she spends time in and out of the community as determined by the major superior and her council, and then a 12-month postulancy, during which she lives in the monastery.[2] Only after the candidate completes the aspirancy and postulancy can the major superior, in

---

2 See CICLSAL, instruction *Cor orans*, April 1, 2018, at http://www.vatican.va/roman curia/congregations/ccscrlife/documents/rc_con_ccscrlife_doc_20180401_cor-orans_en.html.

accord with the institute's proper law, admit the candidate to the monastery's novitiate.

Canon 642

Canon 642 lists the basic qualities a candidate must possess in order to be admitted to the novitiate: sufficient age, appropriate health, suitable character, and sufficient maturity. A candidate's positive qualities must be weighed against the nature, goals, apostolate, and lifestyle of a specific institute/society; does the candidate possess the necessary qualities to embrace the life of this specific institute/society? A significant factor to consider is whether the institute/society is dedicated entirely to the contemplative life or the combination of a contemplative and active lifestyle. It is worth noting that a favorable judgment that results in the candidate's admission only regards the candidate's readiness to begin the novitiate. From this judgment it is not appropriate to conclude that the candidate is necessarily qualified to profess vows. Only after subsequent evaluations during the course of formation can such a determination be made.

In order to assess competently and thoroughly a candidate's health (physical, mental, psychological, etc.), character, and maturity (physical, intellectual, emotional, social, etc.), canon 642 permits institutes/societies to make use of experts. By indicating that experts can be consulted "if necessary," the canon allows for some discretion in this area. However, since the institute/society has the duty and right to ensure that candidates have the requisite qualities to embrace such a life, the institute/society is well within its rights to require medical and psychological examinations as a condition for admission.[3] Of course, having such a requirement does not at all minimize the obligation of the institute/society to limit access to the examinations' results to select personnel (e.g., major superior, vocation director, novice director, vocation councilors, etc.). In this regard, it is noteworthy that canon 642 refers to canon 220, which protects the candidate's rights to a good reputation and

---

3 Since the publication of the 2001 *Procedural Handbook*, psychological testing has become commonplace for those entering religious institutes and societies of apostolic life. In 2008, the Congregation for Catholic Education issued *Guidelines for The Use of Psychology in the Admission and Formation of Candidates for the Priesthood* (http://www.vatican.va/roman_curia/congregations/ccatheduc/documents/rc_con_ccatheduc_doc_20080628_orientamenti_en.html, accessed March 1, 2021), and in 2015 the USCCB's Committee on Clergy, Consecrated Life, and Vocations issued *Guidelines for the Use of Psychology in Seminary Admissions* (http://ccc.usccb.org/flipbooks/cclv-guidelines-psychology-admissions/files/assets/basic-html/page-2.html, accessed March 1, 2021). Although these resources are intended for the admission and formation of seminarians, they have great value for those who work in formation ministry in men's and women's institutes and societies.

privacy. Therefore, even if a candidate authorizes the release of information to select personnel and waives the right to review his/her records, the candidate is not waiving the right to a good reputation or privacy.

In addition to having the necessary qualities, the candidate must also demonstrate that he/she wants to join the institute/society for the right reasons (c. 597 §1). Even if the candidate has all the desired qualities, this vocation is ultimately a calling from God, and so the major superior and vocation director need to discern whether the candidate truly seeks God.[4] It is not sufficient for the candidate to be motivated only or chiefly by human reasons. In such a case, the candidate should not be admitted.

Canon 643

Canon 643 §1 lists the impediments that invalidate admission to the novitiate. It is critical that institutes/societies be attentive to these invalidating provisions. The reason is simple. One who is invalidly admitted to the novitiate cannot complete a valid novitiate, which means he/she cannot validly profess religious vows. The following individuals are impeded from valid admission to the novitiate:

1° one who lacks the minimum age (the minimum age for admittance is 17);

2° one who is bound by an existing marriage bond;

3° one who is bound by an existing sacred bond in a religious institute or secular institute, or an existing bond of incorporation in a society of apostolic life (excepting a case of transfer);

4° one who is entering induced by force, grave fear, or deceit about the essential elements of this life or the institute/society, or one whom the admitting superior is induced to admit by force, grave fear, or deceit (i.e., when a candidate intentionally conceals some fact or asserts a falsehood as fact because he/she thinks admission will be refused if the institute/society knows the truth *and* the institute/society would have rightly refused admission if it had known the truth about a current or past serious illness, past criminal conviction, etc.);[5] and

---

4 See *Rule of St. Benedict* 58, trans. by Anthony C. Meisel and M. L. del Mastro (New York: Doubleday, 1975).

5 For additional reflections on fraud, see William H. Woestman, "Canon 641, §1, 3°: Invalid Admission to the Novitiate Resulting from Fraud," in *CLSA Advisory Opinions on Institutes of Consecrated Life and Societies of Apostolic Life*, ed. Patrick M. Cooney (Washington, DC: CLSA, 2017) 121-123.

5° one who intentionally conceals (i.e., deliberately does not reveal) a previous sacred bond in a religious institute or secular institute or a previous bond of incorporation in a society of apostolic life (this does not regard a novitiate or pre-novitiate program, although these could be objects of deceit).

In accord with canon 643 §2, individual institutes/societies may add other impediments and decide whether they affect the validity of admission.

Canon 644

Canon 644 covers two additional categories of candidates. In neither case does the canon touch upon the validity of admission.

First, a secular cleric (priest or deacon) can only be admitted with the previous knowledge of his bishop. It is important to note that this canon does not require the bishop to consent to the cleric's admission. It only requires that the bishop be consulted. This ensures that the bishop is given an opportunity to inform the major superior about the cleric's suitability for the institute's/society's life and his fidelity to his clerical obligations (see canons 273-289). In the end, the bishop cannot refuse or otherwise prevent the cleric from being admitted. However, if the bishop informs the major superior that the care of souls in his diocese will be seriously harmed unless the cleric's admission is delayed for a brief time (e.g., the bishop needs time to rearrange the distribution of clergy in order to cover the cleric's ministries), the superior would do well to consider deferring the cleric's admission. Such a delay will help to maintain good mutual relations between the bishop and the institute/society as well as between the bishop and the cleric. Since there is no guarantee that the cleric will be permitted to make perpetual profession in the institute (or be definitively incorporated in the society in the manner described in the proper law), which is the point when he would be excardinated from his diocese and incardinated in the institute (or society), it is particularly important to maintain the latter relationship (see canon 268 §2).

Second, candidates with serious financial obligations should not be admitted. Individual institutes/societies can determine the kinds (e.g., student loan debt vs. credit card debt) and amount of debt that they are willing to accept. If an institute/society agrees to assume a debt (e.g., by making monthly payments with a view toward paying it off entirely after perpetual profession), this allows the superior to admit the candidate licitly. Nevertheless, with regard to the debt-ridden, institutes/societies must take care to discern the candidate's intentions. If the candidate is principally or entirely motivated by the prospect of obtaining relief from his/her debts, he/she lacks the right intention and is not to be admitted.[6]

Canon 645

Finally, canon 645 addresses other aspects of the application process, some of which are mandatory while others are optional. Paragraph one requires the candidate to provide proof of baptism (if not baptized as a Catholic, then also proof of reception into full communion with the Catholic Church), proof of confirmation, and the absence of an existing marriage. Paragraph two requires certain applicants to request recommendation letters from specific persons: (1) for a cleric, a letter from his bishop, (2) for one who had previously been admitted into another institute/society (this includes the novitiate but excludes a pre-novitiate program), a letter from the major superior, and (3) for a former seminarian, a letter from the seminary's rector. Paragraph three leaves it to the institute's/society's proper law to determine whether to require recommendation letters from other persons who can attest to a candidate's suitability (e.g., from a pastor, employer, parent, etc.) and/or other proofs of the candidate's suitability and freedom from impediments (e.g., college transcript, record of military service, criminal background check, etc.). Paragraph four is a general clause that gives superiors the freedom to seek out any other information they think is necessary in order to assess accurately a candidate's suitability for admission.

Implementation of the Canons

Building upon the brief exposition of canons 641-645 offered above, this section will outline one way to implement the canons. This outline will consist of two parts, namely, the initial inquiry and the formal application process itself. In this chapter's appendix several sample forms will provide even more specificity to the approach outlined here. At the outset, it is important to note that, although the code speaks only of admission by the major superior, each institute/society should designate a member to conduct an initial inquiry and the admissions process. This member is usually called the vocation director. If possible, the director should be assisted by a council, whose members review the collected documentation and interview each candidate.

---

6 For some helpful approaches to the question of debt, particularly student loan debt, see Eileen C. Jaramillo, "Canon 644: Addressing Debts Before Entering a Religious Institute," and Amy Hereford, CSJ, "Canon 644: Education Loans of Those Entering Religious Communities," both in *CLSA Advisory Opinions on Institutes of Consecrated Life and Societies of Apostolic Life*, ed. Patrick M. Cooney (Washington, DC: CLSA, 2017) 126-129 and 130-131, respectively.

Initial Inquiry

Before permitting an inquirer (i.e., one who has expressed interest to the vocation director about joining the institute/society) to apply, the vocation director needs to make sure the individual is familiar with the institute/society, its history, and its present forms of ministry. Further, the vocation director should become familiar with the inquirer and seek out answers to the following questions.

- What is the inquirer's personal, religious, educational, social, and family background?
- What relationship has the inquirer had with the Church (e.g., parish or campus ministry)? What are the inquirer's spirituality and prayer life? Is he/she a neophyte?
- How has the Lord led the inquirer to this point in his/her life wherein he/she is considering joining this community? What does the inquirer find attractive about this community? If the community is clerical, why is it that the inquirer seeks to be a priest or brother with vows?
- What are the inquirer's expectations of the religious life? What is the inquirer's understanding of the evangelical counsels? What does the inquirer hope to find in community life?
- What are the inquirer's strengths and weaknesses? What are his/her special interests and talents?
- What is the inquirer's dating experience? Was the inquirer ever engaged to be married? Has the inquirer previously been married? What is the inquirer's history in observing chastity?
- Has the inquirer ever been a diocesan seminarian or a member of an institute/society?
- What is the inquirer's current occupation?
- Does the inquirer have any loans?

Having obtained answers to these questions, which do not form a part of the formal application, the vocation director needs to make an initial assessment about an inquirer. Perhaps the director advises the inquirer to apply. Perhaps the director decides that the inquirer is not yet ready to apply but remains in contact in order to assist the inquirer to grow in maturity and virtue with a view toward possibly applying in the future. Depending on the inquirer's age and maturity, this could take several months or even years. Perhaps the director decides that the inquirer is not at all qualified and informs the inquirer that he/she is not advised to apply.

Application Process

Sample Application Guidelines (Appendix A)

If the vocation director advises the inquirer to begin the formal application process, the director needs to provide detailed instructions about the process, including an explanation that the candidate will have to submit several documents as well as undergo medical and psychological examinations, a social media review, and, if required by the institute/society, a criminal background check. It might be helpful to provide the candidate with a checklist of the various components of the application process. The guidelines should also include an explanation of how the institute/society manages the highly confidential information that is collected during the application process.

Sample Application Form (Appendix B)

This form is to be accompanied by a recent copy of the candidate's sacramental records for baptism and confirmation and, if applicable, a marriage certificate and proof that the bond no longer exists. The application should also indicate that the candidate is to have transcripts from undergraduate and graduate institutions mailed directly to the vocation director.

Sample Release Form and Waiver to Review Information (Appendix C)

It is imperative that the confidential information obtained during the admissions process only be made available to select members who are involved in the work of admissions and formation. To that end, this release form will allow the application documents to be shared with, and only with, the members of the vocation council, major superior, and other select formation personnel. Placing these limits on the release of confidential information will help to protect the candidate's right to a good reputation and privacy. Obviously, a vocation director needs to exercise great care when using email or other electronic communication to distribute documents to members of the vocation council. A simple typographical error in an email address can result in very sensitive, confidential information being shared with the wrong person. It is highly advisable that files be encrypted with a password before they are transmitted electronically.

Sample Autobiography Guidelines (Appendix D)

The autobiography is often the first way the candidate introduces him/herself to the entire vocation council and plays an important role in discerning a candidate's readiness for admission. It will provide helpful insights into the candidate's character.

Sample List of References (Appendix E)

The candidate should provide a list of individuals that the vocation director will contact for a letter of recommendation. Those who know the candidate well are best suited to write a letter, such as parents, other relatives, pastor or other priest, former employers, professors, etc. The references should be able to address: (1) the extent of the candidate's motivation by mature faith, (2) the candidate's suitability for religious life (and, if applicable, priesthood), (3) the candidate's honesty, responsibility, and maturity at home, work, school, etc., as well as evidence of his/her capacity for leadership, (4) the candidate's ability to get along with others and engage in teamwork, (5) the candidate's sexual maturity and affective maturity, including his/her responsiveness to the feelings and needs of others and characteristic reactions to stress, and (6) indications of the candidate's ability to grow intellectually, spiritually, emotionally and other qualities related to the mission and charism of the institute/society. Some institutes/societies might decide that the vocation director should personally meet some of the candidate's family members.

Social Media Review (Appendix F)

The vocation director should ask the candidate to disclose his/her social media accounts and then conduct a review of them. Reviewing a candidate's accounts can help to assess a candidate's maturity and suitability.

Finances and Loans

Sample Financial and Loan Statement (Appendix G-1)

This statement will help the institute/society to assess the candidate's maturity, fiscal responsibility, and any possible liabilities it could be assuming if the candidate makes perpetual profession/is definitively incorporated. In this regard, the candidate should indicate not only any outstanding educational loans but any other unpaid bills and loans as well as other financial obligations (e.g., alimony, child support, etc.). The statement should also mention all of the candidate's current assets.

Sample Agreement Regarding Student Loans (Appendix G-2)

If the institute/society is considering accepting a candidate with student loan debt, this agreement will ensure that the candidate understands and accepts how the institute/society will handle his/her debt throughout the time of formation.

Personal Health History

Most often a personal health history form is provided by the doctor when a person goes for a physical examination. It is completed by the candidate before the physical examination and is to be reviewed by the doctor who performs the examination.

Medical Reports

These reports will allow the institute/society to assess whether the candidate has the requisite health to fulfill the duties that the institute/society will expect of him/her. The specifics of the content of these reports are left to the proper law of the institute/society.

- Physical Examination Report
- Immunization History Report
- Tuberculosis Test Report
- HIV Antibody Policy
- Dental Examination Report
- Eye Examination Report
- Covid-19 Test
- Other (as needed)

All reports are to be completed by health care professionals and mailed directly to the vocation director.

Psychological Evaluation Report

It is advisable that each institute/society rely on the services of no more than a few trusted psychologists. Regardless of whether the institute/society relies on a few or many, it must ensure that the psychologists are professionally competent, have some understanding of the nature of an institute/society, and have a Catholic understanding of the human person.

Regarding the psychological testing, the institute/society should see that the psychologist is a person who agrees on evaluating a candidate according to the following criteria so far as possible.

- Wechsler Abbreviated Scale of Intelligence (WASI)
- Bender Visual Motor Gestalt Test
- Minnesota Multiphasic Personality Inventory (MMPI-2)
- Millon Clinical Multiaxial Inventory-III (MCMI-III)
- Rorschach Inkblot Test

- Thematic Apperception Test (TAT)
- Incomplete Sentences Blank
- Projective Drawings

Before the vocation director and council meet to discuss a candidate's completed application, the director should arrange, insofar as possible, to have the psychologist available by telephone in case any questions arise about the assessment report.

Criminal Background Check

If it is the institute's/society's policy, the vocation director should ask the candidate to submit to a criminal background check.

Conclusion

The vocation director has the monumental task of guiding candidates through a very demanding screening process. Yet, in the end, it is not the director, the applicant's references, or any of the health professionals who admit the candidate. That decision is left to the major superior/competent superior according to the provisions of the proper law of the institute/society. It is for the vocation director, then, to make sure that all of the relevant information is collected and disclosed to the competent superior, so that he/she can make an informed decision about a candidate's application.

Appendices

The admissions process outlined above, which is just one way to implement canons 641-645, is designed to assure that the novitiate is not a debilitating experience for the institute/society or the novice. This is not to suggest, however, a one-size-fits-all approach to admissions. In accord with canons 641-645[7] and its own proper law, each institute/society must develop its own process that meets its own particular needs. The sample forms are provided below to assist institutes/societies in crafting an admissions process that will strive to ensure, as best as possible, that only suitable candidates are admitted to the novitiate. The institute/society might also want to consult the following national organizations as well as others for assistance regarding additional forms that might be helpful.

- National Religious Vocation Conference (NRVC) - nrvc.net
- Religious Formation Conference (RFC) - relforcon.org
- Resource Center for Religious Institutes (RCRI) - trcri.org

---

7 Canon 735 §2 states that the conditions in canons 642-645 are to be observed by societies of apostolic life, so these Appendices can be adapted by societies.

Appendix A
Sample Application Guidelines

(Note: Each institute/society has its own proper law. This appendix is one approach of how an institute/society might develop its own distinctive way of designing the formal application process.)

On behalf of the institute/society, we are delighted that you have begun the formal application for admission to our novitiate. The purpose of the following guidelines is to help you to complete the steps of the application process and to present to you our policies with regard to the management and confidentiality of the information submitted in your application. Our application process is necessarily intense, thorough, and time-consuming. It will take particular diligence on your part to move through all of the required components. Although the vocation director will guide you through the application process, s/he and the vocation committee, together comprising the vocation council, are first of all agents of the Church and of the institute/society. The members of the committee will conduct face-to-face interviews with you as will a psychologist. In this regard, your completed autobiography must be submitted to the vocation director at least two weeks prior to your interviews. You should communicate as soon as possible with the vocation director regarding the dates of your interviews. It is important that you understand the complete application process and the management of your personal and confidential information. If at any time you require clarification, please contact the vocation director. Please submit each part of the application as it is completed.

Management of Confidential Information

The application process involves highly confidential data since psychological, psycho-sexual, intellectual, and health data is gathered to determine your suitability and readiness for acceptance. Your full and complete disclosure is essential to the process and must be the result of your own free choice. Confidential data pertinent to your application is reserved to members of the vocation council, those associated with your psychological evaluation, and the major superior. When the vocation director presents the results of the vocation council's deliberations to the major superior, only the information that is necessary to make a decision is discussed. However, the vocation director is obliged to answer with candor any questions asked of him by the major superior.

If you are accepted, all original documents will be retained in your permanent personnel file in the major superior's office. An executive summary and your clinical data, both medical and psychological, will be shared with the novice director at the appropriate time. If you are not accepted, only the psychological report and the criminal background check will be retained in the files of the major superior's office. If you are not accepted or are accepted and leave the institute/society, by signing the

Release Form you agree that any information in your personnel file in the major superior's office may be shared with a diocese or religious institute/society upon their request should you desire to enter elsewhere.

Finances

Those admitted to the novitiate are asked to contribute *(mention amount here)* or any part of it towards the expenses of the novitiate year. If your means are limited, any contribution is appreciated. Those admitted to the novitiate are expected to provide their own health insurance for that year. Upon profession of vows at the end of the novitiate (or temporary/definitive incorporation into the society at the end of the probationary period), the member is incorporated into the insurance plan of the institute (or society). If you are without the means to cover even this year, please speak with the vocation director. *(If applicable: It is the policy of the institute/society not to admit candidates with any financial debt. These circumstances need to be discussed with the vocation director.)*

Notice of Acceptance

The institute/society accepts responsibility before God and the Church to determine, as best as we are able, your readiness to enter the novitiate. When the process is completed, the vocation director and council will meet and thoroughly review your application and autobiography, the recommendation letters written on your behalf, and the submitted medical and psychological reports to assess your suitability for the novitiate. The results of that discussion will be communicated to the major superior whose responsibility it is to accept candidates to our novitiate. Only then will the vocation director notify you as to the major superior's decision.

Appendix B
Sample Application Form

(Note: The canons that are listed on this form assist the institute/society in understanding what is required for a particular institute/society.)

Please print out this application form and type or clearly print all of your information. The following questions are required by Church law and the laws of the institute/society. (*Note: c. stands for canon, and cc. stands for canons.*)

Please submit a color photograph with this application.

1. General Information

Name:

Last *First* *Middle*

Date of Birth (c. 643 §1, 1º):

Place of Birth:

(city, state)

Country of Citizenship:

Home Address:

Mailing Address:

(if different)

Telephone:

Email Address:

Social Security Number:

Applying for (*in clerical communities*): Priesthood Brother

2. Sacramental Background (c. 645 §1)

Baptism

Date:

Name and Address of Church:

Roman Catholic or Eastern Catholic?

If a non-Catholic baptism, please specify:

If you entered the Roman Catholic Church from another Christian faith, please indicate the date and place of reception:

Confirmation

Date:

Name and Address of Church:

If you were ever a member of a non-Catholic religion, give the name of the religion and the date(s) of membership:

Religion/Denomination	Beginning	Ending

Following Baptism in (or reception into) the Roman Catholic Church, have you ever *formally* and *publicly* fallen into apostasy, promoted heresy, or joined a schismatic community? Yes No

Have you ever fallen or drifted away from the practice of your Catholic faith? Yes No

If you have answered yes to either of the two previous questions, please explain when, how long, and the circumstances surrounding your return to the faith.

Note: *Baptismal and Confirmation certificates issued within the last six months, along with appropriate certificates testifying to reception into the Church, must be submitted. Write directly to the respective churches for these certificates and have them sent directly to the vocation office.*

Marriage (cc. 643 §1, 2°; 1041, 3°; 1042, 1°)

Are you or have you been married, even in a civil ceremony?
Yes No

Note: If you answered yes, please submit a marriage certificate and proof of annulment, dissolution, or your spouse's death. (c. 645 §1)

Do you have any children? Yes No

If yes, please give the name, address, and age of each.

Name	Address	Age

What financial arrangements have you made for them?

Is anyone (including parents, grandparents, children, etc.) dependent on you or likely to be dependent on you for their upkeep? (cc. 285 §4; 644)

3. Family Background

Father's full name:

Age:

Place of Birth:

If deceased, date of death:

Address:

Occupation (indicate if retired):

Religion:

Is he a member of an Eastern Catholic Church? Yes No

If so, please indicate which one:

If a neophyte to the Roman Catholic Church, what was his previous religious affiliation:

Mother's full maiden name:

Age:

Place of Birth:

If deceased, date of death:

Address:

Occupation (indicate if retired):

Religion:

Is she a member of an Eastern Catholic Church? Yes No

If so, please indicate which one:

If a neophyte to the Roman Catholic Church, what was her previous religious affiliation:

Date of parents' marriage:

Name and Address of Church:

Current marital status:

If divorced, date of divorce:

Please list, giving full name and age, all your brothers and sisters, both living and dead. List them according to their birth order along with their age, occupation, and marital status. Include yourself.

Name	Age	Occupation	Marital Status

Do you have any close relatives who are priests or religious?

If yes, please explain:

4. Personal Information

Are you choosing to enter the institute/society without constraint of any kind? (cc. 643 §1, 4°; 645 §1) Yes No

Have you ever been a seminarian?

(Arch)diocese:

Dates:

Reason(s) for leaving:

Were you ever a postulant, a novice, or professed religious of this institute/society or any other community? (cc. 643 §§3 and 5) Yes No

Institute/Society/Other:

Dates:

Reason(s) for leaving:

If, as a seminarian or a member of an institute/society, you received any ecclesiastical ministries or Orders, please list them and the dates they were received:

If you are a cleric, has your diocesan bishop been consulted?
Yes No

Have you ever withdrawn an application or been refused admission to this institute/society, any other institute/society, or any seminary?
Yes No

Institute/Society:

Dates:

Reason(s) for withdrawal or refusal:

Were you ever in the US Military Service? Yes No

If yes, give specific information on a separate sheet of paper.

Are you presently registered for Selective Service? Yes No

Employment History:

Employer	Position	Dates	Reason(s) for leaving

Volunteer History:

Organization	Position	Dates	Reason(s) for leaving

Information concerning your most recent job (if applicable):

Employer:

Address:

Dates of Employment:

Job Title and Description of Duties:

Hours per week:

Hourly Wage/Annual Salary: $

Do you or your parents belong to any professional or fraternal organizations? Yes No

If yes, please explain:

List hobbies and outside of school/work interests:

What kind of reading do you do in your free time? Name some favorite authors.

Are you currently dating? Yes No

Have you ever been engaged? Yes No

How old were you when you first thought of religious life or priesthood?

Have you discussed your decision with both of your parents? Yes No

Is anyone opposed to your decision? Yes No

If yes, whom?

If you were not to join this institute/society, what else might you do with your life?

What are some aspects of being a member you find appealing?

If you answer yes to any of the following questions, please explain on a separate sheet of paper.

Have you ever been arrested? Yes No

Have you ever received a background check by civil authorities?
Yes No

Have you ever been convicted by a civil, criminal, or military court?
Yes No

Are you liable for prosecution by a civil, criminal, or military court at this time? Yes No

Have you ever committed a voluntary homicide (c. 1041, 4°)?[8]
Yes No

Have you ever cooperated in the procurement of an abortion (c. 1041, 4°)? Yes No

Have you ever gravely and maliciously mutilated yourself or another (c. 1041, 5°)? Yes No

Have you ever attempted suicide (c. 1041, 5°)?
Yes No

Have you ever suffered from any physical, mental, or psychological disorders or disabilities which required professional intervention (cc. 1029; 1041, 1°)? Yes No

Have you ever joined a non-Catholic religion, including any Masonic, theistic, atheistic, or another secret society (c. 1041, 2°)?
Yes No

Have you ever had any history of substance abuse (alcohol, drugs, etc.)?
Yes No

Are you allergic to wheat? Yes No

Are you allergic to bread? Yes No

Are you allergic to wine? Yes No

Are you allergic to grape juice? Yes No

8 This question and the next five are specifically required for ordination, but institutes/societies may find them helpful for other reasons as well.

5. Education

Educational History: List the educational institutions you have attended beginning with primary school. When applicable, indicate degree(s) and major(s).

School/Institution	Location	Dates	Degree/Major

Note: *Have each college or university send an official transcript directly to the vocation office. If you are in your final year, arrange now for a final official copy to be sent to the vocation office upon graduating.*

6. Financial and Loan Information

Please be sure to submit the Financial and Loan Statement and the requisite documentation.

Do you have any outstanding education/student loans (c. 644)?
Yes No

Amount: $

Have they been refinanced? Yes No

Are you carrying any other debt (credit card, automobile, etc.) (c. 644)?
Yes No

Amount: $

Are you an administrator and/or bound to account for any trust?
Yes No

Are you now, or will you be in the future, financially responsible for anyone (cc. 285 §4; 644)? Yes No

If yes, explain:

7. Medical Background

When (approximately) was your last physical exam?

Who is your personal physician? Address:

List any physical disabilities or limitations (c. 642):

List any serious illness you have had and your age at the time (c. 642):

List any serious surgeries you have had and your age at the time:

List any serious accidents you have had and your age at the time:

Approximately how many days of work/school have you missed in the last year due to illness? Cause?

Do you drink alcohol? Yes No

If yes, what kind and how much per week?

Have you ever used drugs of any kind? Yes No

If yes, what kind and how often?

If yes, when was the last use?

Is there a history of mental illness, alcoholism, and/or drug addiction in your family (c. 642)? Yes No

If yes, explain briefly on a separate sheet of paper.

Have you ever received psychological or psychiatric counseling (c. 642)? Yes No

If yes, explain briefly on a separate sheet of paper.

Have you ever had a psychological evaluation? Yes No

If yes, explain briefly on a separate sheet of paper.

If yes, will you release these results to the vocation director?
Yes No

Are you currently covered by medical insurance? Yes No

If yes, give details. If no, please explain.

8. Signature

I, ______________________, have answered all of the above questions to the best of my knowledge and ability, truthfully and without reservation.

____
Applicant's Signature

____
Date

Appendix C
Sample Release Form and Waiver to Review Information

Name of Institute
Vocation Office
(street address)
(city, state, zip code)
(telephone number)
(email address)

(Note: This sample release form contains very important content. Since it is not lengthy, an institute/society may want to make adjustments. It is recommended that a civil attorney who is familiar with institutes/societies review the form that will be used.)

I, (name) the undersigned Applicant, release the contents of the psychological evaluation prepared by the consulting psychologist that the institute/society has assigned to me as part of the admissions process, to the vocation council, formation team and major superior of the institute/society.

I also give them the right to review the contents of all the materials submitted to the vocation director for the application process.

I also waive my right to review the letters of recommendation which will be included as part of the application to enter the novitiate of the same institute/society.

____
Applicant's Signature

____
Applicant's Name (Printed)

____
Address

____
City

____
State and Zip Code

____
Date

____
Witness's Signature

____
Witness's Name (Printed)

____
Address

____
City

____
State and Zip Code

____
Date

Appendix D
Sample Autobiography Guidelines

Your autobiography will require careful and prayerful attention on your part. Hopefully the experience will be beneficial to your ongoing consideration of a vocation to the institute/society. It will probably help to clarify your understanding of some aspects of your own history. What you share will play a crucial role in helping the vocation director and vocation council to get to know you and to discern your readiness to continue in the application process with the institute/society. You may find it helpful to discuss your autobiography with your spiritual director as you begin and as you continue to work on it.

Formatting

This is determined by the institute/society.

Content

Your autobiography should cover the nine sections outlined below, in this particular order, question-by-question. Please do not write the autobiography in a narrative style; simply answer each question.

1. Basic Biographical Information

A basic introduction of who you are (include your name, date of birth, basic family information), where you are from, educational background, where you are currently living and what you are currently doing.

2. Spiritual Development and Vocation Discernment

Describe pertinent elements of your spiritual development and vocation discernment. What experiences have led you to consider a vocation to the religious life and/or priesthood? Speak about your relationship with Jesus Christ and the Church. Describe typical elements of your prayer life. Touch upon any involvement you have had in your parish or faith community.

3. Relationship with the Institute/Society

Describe in general detail any experiences which have moved you to consider the institute/society. Mention members you have met, communities you have visited, and what particular aspects of the institute's/society's life and ministries that attract you.

4. Familial and Personal Relationships

Discuss separately your relationship to your father, your mother, and your siblings as well as any others who have played a major role in shaping the person you are today. How have your relationships with your parents changed over the years? Describe experiences, values, and facets of your upbringing which were significant to you.

5. Emotional, Intellectual, and Social Development

Touch upon your social life whether in or outside of religious circles. Discuss your capacity to form meaningful and close friendships, dating relationships you have had, and what a mature sexual identity has to do with entering into religious life. What evidence is there to suggest that living a life of chaste celibacy is a realistic option for you?

6. Work and Volunteer Experiences

Give examples that taught you the value of hard work and discuss the types of jobs you have had, as well as any volunteer or ministerial work you have done.

7. A Personal Success

Describe one personal success in your life which helped you to see more clearly the type of person you are, to identify purpose in your life, or to see more clearly how you wish to live.

8. A Personal Failure

Describe one personal failure in your life which helped you to see more clearly the type of person you are, to identify purpose in your life, or to see more clearly how you wish to live.

9. Chronology of Important Life Events

Attach to your autobiography an appendix which lists in chronological order all the important events of your life from birth to the present. Include a very brief description where necessary.

Submitting your Autobiography

This is determined by the institute/society.

Appendix E
Sample List of References

You will need to contact five (5) people who know you well and are able to comment on your suitability for religious life and/or priesthood.

- One letter of recommendation (and only one) must be from an immediate or extended family member. A parent is preferable insofar as possible.
- If possible, one letter of recommendation should be from your pastor, chaplain, or campus minister (priest), or another priest who knows you well.
- Try to include letters of recommendation from various parts of your background (educational, professional, religious, etc.).
- If you are a seminarian or former seminarian, one letter of recommendation is to be from the seminary's rector.
- If you had been admitted into another institute or society (this includes the novitiate but excludes a postulancy or other pre-novitiate program), one letter is to be from the major superior.
- If you are a diocesan priest or deacon, one letter of recommendation is to be from your bishop.
- (Note: Women's institutes/societies often request references from a member of the institute.)

Please fill out the form below and email it to the vocation director with the following information for each reference:

- Full name and title (if applicable)
- Relation to you
- Mailing address
- Phone number
- Email address

This information should be sent to the vocation director as soon as possible. He/She will contact each reference and ask him/her to compose a letter of recommendation. You should tell your references to expect a letter from the vocation office.

Applicant's Name: ______________________________

Reference #1
Name: ______________________________
Relation: ______________________________
Mailing address: ______________________________
Email address: ______________________________
Phone number: ______________________________

Reference #2
As above.

Appendix F
Sample Social Media Review

Applicant's Name:

Please mark with an "x" the social media platforms for which you have a personal or "public figure" account:

Platform	Username/Channel
Facebook	
Twitter	
Instagram	
LinkedIn	
YouTube	
Pinterest	
Tumblr	
Flickr	
Reddit	
Google+	
Website/blog	
Other: (specify)	

In addition to these platforms and websites, a general internet search on you will be performed.

Are you aware of any possible derogatory content on any of these platforms or websites? Yes No

If yes, please explain on an attached sheet of paper.

By signing this form, you consent to the vocation office of this Institute/Society to review any and all of your publicly available social media platforms and websites.

____

Applicant's Signature

____

Date

Appendix G-1
Sample Financial and Loan Statement

Name:

Assets

Please indicate the amount of money you currently have on account:

Please indicate the property you own (its nature and approximate value):

Student Loan Information

_____ I do not have any student loans.

_____ I do have student loan(s) and have completed the requested information below:

Current total balance of loan(s): $

Please attach the latest available bank and/or loan statements.

Interest rate(s):

Are loans in deferment? Yes No

If you have not attached the latest statement for each loan, please explain:

Other Debts

Amount of indebtedness: $

To whom is it owed?

When is payment due on these debts?

What plans have you made for retirement of these debts?

Please attach the latest available bank and/or loan statements.

(Note: The following could also be included: During the novitiate the community will pay ordinary expenses, e.g., room and board, etc. Novices are expected to maintain their own medical insurance during the time they are in the novitiate. If you do not have any other policy (e.g., through your family), adequate coverage must be obtained before coming to the novitiate. Also, the community asks each novice to contribute *(mention amount here)* toward his support during the novitiate year.)

____
Applicant's Signature

____
Applicant's Name (Printed)

____
Date

Appendix G-2
Sample Agreement Regarding Student Loans[9]

Agreement between the ____________________ (institute/society) and ______________ (candidate) concerning the financial arrangements regarding the candidate's education loan.

(1) A copy of the loan agreement and recent statement of the account is attached hereto.

(2) The candidate will continue to service the loan while s/he is financially independent.

(3) When the candidate ceases to have personal income, and as long as s/he remains a novice or a professed member of the institute/society, the institute/society will service the loan.[10]

(4) If the candidate should leave the institute/society at any time, for any reason, s/he will still have primary responsibility for paying off the loan.

(5) XX years after the member makes final profession (or is definitively incorporated), the institute (or society) may, in its sole discretion, completely pay off the loan.

____

Applicant's Signature

____

Applicant's Name (Printed)

____

Date

9 This form is adapted from Amy Hereford, CSJ, "Canon 644: Education Loans of Those Entering Religious Communities," 130-131. Used with permission from the author.

10 Alternatively, the institute/society might prefer that the candidate apply for a student loan deferment that would cover all or part of the period of formation.

CHAPTER FIVE

FORMATION: CANONS 646-661

Rose McDermott, SSJ[1]

Novitiate

Life in a religious institute begins with the novitiate (c. 646). The novitiate initiates a life-long formation of the person, i.e., his or her human, spiritual, intellectual, and pastoral qualities in a specific institute for life and service in the Church. Canons on the novitiate focus on the time, place, personnel and content of the initial formation or novitiate program. A prolonged absence can interfere with this formation process and render the novitiate invalid (c. 649 §1).

The Novitiate House

> Can. 647 §1. The erection, transfer, and suppression of a novitiate house are to be done through a written decree of the supreme moderator of the institute with the consent of the council.

Just as seminaries in dioceses provide a separate, suitable place for the systematic formation of men preparing for the priesthood (c. 235 §1), religious institutes provide novitiate houses for women and men beginning their formation in religious life (c. 646). Canon law provides that only the supreme moderator (highest superior) in a religious institute has the authority to erect, transfer and suppress a novitiate house with the consent of the council (c. 127 §1) through a written decree. The novitiate is separate from other houses in the institute[2] in order that the novices receive—without distraction or interference—a systematic formation from a qualified director (and assistants, if necessary) in

---

1 Rose McDermott, SSJ, was the original author and also revised this chapter. She noted that Rev. Jonathan DeFelice, OSB, contributed to the original chapter. The revision includes text from the original version along with new text.

2 "Besides being a program, the novitiate is also a place." Rosemary Smith, SC, "The Formation of Candidates and the Formation of Members," in *New Commentary on the Code of Canon Law,* eds. John Beal, et al (New York/Mahwah, NJ: Paulist Press, 2000) 813, commentary on c. 647. The canon does not specify whether the novitiate needs to be a separate canonical house, a separate physical house, or merely a separate space or area of a larger building, but only that it be "made in a house properly designated for this purpose" (c. 647 §2).

order to understand the patrimony (c. 578), lead the life, and carry on the apostolate of a specific religious institute.

If the decision is to transfer the novitiate, the written decree should indicate the place from which (*a qua*) and the location to which (*ad quam*) the novitiate is transferred. The novitiate need not be a separate house; often it is established within the generalate or provincialate of the institute. The important issue is providing a secure, separate house for the initial formation of those beginning religious life in a specific institute.

EXAMPLE DECREE OF ERECTION OF A NOVITIATE
I, ____________________ Supreme Moderator (or other title for highest superior of the institute), having obtained the consent of the council, establish (transfer or suppress) the novitiate house of our institute located at ______________ (site of novitiate), on ______________ (date). ______________________ Supreme Moderator

A Valid Novitiate – Place and Time

> Can. 647 §2. To be valid, a novitiate must be made in a house properly designated for this purpose. In particular cases and as an exception, by grant of the supreme moderator with the consent of the council, a candidate can make the novitiate in another house of the institute under the direction of some approved religious who acts in the place of the director of novices.

A novitiate is to be made in the proper house so designated. Exceptions in particular cases may occur: a person who departed another religious institute after profession, a diocesan priest or person with an advanced theological degree, or a person with English as a second language. Such persons would need a modified program to meet their particular needs. Applicants may already have well-formed backgrounds for living religious life; a capable member in another house of the institute could be appointed to instruct such a person in the nature, purpose, spirit, and character of the institute (c. 578).

> Can. 647 §3. A major superior can permit a group of novices to reside for a certain period of time in another house of the institute designated by the superior.

At times, the major superior (general or provincial) may decide that the community of novices can reside in a retreat or vacation house of the institute. These dwellings afford the novitiate community the experience of a special place for a time of extended prayer, or rest and relaxation. Note the norm stipulates it is the community of novices and another house of the institute. The novices may be on retreat or enjoying recreation in a designated house of the institute. Such periods would contribute to the well-being of the novices without jeopardizing their experience of community life in the institute.

> Can. 648 §1. To be valid, a novitiate must include twelve months spent in the community itself of the novitiate, without prejudice to the prescript of canon 647 §3.

This wise provision affords a stipulated time (twelve months) for a systematic formation in communal life with formal studies, directed by capable members of the religious institute without interference from well-meaning members. While the novice director and, assistants, if necessary, engage the novices in the important ministry of formation (cc. 651 §1, §2; 652 §3), other members of the institute have their significant roles of prayer and example (c. 652 §4).

In recent years, with the scarcity of vocations to religious institutes and the singular importance of communal living in the novitiate, the Congregation for Institutes of Consecrated Life and Societies of Apostolic Life (CICLSAL) has granted indults permitting religious institutes sharing the same patrimony (c. 578) to have a common novitiate house. The major superiors of these institutes agree to the place of the novitiate, the director of novices, and, if need be, assistants in accord with canons 651 and 652 §§1-2. The director is responsible to render an account of the progress and suitability of each novice to the major superior of the respective institutes.

A sample petition for a common novitiate follows for institutes which may be contemplating making such a request.

EXAMPLE
PETITION FOR A COMMON NOVITIATE HOUSE

Date:

[Name of Prefect]
Prefect
Congregation for Institutes of Consecrated Life
and Societies of Apostolic Life
Piazza Pio Xii 3
00193 – Rome, Italy

Dear [Name of Prefect],

Recently the following religious institutes sharing the same patrimony (c. 578) have been receiving less than three (3) candidates for admission to their respective religious institutes:

(List the generalates/provincialates and location in arch/dioceses)

Because of this scarcity of vocations and the singular importance of community life for those beginning religious life (c. 607 §2), the major moderators of these institutes petition permission to erect a common novitiate with a director of novices responsible for the initial formation of these women in the charism of the religious institutes. The director of novices, appointed after agreement among the major superiors, will be accountable to the major superiors of each religious institute for the progress of their respective novices during the canonical novitiate year. We understand that the major superiors and their successors reserve the right to provide for the novitiate formation of any candidate entering their particular religious institute (641).

Thank you, your Eminence, for your kind attention to our petition and for all of your efforts for those in consecrated life throughout the world.

Sincerely yours in the Lord,

____

(Signed by major moderators of the religious institutes petitioning for the common novitiate)

Length of the Novitiate

> Can. 648 §2. To complete the formation of novices, in addition to the period mentioned in §1, the constitutions can establish one or more periods of apostolic exercises to be spent outside the community of the novitiate.
>
> §3. The novitiate is not to last longer than two years.

The law wisely puts parameters around the novitiate, while providing for the novices to experience the apostolate of the institute prior to first profession. In this way, novices will experience the apostolic works of the particular institute prior to first profession. While the canonical novitiate must last twelve months spent in the community of the novitiate (c. 648 §1), many institutes, particularly apostolic institutes, provide a "mission year" in the proper law or formation statutes for novices to experience life in a mission community and the institute's proper works prior to first profession.

During this year, periodic reports are sent to the director of novices by the local moderator regarding the adaptation of the novice to the institute's mission, both communal and apostolic. However, the time of the novitiate is not to last longer than two years. Only in an individual case and by way of exception can the novitiate be extended for another six months (c. 653 §2). This is a wise provision, since both the novice and the competent authority in the institute must decide whether the novice is to advance to the next step, i.e., temporary profession, or depart the institute.

Absences from the Novitiate House

> Can. 649 §1. Without prejudice to the prescripts of can. 647 §3 and can. 648 §2, an absence from the novitiate house which lasts more than three months, either continuous or interrupted, renders the novitiate invalid. An absence which lasts more than fifteen days must be made up.

This norm applies to the canonical novitiate which lasts twelve months. It is extremely important that there be no extended interruptions in this year. The law wisely provides for the avoidance of lengthy absences from the novitiate house. An absence lasting more than fifteen days must be made up, while an absence lasting more than three months, whether continuous or interrupted, renders the novitiate invalid.

Departure, Dismissal of a Novice

> Can. 653 §1. A novice can freely leave an institute; moreover, the competent authority of the institute can dismiss a novice.
>
> §2. At the end of the novitiate, if judged suitable, a novice is to be admitted to temporary profession; otherwise the novice is to be dismissed. If there is doubt about the suitability of a novice, the major superior can extend the time of probation according to the norm of proper law, but not beyond six months.

Admission to a novitiate demands a great deal of preparation on the part of both the candidate and the admitting major superior of a religious institute:

a) reports of the physical, psychological, and academic aptitude of the candidate,

b) canonical documents for valid admission, and

c) other references/proofs required for suitability by the proper law of the institute or the respective religious superior (cc. 641-645).

Therefore, a decision to leave on the part of the novice, or a decision to dismiss on the part of the competent authority of the institute should be done only after prayer, careful discernment, and charity.

If a novice decides to leave the institute at any time, he or she should be encouraged to bring the decision to prayer and wise counsel from a confessor, spiritual director, novice director and/or the major superior of the institute. If the decision is made to depart, a notation of the date and reason for the departure should be recorded in the files of the institute in the event the departing novice eventually decides to seek readmission or enter another religious institute. The reason(s) for departing would prove helpful in such instances.

The novice is not yet a member of the institute (c. 654); therefore, the decision to dismiss is not the complex canonical dismissal of a member in perpetual profession (cc. 694-701). Nevertheless, this serious decision should be made by the legitimate superior only after prayer and counsel from those in charge of the formation of the novice and the council in accord with proper law. Charity should always accompany such a dismissal, so that the novice departs the institute with greater confidence and aptitude to embrace the lay vocation than before entrance to the novitiate. Again, an account of and reason(s) for the dismissal should be kept on file in the event the person seeks readmission or admission to another religious institute.

Temporary Profession

Validity of Temporary Profession

Can. 656. For the validity of temporary profession it is required that:

1° the person who is to make it has completed at least eighteen years of age;

2° the novitiate has been validly completed;

3° admission has been given freely by the competent superior with the vote of the council according to the norm of law;

4° the profession is expressed and made without force, grave fear, or malice;

5° the profession is received by a legitimate superior personally or through another.

It is important that the above five provisions be met since they are required for the validity of temporary profession.

Since a person completed seventeen years of age at admission to a religious institute, and the time of a valid novitiate must include twelve months spent in the novitiate community, the person would have completed the required age of eighteen for temporary profession. In many countries today, persons entering religious life are much older than seventeen years of age so age for temporary profession is not an issue.

The twelve months spent in the novitiate community with the exceptions permitted in the law (cc. 647 §3; 648 §2; 649) are necessary for a valid novitiate. This time has been discussed above.

The competent superior with the vote of the council must give permission for a novice to make temporary profession. Proper law would indicate the proper superior (general or provincial) and whether the vote of the council is deliberative or consultative (c. 127 §1),

The profession is expressed publicly during the Rite of Religious Profession and made without force, grave fear, or malice. Many religious institutes require that novices express this request in their own handwriting prior to publicly voicing it during the rite. This written petition is kept in the personal file of the novice. It is similar to that required of men prior to ordination to the diaconate (c. 1036).

Today, men and women seeking admission to religious institutes are older, and there seems to be no danger of force or fear, particularly on the part of women. Malice could be an issue if the candidate deliberately conceals the fact that he or she was married, bound by vows or sacred bonds in another institute, or suffers from a serious illness (c. 643 §1, 2°-5°).

The proper law should state the competent superior who receives the profession. It may or may not be the same superior who admitted to profession. At times, particularly in missionary or international institutes, the profession is received by another person delegated by the legitimate superior (c. 656, 5°) unable to travel at the particular time for the profession.

Renewal of Profession/Perpetual Profession

> Can. 657 §1. When the period for which the profession was made has elapsed, a religious who freely petitions and is judged suitable is to be admitted to renewal of profession or to perpetual profession; otherwise, the religious is to depart.

Profession made for a period of time is part of the formation process, during which the young religious experiences living the vowed life in the institute. Ordinarily, temporary profession is made for a period no less than three years, but no longer than six years (c. 655). Some institutes provide in the proper law that temporary profession is made annually. In this way, there is a time at which both the young religious and the competent superior can evaluate the temporary professed religious' quality of life before he or she makes subsequent profession.

If the religious decides to depart at the end of the year or years in temporary profession, she or he is free to do so (c. 688 §1). Likewise, the religious in temporary profession can also request to depart during the time of temporary profession. Such a decision should be made only after prayer, spiritual direction and counsel from a wise and experienced person.

If the religious is still bound by temporary profession in an institute of pontifical right, the supreme moderator can issue an indult of departure; if the institute is of diocesan right, the diocesan bishop of the house of assignment must confirm the indult for validity (c. 688 §2). Such an indult granted legitimately and made known to the member dispenses from the vows and all other obligations arising from profession (c. 692).

Extension of Temporary Profession

> Can. 657 §2. If it seems opportune, however, the competent superior can extend the period of temporary profession according to proper law, but in such a way that the total period in which the member is bound by temporary vows does not exceed nine years.

This provision seems a rather extensive period of time for one to decide on a permanent vocation in the Church. Note that the provision must be stated in the proper law of the institute, and the total period of time in temporary profession cannot exceed nine years. In other words, if temporary profession is ordinarily made for six years, and the proper law permits nine years, the competent superior can grant three more years.

Here again, it is unjust to permit temporary profession to continue unchecked for a period of years. Proper law can provide that temporary profession be made annually with yearly evaluations from those responsible for the young religious. Experience has taught major superiors that allowing a member to make temporary profession for a number of years without periodic evaluations is unjust to both the individual religious and the institute. To permit one to continue in temporary profession for nine or even six years only to refuse him or her perpetual profession without having significant evidence for the refusal through evaluations and even counseling is both cruel and unjust. Not only does the person seem unfit for religious life, but he or she has lost contact with the life of a lay person in society.

Perpetual Profession

Validity of Perpetual Profession

> Can. 658. In addition to the conditions mentioned in can. 656, nn. 3, 4, and 5 and others imposed by proper law, the following are required for the validity of perpetual profession:
>
> 1° the completion of at least twenty-one years of age;
>
> 2° previous temporary profession of at least three years, without prejudice to the prescript of can. 657 §3.

Three of the requisites for a valid temporary profession are likewise required for perpetual profession: 1) admission freely given by the competent superior, 2) profession expressed, free of force, grave fear or malice, and 3) the legitimate superior or one delegated by the same superior receiving the profession. These requirements have already been addressed under canon 656.

In addition, the member must have completed twenty-one years of age, and made temporary profession for at least three years (c. 655), without prejudice to the provision of canon 657 §3. This latter norm permits the anticipation of perpetual profession up to three months.

Again, age would not seem to be an issue. For first profession, the candidate must be at least eighteen years of age, and temporary profession must extend for at least three years (cc. 655; 656 1°), the candidate for perpetual profession would seem to have competed twenty-one years of age. This does not seem an issue in most developed countries today, since candidates applying to religious institutes tend to be much older.

The exception to the full three years minimum required for perpetual profession would be the three months that perpetual profession can be anticipated for a just cause in canon 657 §3. Such just causes could be: a religious being assigned to a missionary country with an early departure, relatives of the religious or the major superior traveling distances for the perpetual profession, or a particular solemnity/feast of the Church that has special significance for the religious institute anticipating the profession.

Again, it must be stated that it is wise to have temporary profession made annually or at intervals prior to perpetual profession. This allows for periodic evaluations with written reports from formation personnel and/or local superiors kept on file. These reports demonstrate the aptitude of the candidate for the vowed life, communal living, and the apostolic works of the institute, as he or she advances to perpetual profession. Again, it must be emphasized that to permit a member in temporary profession to continue in temporary profession for three, six or nine years (c. 657 §2), without evaluations from formation personnel and local superiors, only to be denied perpetual profession, is unjust and cruel on the part of those responsible for admitting to profession.

Ongoing Profession

Formation after First Profession

> Can. 659 §1. In individual institutes the formation of all the members is to be continued after first profession so that they lead the proper life of the institute more fully and carry out its mission more suitably.
>
> §2. Therefore, proper law must define the program of this formation and its duration, attentive to the needs of the Church and the conditions of people and times, insofar as the purpose and character of the institute require it.
>
> §3. Universal law and the program of studies proper to the institute govern the formation of members who are preparing to receive holy orders.
>
> Can. 660 §1. Formation is to be systematic, adapted to the capacity of the members, spiritual and apostolic, doctrinal and at the same time practical. Suitable degrees, both ecclesiastical and civil, are also to be obtained when appropriate.
>
> §2. During the time of this formation, offices and tasks which may impede it are not to be entrusted to the members.

Each religious institute must describe its own formation program. Such a program cannot be adequately described in the proper law of the institute; formation must have its own statutes. The statutes should contain the prerequisites and impediments to admission as well as provisions about formation—during novitiate, following first profession, and the ongoing formation throughout the life of the members—in accord with the life and mission of the institute. Clerical religious institutes would include in the formation statutes prescriptions required in universal law and other documents required for the formation of men aspiring to ordination.

The canon wisely cautions against assigning offices or works impeding such formation and professional preparation, particularly for temporary professed religious. This is to insure the young religious' confidence in his or her vocation and profession. This investment of time and expense on the part of the institute for young religious should not be disrupted by placing too much responsibility on a young religious prior to perpetual profession. While a young religious may have excellent professional potential, his or her vocation may be lost due to demanding apostolic responsibilities during the delicate formative period in religious life. Instruction in spiritual development continues, as members are sent on for studies and advanced degrees in fields of education, health care or social services in accord with the purpose of the institute. Apostolic religious need constant updating so as to meet the civil requirements demanded in their various areas of specialization.

Sui iuris monasteries, due to their small size, often unite with other monasteries of their federation in order to devise a quality formation program for their members in keeping with the contemplative way of life. Formation, particularly in theology and spirituality, is a *sine qua non* for these members dedicated to a contemplative lifestyle.

Ongoing Formation of Religious

> Can. 661. Through their entire life, religious are to continue diligently their spiritual, doctrinal, and practical formation. Superiors, moreover, are to provide them with the resources and time for this.

The canon places the responsibility of ongoing formation throughout the life of a religious on the shoulders of both the individual member and major superiors. Retreats, spiritual direction, professional updating in accord with one's age, health, and competence for service in the Church would be included in the statutes describing ongoing formation (c. 670).

Members of religious institutes, like all men and women, encounter the ordinary phases of human development. These stages coupled with illness, death of loved ones, failures, or disappointments in professional life, etc., that all persons inevitably encounter, take their toll with varying effects on the well-being of religious physically, psychologically and spiritually. Such challenges have to be met with understanding on the part of both the individual member and his or her major superiors. Professional lectures, workshops, as well as counseling in individual cases often assist individual religious, as they face such issues as part of their human journey. However, little can be accomplished unless the religious understands the effects such situations take on his or her person and willingly accepts assistance offered by major superiors.[3]

The Temporal Goods of Religious

Canon 668 §§1-5

One should carefully note the placement of the one canon (c. 668) addressing the temporal goods of individual religious, as distinct from the seven canons (cc. 634-640) of the temporal goods of religious institutes, public juridic persons in the Code of Canon Law. The temporal goods of individual religious are addressed in Chapter IV, The Obligations and Rights of Institutes and Their Members. The temporal goods of individual religious have implications for the vow of poverty.

> Can. 668 §1. Before first profession, members are to cede the administration of their goods to whomever they prefer and, unless the constitutions state otherwise, are to make disposition freely for their use and revenue. Moreover, at least before perpetual profession, they are to make a will which is to be valid also in civil law.

Paragraph one of the canon addresses the obligations of the vow of poverty once the member makes first profession in a religious institute. The man or woman becomes a member of the religious institute, lives common life in community, and has certain rights and obligations resulting from first profession (c. 654). The religious devotes himself/herself to the apostolic commitments of the religious institute. Therefore, the religious cannot be distracted from his or her communal life and ministerial undertakings with the administration of personal goods. Likewise, the institute is bound by law to provide for the

---

3 Following the Second Vatican Council, papal and curial documents have addressed the important topic of initial and ongoing formation in religious institutes. For religious institutes in general, see Pope John Paul II, *Vita consecrata* 64-71 and CICLSAL, *Potissimum institutioni*. Members of *sui iuris* monasteries of women religious should study Pope Francis, *Vultum dei Quaerere* 13-15 and CICLSAL, *Cor Orans* chapter four.

member all that is necessary to achieve his or her vocation in accord with the constitutions (c. 670). Therefore, prior to first profession, he or she must yield the administration of personal goods to whomever preferred, unless the constitutions of the institute state otherwise.

Note that it is the administration of personal goods, not the ownership, that must be given over to another. The professed member retains ownership but yields the administration of the personal goods to whomever he or she wishes. It would be well if the member seeks financial advice at this point, particularly if he or she has a great deal of assets. The religious is still in a temporary status in the religious institute until final profession. If he or she departs or is dismissed, it is important that the personal goods of the individual are protected in the event of a return to secular life.

Some religious institutes, if requested, accept this responsibility. However, the temporal goods of members have to be administered separately from the temporal goods of the institute. It should be remembered that personal goods are subject to taxation. All of this should be explained to the individual prior to first profession, so the novice will make an informed decision regarding the administration of his or her personal goods. The act of cession should be made in keeping with the novice's provisions regarding the use of personal property and the interest derived from such goods. A copy of the document should be kept in the individual's file. The religious should choose a trustworthy administrator, one who would give an annual account to the religious. If the institute is chosen as administrator, the finance officer should give an account to the religious.

Ceding the administration of personal goods frees the religious to focus on his or her vocation, i.e., communal living and apostolic service. If the member owns property, the religious decides if it will be rented and if money from the rent will be applied to his or her savings. If there is interest from capital savings, etc., the religious decides whether it will redound to the capital or be distributed in some way. For example, a person entering religious life may have a pension and specify it will go to his or her aging parent for use and maintenance. All of this should be discussed with the administrator and be finalized in a legal binding document.

Paragraph one of the same canon also provides for a will, since the status of the person has changed with first profession from a lay person to a religious. Again, the religious is free to dispose of personal possessions in the will (*mortis causa)* as he or she chooses. The change in status from a lay person to a religious may or may not have any implications for the person's will. If the person departs religious life or is dismissed, the will can be changed.

It is not wise for a religious institute to accept a gift of temporal goods from a novice or one in temporary profession. Neither the person nor the major moderators of the institute know if the temporary professed will persevere in religious life. Therefore, it is wise that the personal goods are dealt with to the advantage of the religious. The institute is interested in the quality of the vocation of the member, his or her progression in the life and mission of the institute, not in the personal possessions of the individual.

> Can. 668 §2. To change these dispositions for a just cause and to place any act regarding temporal goods, they need the permission of the superior competent according to the norm of proper law.

Changes resulting from favorable or tragic circumstances occur in everyone's life; no one escapes them. A needy parent or sibling, a physically or mentally challenged niece or nephew, or even an inheritance may prompt the need for a change in either the administration of one's temporal goods or a change in the will (*mortis causa)* of the temporary professed. Likewise, the administrator of the religious may prove incompetent, may move or die; there may be other reasons prompting changes in the status of the administrator, the administration of personal goods, and/or the will of the religious.

To make such changes requires the permission of the competent superior, an obligation due to the vow of obedience. This permission would not be refused for a just cause. Again, it would be wise for the religious to seek financial advice from a competent person before making such significant changes.

> Can. 668 §3. Whatever a religious acquires through personal effort or by reason of the institute, the religious acquires for the institute. Whatever accrues to a religious in any way by reason of pension, subsidy, or insurance is acquired for the institute, unless proper law states otherwise.

While paragraphs one and two of canon 668 address the rights of the individual religious regarding personal goods, paragraph three describes the responsibilities of the professed member towards the religious institute. As noted above, the religious institute accepts the responsibility of caring for the religious once he or she makes profession (c. 670). For his or her part, the religious agrees that whatever he or she acquires through personal effort or by reason of the institute is acquired for the institute. Personal effort would include royalties from publications, payments for artwork, etc. A stipend/salary received for an assigned apostolate or ministry is received by reason of the institute.

Likewise, any subsidy, insurance, pension, etc. accruing to the religious as a professed member belongs to the religious institute.

> Can. 668 §4. A person who must renounce fully his or her goods due to the nature of the institute is to make that renunciation before perpetual profession in a form valid, as far as possible, even in civil law; it is to take effect from the day of profession. A perpetually professed religious who wishes to renounce his or her goods either partially or totally according to the norm of proper law and with the permission of the supreme moderator is to do the same.

Paragraph 4 divides into two sentences and addresses the concept of renunciation. The first sentence deals with the vow of poverty of a religious in an institute which by its nature requires the renunciation of personal goods prior to perpetual profession. Before perpetual profession, the member renounces or freely gives his or her personal goods to whomever he or she pleases in a document acceptable in civil law.

The second sentence addresses members in a religious institute that does not require such a renunciation. These religious may freely choose at any time during perpetual profession to renounce personal goods in whole or in part in accord with the proper law of the institute and with the permission of the highest superior of the institute. The religious does not lose the capacity to acquire other temporal goods in the future. Note that this provision must be stated in the proper law of the institute, and the permission can only be given by the highest superior. Many religious institutes discourage such a renunciation because the religious may decide to depart the institute or there may be a family member in need of monetary assistance from the professed religious.

> Can. 668 §5. A professed religious who has renounced his or her goods fully due to the nature of the institute loses the capacity of acquiring and possessing and therefore invalidly places acts contrary to the vow of poverty. Moreover, whatever accrues to the professed after renunciation belongs to the institute according to the norm of proper law.

Paragraph five describes the condition of a professed religious renouncing personal goods in accord with the nature of the institute. This religious does not lose the fundamental right to goods, but the capacity to acquire or possess temporal goods in accord with the nature of the institute. Civil law does not always recognize such a renunciation. In accord with the proper law of such religious institutes, any temporal goods accruing to the religious in any way after perpetual profession (bequest, inheritance, etc.) belong to the institute.

From this very detailed canon, one can see how important it is that the proper law of each religious institute describe precisely the requirements and effects of the vow of poverty in accord with the nature of the institute.[4]

EXAMPLE
AN ACT OF CESSION OF ADMINISTRATION

This is an agreement between (the legal name of the novice), party of the first part, and (legal name of the administrator/religious institute), party of the second part (the religious institute, if the major superior agrees to permit the institute to accept this responsibility).

In accord with the provisions of admission to first profession, the party of the first part will depend on and receive the necessities of life from the religious institute (name). Canon 668 of the *Code of Canon Law* binds those about to make first profession in an approved religious institute of the Catholic Church as follows:

1. The party of the first part agrees to render freely his/her services and labor to the religious institute.

2. The party of the first part retains ownership of all property, real and personal. However, provision is made for such property as follows:

a) The party of the first part cedes the administration of his/her property, real and personal, that he/she owns during the time of profession and appoints ______________________ as the administrator.

b) The use and interest of said property shall be disposed as follows:

(provisions for use and interest indicated here)

c) If the profession of vows ceases in any way whatsoever, this agreement becomes by that fact null and void.

The parties declare that they intend to be legally bound by this agreement made on ______________________(date).

____
Legal Name//Party of the First Part

____
Administrator /Party of the Second Part

____
Notary and Seal

4 See *Exegetical Commentary on the Code of Canon Law,* ed. Ernest Caparros et al (Montreal: Wilson & Lafleur/Chicago: Midwest Theological Forum, 2004) II/2: 1783-1788.

EXAMPLE
LAST WILL AND TESTAMENT

I (legal name), a resident of (city, state, county), being of sound mind, memory and understanding, do make and declare this to be my last Will and Testament.

FIRST: I direct that all my funeral arrangements, including time, place, and manner of viewing be determined and financed by (religious institute) in accord with its traditions and customs.

SECOND: I hereby direct that my patrimony, which in accord with canon law includes all assets, real and personal, which I own in my individual capacity and received through inheritances, bequests and gifts made specifically and unequivocally to me during my life and after my death, be distributed in the following manner:

(Provisions)

THIRD: I hereby acknowledge that all income (principal, interests, royalties, etc.) and assets accrued as a result of my work, work products, and efforts, whether these efforts be in my official ministry or otherwise, rightfully belong to (religious institute). Accordingly, I direct that said assets remain with the said (religious institute).

FOURTH: I hereby acknowledge that my ownership of property, real and personal, is subject to civil law and the canon law of the Roman Catholic Church and the laws of the religious institute to which I belong.

I direct that my specific intent in the dispositions made in this Will be governed by my general intent to conform to the law of the Roman Catholic Church and the proper law and customs of my religious institute (name religious institute).

IN TESTIMONY WHEREOF, I have hereunto subscribed my name and affixed my seal this __________ day of _________ in the year_________ .

____

Signature of Religious

______________________ ______________________

Signature of Witness Signature of Witness

____

Notary and Seal

NOTE: Check the legal requirements in the state in which the will is being executed to make sure all formalities are met. Assistance of a knowledgeable attorney is recommended.

EXAMPLE

ADVANCE DIRECTIVE FOR HEALTH CARE

I, ______________________________, being of sound mind, willfully and voluntarily make this declaration to be followed if I become incompetent, i.e., if I lack sufficient capacity to make or communicate decisions concerning myself. This declaration reflects my firm commitment to refuse life-sustaining treatment under the circumstances indicated below.

I direct my attending physician to withhold or withdraw life-sustaining treatment that serves only to prolong the process of my dying, if I should be in a terminal condition or in a state of permanent unconsciousness.

I direct that treatment be limited to measures to keep me comfortable and to relieve pain, including any pain that might occur by withholding or withdrawing life-sustaining treatment.

In addition, if I am in the condition described above, I feel especially strong about the following forms of treatment:

1 (___) do want (___) do not want cardiac resuscitation.
1(___) do want (___) do not want mechanical respiration.
I (___) do want (___) do not want tube feeding or any other artificial or invasive form of nutrition (food) or hydration (water).
I (___) do want (___) do not want blood or blood products.
I (___) do want (___) do not want any form of surgery or invasive diagnostic tests.
I (___) do want (___) do not want kidney dialysis.
I (___) do want (___) do not want antibiotics.

I realize that if I do not specifically indicate my preference regarding any of the forms of treatment listed above, I may receive that form of treatment.

Other Instructions:

I designate the following person as my surrogate to make medical treatment decisions for me if I should be incompetent and in a terminal condition or in a state of permanent unconsciousness.

The name and address of such person is: ______________________________

(Name of Superior General/Congregational Minister/President)

______________________________ (religious institute)

______________________________ (address)

The name and address of the successor in office of the above-named person, upon assuming this office in the religious institute, is likewise competent to make these decisions for me.

I made this declaration on the _____day of ______, 20________ .

____
Signed

____
Address

____
City, State

The Declarant, or the person at the direction of the Declarant knowingly and voluntarily signed this document by signature or mark in our presence. We, the witnesses, hereby certify that we: (1) are not related to the Declarant by blood, marriage or adoption; (2) are not entitled to any portion of the Declarant's estate by will or intestacy; (3) do not have a present or inchoate claim against the estate of the Declarant; (4) do not have final responsibility for declarant's medical care; or (5) are not employees of, and do not have controlling interests in, a hospital or health care facility in which Declarant is a patient.

______________________	______________________
Witness	Address
______________________	______________________
Witness	Address

NOTE: *Nearly every U.S. state now has a statutory living will form. Some states require their use. Most are readily available online by searching for the name of the state and "living will form." These forms should be used, and attention should be given to their compliance with Catholic social teaching related to medical matters. Similarly, other types of health care directives such as surrogacy and powers of attorney for health care should be discussed with knowledgeable persons to make sure that they contain what is required by applicable civil law and are properly executed.*

CHAPTER SIX

MEMBERSHIP: FULLY INCORPORATED MEMBERS

Phillip J. Brown, PSS[1]

Introduction

This chapter is an effort to identify and explain in practical, non-technical terms the canonical consequences that result from full incorporation in three separate and distinct kinds of committed life or intentional communities: religious institutes, secular institutes, and societies of apostolic life. The first two of these are different forms of *consecrated* life, in contrast to *apostolic* life in the third. Membership in each of these communities represents an opportunity to live a well-ordered, committed, purposeful Christian life in community with others who desire the same. This opportunity is made available by the Church to those who have found meaning and purpose for their lives as members of the Christian faithful and who want to devote their lives to the ends of the specific intentional community to which they have chosen to present themselves for membership. This is done in a particular way, according to the norms of canon law and the constitutions and proper law of the religious institute, secular institute, or society of apostolic life. The rights and obligations that flow from membership in an institute of consecrated life or society of apostolic life are a consequence of that membership status.

---

1 This chapter was written by Emmett J. Gavin, OCarm, and Elissa Rinere, CP, for the 2001 edition of the Procedural Handbook. Father Phillip Brown, PSS, revised this chapter on membership. The revision includes text taken directly from the original version along with new text.

Stages of Incorporation

As a general rule the Code of Canon Law contains more specific norms for admission to a religious institute than for secular institutes or societies of apostolic life, the latter to be established by the institute's constitutions or the society's proper law. In order to ascertain whether all of the rights and obligations pertaining to membership in a religious institute have been acquired through perpetual profession, and what those rights and obligations are, one should consult the code and the constitutions and other proper law of the institute itself. For secular institutes, one should consult the code more generally and the constitutions and proper law of the institute. For societies of apostolic life, one should consult the code generally and the proper law of the society more specifically.

Membership in each of these forms of intentional communities is normatively acquired in stages.

- *Religious Institutes*: Conditions for inclusion in a religious institute are covered in canons 642-645. The first stage of membership in a religious institute is the "novitiate" (c. 646), leading to temporary profession of vows (c. 655), which can include a renewal of temporary profession in accordance with the proper law of the institute (but not to exceed nine years in temporary vows) and culminating in perpetual profession (c. 657).
- *Secular Institutes*: The code speaks of stages of "incorporation" with respect to secular institutes (c. 723), according to the constitutions of the institute (c. 720). The stages of incorporation are to include a period of probation, ordered in a way that the candidates understand more fittingly their own divine vocation and that which is proper to the institute. During that time they are trained in the spirit and way of life of the institute (c. 722). Next comes "first incorporation," which should be temporary and at least of five-years duration, according to the norm of the constitutions (c. 723 §§1, 2). Perpetual or definitive incorporation is available if the candidate is judged suitable, with "temporary bonds that are always to be renewed" (c. 723 §3). Definitive incorporation "is equivalent to perpetual incorporation with regard to the specific juridic effects established in the constitutions" (c. 723 §4).
- *Societies of Apostolic Life*: The code also recognizes stages of "incorporation" with respect to societies of apostolic life (c. 735). The "proper law of each society determines the admission, probation, incorporation and formation of members" (c. 735 §1), but the conditions that apply to the admission of members to a religious

institute (cc. 642-645) are to be observed in the admission of candidates to these societies (c. 735 §2). This includes standards of suitability, submission of the required documentation, absence of the identified impediments, no admission of secular clerics without consulting their proper ordinary, and no admission of candidates who are burdened by debts they cannot repay.

Nature and Ends of Institutes and Societies

Members of both institutes and societies are to strive for the perfection of charity, but how they do so is conceptualized by the code in different ways for members of religious institutes, secular institutes, and societies of apostolic life. For religious it is living out the evangelical counsels through common life separate from the world; for secular institutes, it is by living out the evangelical counsels "in the world;" and for members of societies, with or without vows, it is by pursuing the apostolic purpose of the society through living common life and the observing the constitutions.

When seeking to interpret and understand the specific rights and obligations that pertain to religious institutes, secular institutes, and societies of apostolic life, it is important to remember that essential differences exist with respect to the nature and ends of these distinctive forms of committed life. Also, the rights and obligations that accrue to members of institutes of consecrated life upon perpetual profession and to members of societies of apostolic life upon definitive incorporation do not exclude the rights and obligations they possess in virtue of their baptism as members of the Christian faithful (see cc. 204-205 and 208-223), including those specific to laypersons (cc. 224-231) and clerics (cc. 273-289). These other rights and obligations might, however, be modified, restricted, or expanded by the approved constitutions of the institute or society.

Nature and Ends of Institutes of Consecrated Life

Institutes of consecrated life represent "a stable form of living" by which members "foretell the heavenly glory" by "following Christ more closely under the action of the Holy Spirit" (c. 573 §1). Through the profession of the evangelical counsels, members are "totally dedicated to God . . .[as] they strive for the perfection of charity in service of the kingdom of God" and are made an outstanding sign in the Church (c. 573 §1). They assume this way of life freely and live in institutes of consecrated life erected by competent authority (c. 573 §2).

To protect the proper vocation and identity of each institute, each is to have a fundamental code or "constitutions" that contain everything that is to be observed (see c. 578), as well as the fundamental norms "regarding governance of the institute, the discipline of members, incorporation and formation of members, and the proper object of the sacred bonds" through which one becomes incorporated (c. 587). Thus, the fundamental code or constitutions is, along with relevant provisions of the Code of Canon Law, the fundamental source of the rights and obligations of members. This pertains to both religious and secular institutes.

Institutes may be either clerical or lay, although by its nature, the state of consecrated life itself is neither clerical nor lay (c. 588). That is, consecrated life itself is unique, and one's status as a cleric or a layperson is independent of one's status as being in consecrated life. Likewise, one does not forfeit one's rights nor lose the obligations that come from being a cleric or a lay person in the Church by virtue of incorporation in a religious or secular institute, although those rights and obligations may be qualified, limited or expanded in virtue of membership in the institute. The rights and obligations that stem from being a member of the Christian faithful (cc. 208-223), a lay member of the faithful (cc. 224-231), or a cleric (cc. 273-289) remain intact as long as they are not at variance with the specific rights and obligations of one in perpetual profession or definitive incorporation in a religious or secular institute. Rights and obligations specific to membership in the institute, however, do qualify and may limit or expand those other obligations and rights.

Differences between Religious Institutes and Secular Institutes

There are two forms of institutes of consecrated life: religious institutes and secular institutes. Members of both religious and secular institutes profess the evangelical counsels (c. 573). What, then, distinguishes a religious institute of consecrated life from a secular institute of consecrated life? The answer lies primarily in the life in common of their members and the "separation from the world" proper to the character of the institute (c. 607 §3).

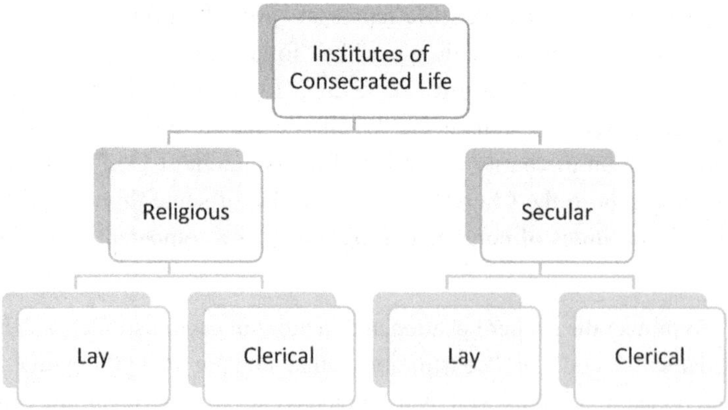

A religious institute is "a society in which members . . . pronounce public vows, either temporary or perpetual . . . and lead a life of brothers or sisters in common" (c. 607 §2). Religious life in an institute involves a consecration of the whole person, manifesting to the Church what the code calls "a wonderful marriage brought about by God and a sign of the future age" (c. 607 §1). A religious "brings to perfection a total self-giving as a sacrifice offered to God, through which his or her whole existence becomes a continuous worship of God in charity" (c. 607 §1). This "entails a separation from the world proper to the character and purpose of the institute" (c. 607 §3) as the member assumes life in common in a legitimately established house under the authority of a superior (c. 608). All members of institutes of consecrated life profess the evangelical counsels (c. 573) and not only must observe them fully and faithfully but also must arrange their lives according to the proper law of the institute, thereby striving for the perfection of their state.

Thus, the exercise of rights and the fulfillment of obligations by members of religious institutes should be ordered to the primary apostolate in relation to other charisms or apostolates in which the religious institutes engage. For those religious institutes dedicated to works of the apostolate, the whole life of the members should be imbued with an apostolic spirit, even as the whole of their apostolic action is informed by a religious spirit (c. 675).

Members of secular institutes, on the other hand, strive for the perfection of charity and contribute to the sanctification of the world by living "in the world" (c. 710). In contrast to religious institutes, norms regulating the lifestyle of members of secular institutes are expected to be set forth in the constitutions (c. 714); members of secular institutes have a positive canonical obligation in the code to devote themselves diligently to prayer, to the reading of sacred scripture, to an annual retreat, and to whatever other spiritual exercises are required by particular law (c. 719 §1). Likewise, they are to celebrate the Eucharist daily, if possible, approach the sacrament of penance freely and frequently, and freely seek out spiritual direction (c. 719 §§2, 3 and 4).

In practice, aside from other signs of membership in a religious institute—such as wearing distinctive dress (c. 668 §1; see also c. 284)—the distinction between these two forms of consecrated life would not always be obvious to outside observers since religious often engage in works of the apostolate that are embraced or permitted by the institute, which works appear to involve living and working "in the world." But, while members of religious institutes do engage in works of the apostolate, the first apostolate of religious is the witness of their consecrated life itself, to be fostered by prayer and penance (c. 673). The life of religious remains anchored in the formally erected community life of the institute and its houses as providing for a life separate from the world.

Some institutes of consecrated life are dedicated to contemplation, and their members therefore cannot be summoned to assist in pastoral ministries, however much the needs of the active apostolate might encourage it (c. 674). Lay institutes, on the other hand, are presumed to participate in the pastoral function of the Church through spiritual and corporal works of mercy and by offering diverse services to people (c. 676).

Nature and Ends of Societies of Apostolic Life

Societies of apostolic life resemble institutes of consecrated life, but by their nature do not involve the profession of religious (e.g., public) vows (c. 731 §1). Rather, members pursue the apostolic purposes of the society without religious vows (unless required by the constitutions of the particular society), while living a common life as brothers or sisters (according to the proper manner of doing so) and striving for the perfection of charity through the observance of the constitutions of the society (c. 731). There is no presumed form of common life for members of such societies. The defining feature of societies is their apostolic purpose, not formal witness to the evangelical counsels and the perfection of charity through the profession of vows and common life (c. 731). It would not be a mistake to describe societies of apostolic life as hybrid in principle, resembling both religious and secular institutes, in virtue of the elements of the particular society's constitutions. The code provides for much greater creativity in defining the nature, apostolic purposes, and manner of life of societies of apostolic life than in the case of either religious or secular institutes.[2]

The essential contextualizing elements of the rights and obligations of the members of a society of apostolic life are (1) the apostolic purposes of the society, and (2) the way the constitutions identify and define the manner of life of the society and how it is to be lived in concrete circumstances (c. 731). Members of societies of apostolic life who do not profess religious vows are not required by the code to make any special commitment to observe the evangelical counsels. The code does provide that a particular society may require in its constitutions that its members assume the evangelical counsels by some

---

2 See Phillip J. Brown, "Societies of Apostolic Life: The Evolution of a Canonical Institute" in *Essays in Honor of Sister Rose McDermott, S.S.J.: Service for Union with God and With One Another*, ed. Robert Kaslyn, 1st ed. (Washington: The Catholic University of America, 2010) 201-234.

prescribed bond (c. 731 §2). However, no such special commitment is required for members if not specified in the constitutions of the particular society.

The rights and obligations enjoyed upon definitive incorporation for members of a society of apostolic life are determined by the constitutions, not the Code of Canon Law. The canons concerning societies do not contain the same specificity as the ones for institutes of consecrated life—religious or secular.

Select Norms Related to Institutes and Societies

It is not the purpose of this chapter to deal with the broad universe of rights and obligations set forth in the Code of Canon Law. Many of these rights and obligations are addressed in other chapters of this book and will not be addressed here unless especially pertinent to rights under discussion that derive from membership. This chapter is focused on specific rights and obligations acquired by members of institutes (through perpetual profession) and societies (through definitive incorporation) and on activities restricted by or inconsistent with membership.

All institutes of consecrated life, lay and religious, are subject to common norms set forth in canons 573-587. The code then goes on to distinguish clerical from lay institutes (c. 588), pontifical vs. diocesan (c. 589), exempt institutes (c. 591), and the eremitical life and that of consecrated virgins (cc. 603 and 604); it also foresees the possibility of new forms of consecrated life (c. 605). The common norms apply to all forms of consecrated life except as qualified by the nature of a given form of life or the constitutions of institutes and societies that have them. The nature of consecrated life has already been considered as context for the acquisition and exercise of rights and obligations by those who have definitively adopted the specific forms of consecrated life under consideration. The common norms discuss the ecclesial dimension of consecrated life, the variety of gifts exhibited by the different forms, and the duty of members to be faithful to the spiritual patrimony of the form of life to which they adhere (c. 578).

General Norms Supporting the Consecrated Life of Members of Religious Institutes

Religious institutes have the longest history of the three canonical forms of committed life under consideration in this chapter and, in many ways, they have influenced canon law as the "template" for all institutes of consecrated and even societies of apostolic life.[3] In this section, norms on the following topics will be discussed briefly in relation to religious institutes:

- Governance and relationship to authority
- Common life
- Cloister
- Living outside community
- Formation and support of members
- Restricted activities and activities inconsistent with membership
- Departure, transfer, and dismissal

Governance and Relationship to Authority

The members of the leadership team of a religious institute, whether pontifical or diocesan, have an obligation to see to it that the institute and its houses have been properly erected by the competent authority (cc. 579-585; 608-616). Only thus can the rights of members be properly secured and their obligations fulfilled. Not all functioning communities have been properly erected canonically, which can lead to serious difficulties when members seek to have their rights respected or superiors attempt to call forth fulfillment of obligations of members. Thus, leadership should take pains to assure proper erection and that proper constitutions have been written and promulgated (cc. 587 and 598; see also c. 86). Furthermore, institutes are entitled to a just autonomy of life, especially in governance (c. 586).

The constitutions are to define in particular the manner in which the evangelical counsels of chastity, poverty, and obedience are to be observed in the institute, acknowledging both the obligation of members to do so and their rights with respect to them (c. 598). Canon 601 addresses the very delicate matter of the obligation of obedience which requires the submission of the will to legitimate superiors who, the canon states, "stand in the place of God when they act according to the proper constitutions" (c. 601).

Balanced against this awesome power of superiors is the fundamental equality regarding dignity and action by which all the Christian faithful cooperate in the building up of the Body of Christ according to each one's own condition and function (c. 208). In governing their institutes, therefore, superiors

3 For an overview of the manner in which the canonical norms governing religious institutes have served as a template for the treatment of societies of apostolic life see Brown, "Societies of Apostolic Life."

are obliged to recognize and respect the dignity of each member even when exercising the considerable power conferred upon them by canon 601. The tendency to condescend to members, even to "infantilize" sometimes exhibited by religious superiors ought to be rejected by all and be seen as a violation of the fundamental right to have one's dignity recognized and respected and to be treated as an adult. In that way, the perfection of charity can be achieved and exhibited to all, as contemplated by the very nature of religious life and as supported by the norms of the Code of Canon Law. More particularly, canon 618 exhorts superiors to exercise their authority in a spirit of service, stating:

> Therefore, docile to the will of God in fulfilling their function, they are to govern their subjects as sons or daughters of God and, promoting the voluntary obedience of their subjects with reverence for the human person, they are to listen to them willingly and foster their common endeavor for the good of the institute and the Church, but without prejudice to the authority of superiors to decide and prescribe what must be done.

Common Life

It is the responsibility of both the individual religious and the religious institute to assure that a lifelong commitment to the vowed life in community can be achieved in a meaningful and fruitful way (cc. 607 §2 and 608-616). This must take appropriate account of both the charism of the community and the norms of proper and universal law. Those who establish a religious house have an obligation to suitably provide for the needs of the members (c. 610 §2). The consent of a diocesan bishop for the erection of a house entails the right of the members (1) to lead their lives according to the character and proper purposes of the institute; (2) to exercise the works proper to the institute according to the norm of law; and (3) with respect to clerical institutes, to perform sacred ministries observing the requirements of the law (c. 611).

Canons 602, 607 §2, and 665 §1 establish the principles which govern and define the obligation of members of religious institutes to live in common. The requirements flowing from these general canonical norms should be reflected in the proper law of religious institutes and should be quite explicit with regard to the obligation of members to live in community in a religious house of the institute. At the same time, as a practical matter these obligations are today often tempered in practice by the current and evolving realities of the apostolate and contemporary demands on religious and religious life. The demands of today are demonstrably very different from those that gave birth to the norms enshrined in the law of the Church and in the proper law of religious institutes. Therefore, at this point in history, any discussion of common life and its requirements must include the creative and sincere efforts of many religious institutes to adapt the spirit of the law governing common life to contemporary realities.

Canon 602 is one of the norms common to all institutes of consecrated life (see cc. 573-606). Because it applies to secular as well as religious institutes, its reference to "*vita fraternal*" as a norm of life must be understood in proper context with respect to the kind of institute being considered. It should not therefore be construed as meaning common as such. Rather, it is meant to describe a life of shared ideals and commitment which, for members of religious institutes, finds its most authentic expression in the context of community life.

On the other hand, the obligation of religious to live in common with other members of the same institute is addressed quite explicitly in canons 607 §2 and 665. Life in common is specified in those canons as one of the defining characteristics of religious life. At the same time, while traditional common life is clearly the ideal and an expectation held up by the law of the Church as a defining norm for religious life, efforts are being made today in many religious communities to take into consideration their lived experience of efforts to further the apostolic priorities of the community and how to conceive of "common life" in ways that better support those efforts. This openness to conceiving common life in creative new ways is an effort to allow room for creative experiences of communal involvement and accountability. For example, it is not uncommon today that some members of an institute live on their own in proximity to individual apostolic commitments, coming together only on a periodic basis with other members of the community for prayer, discussion and community business and sharing.

In other instances, sharing is done on an intercommunity basis that may be in lieu of more regular involvement with members of one's own community. Practical issues such as distance and expense may dictate that some of these arrangements be employed, but they also sometimes come about because of common apostolic commitments. Such variations on more traditional communal living arrangements are becoming more common, especially among religious women, who today often work in individual apostolates rather than together in institutional ministries, frequently out of financial necessity. The dispersion of personnel reflected in such shifts in apostolic priorities often lead to creative living and communal relationships being considered as necessary. In this era when religious life is evolving, and its future direction and dimensions are so uncertain, such innovations and variations of traditional common life are perhaps not only inevitable but necessary.

It must be acknowledged that the Holy See and some canonical commentators disapprove of the growing incidence of members of religious institutes living apart from their communities, often even on an open-ended basis and for reasons unrelated to apostolic or communal needs or traditions. The consensus of these commentators is that this is an unhealthy aberration at odds with the traditions of the Church and the explicit requirements of the law, including the proper law of the affected institutes themselves.[4] There have no doubt been excesses in these practices. The avoidance of excesses and the need for careful ongoing supervision of non-traditional expressions of "common life" urgently require that norms governing such living arrangements be developed in all communities that permit members to live and form community in non-traditional ways, while safeguarding the underlying principles and values of the common life. Such norms should, with appropriate canonical advice, take due account of the spirit and letter of universal and proper law. They should also include clear criteria of accountability on the part of members and superiors, and provide for regular, periodic reassessment. Every effort should be made in the canonical norms to maximize both opportunities and the requirements for regular occasions of traditional life in common. Common life remains integral to religious life. There is a clear need today to preserve the best of its traditional values and structures. At the same time, creative innovations that retain the values and ideals that give meaning to religious life must not be stifled, lest the ability to adapt and grow in a changing world is foreclosed.

Cloister

A space apart from the demands of the apostolate and the encroachments of the outside world is regarded as a fundamental right of religious and a necessary element of life in common. Both the individual religious and the community which shares a religious house are seen as requiring this assurance of a minimum of separation from the demands and distractions of non-members.

Recognition of this right is expressed in canon 667 §1 which, while deferring to proper law and the character and mission of the institute to determine the specifics of what is appropriate, requires that all religious houses provide for some space not open to non-members. The space so designated should be ample enough to assure that the members of the community can engage in private prayer and rest in an undisturbed atmosphere and also enjoy leisure activity with other members without outside intrusion.

---

4 See *CLD* 9: 446-452; *Origins* 23, 693-712; *The Canon Law: Letter and Spirit* (Collegeville, MN: The Liturgical Press, 1995) 331, 335.

In larger houses this should present no difficulty. In the kind of smaller communities that are so typical today, this canon would seem to require at a minimum that the sleeping quarters of the members be reserved as a private area and also, if possible, that there be a common or recreation room where members can gather in private for community sharing and leisure activities together.

Space apart is especially crucial and essential to the nature and identity of contemplative religious institutes. Canon 667 recognizes this by laying down explicit requirements governing cloister in these communities. Men's contemplative communities are enjoined in canon 667 §2 to observe a "stricter discipline of cloister" than the minimalist requirements of canon 667 §1. It is then left to the proper law of the community to prescribe the nature and restrictions of the "stricter discipline" which are needed.

A different standard is applied to contemplative communities of women religious. Tracking the restrictive and highly supervised criteria set forth in the 1969 instruction *Venite seorsum,* canon 667 §§3 and 4 provide for very little discretion in the observance of cloister in women's contemplative communities.[5] "Papal cloister" is prescribed for women's communities that are dedicated to the contemplative life. This simply means that the Apostolic See is vested with the authority to regulate the terms and conditions of the requirements of cloister in such communities (c. 667 §3).

The actual supervision of the observance of papal cloister is entrusted to the diocesan bishop. For a just cause, the ordinary of a diocese in which such a monastery of nuns is located has a right of access to the cloister; for an appropriately grave reason, with the consent of the superior, he can also permit others to enter as well (c. 667 §4). For example, the need for emergency medical treatment, for pastoral services, or the repair of monastery facilities would be typically serious reasons justifying entry to the cloister. Also, where the reason is considered serious enough, such as to receive medical treatment or to exercise the right to vote, the ordinary can permit nuns to leave the cloister for whatever period of time is reasonably necessary to accomplish the approved objective, with the consent of the superior.

It is interesting to note that, despite the restrictions governing entry to and departure from the cloister, the 1983 code does not prescribe any penalties for violation of cloister. This stands in marked contrast to the 1917 code which

5 Sacred Congregation for Religious and Secular Institutes, instruction *Venite seorsum*, *AAS* 61 (1969) 674-690.

prescribed severe penalties, including in some cases excommunication, for a violation of cloister.

Also of considerable note with regard to contemplative monasteries of nuns are the provisions of two documents issued by Pope Francis in recent years: *Vultum Dei quaerere*[6] and *Cor orans*.[7] These two important documents have been challenging with respect to their implementation and, as one canonist who has written and spoken extensively on the documents has noted, are a "force to be reckoned with."[8] *Vultum Dei quaerere* is a 2016 apostolic constitution that gives a general overview of the areas of monastic life on which Pope Frances is focused. Two years later, the Congregation for Institutes of Consecrated Life and Societies of Apostolic Life followed it with the instruction *Cor orans*, which gives more specific details about how these concerns of Pope Francis are to be addressed.

Cor orans derogates from several provisions of canon law, in particular those dealing with certain aspects of the cloister. For example, the dispensation of a member from the cloister now rests solely with the major superior and no longer requires the involvement of the diocesan bishop or religious ordinary (*Cor orans* art. 174, 175). The law regarding single monasteries and monastic congregations of nuns represents an area regarding which a community's leadership team and those working with such communities of women should diligently seek out the expertise of knowledgeable canonists familiar with the implementation of these and other critical documents.

Living outside the Community

Universal law sets forth criteria for the terms and conditions that may justify living apart from community for members of religious institutes (c. 665 §1). Exclaustration[9] (cc. 686-687) and a similar process applicable to members of societies of apostolic life are processes that not only allow but require living outside community. They are covered in greater detail in chapter seven of this

---

6 See Pope Francis, apostolic constitution *Vultum Dei quaerere*, June 29, 2016 (Vatican: Libreria Editrice Vaticana, 2016). Available at http://w2.vatican.va/content/dam/francesco/pdf/apost_constitutions/documents/papa-francesco_costituzione-ap_2016 0629_vultum -dei-quaerere_en.pdf.

7 See Congregation for Institutes of Consecrated Life and Societies of Apostolic Life, instruction *Cor orans*, April 1, 2018 (Vatican: Libreria Editrice Vaticana, 2018). Available at http://www.vatican.va/roman_curia/congregations/ccscrlife/documents/rc_con_ccscrlife_doc_20180401_cor-orans_en.html.

8 Nancy Bauer, OSB, "*Cor Orans*: Implementing New Papal Norms for Nuns," in *CLSA Proceedings 2019* (Washington, DC: CLSA, 2020) 60.

9 *Cor orans* articles 177 and 178 also made changes to canon 686 §2 with respect to exclaustration of nuns.

handbook on "Separation of Members," as is canon 703, which, in particularly serious circumstances, permits the major superior to expel a member of a religious institute from a house. In this chapter we will address principally the norms and criteria governing non-communal living for fully incorporated members in good standing who are permitted to live apart from the institute or society for a time.

Authorization by the competent superior must be obtained for a member of a religious institute to be absent from common life. The local superior would normally be the appropriate one to authorize routine brief absences, such as vacations or perhaps even absences of a few months' duration for spiritual or apostolic purposes. A "lengthy" absence, however, typically requires the permission of the major superior and his or her council. In accordance with canon 665 §1 such absences are not to exceed one year and require a "just cause." What makes an absence "lengthy" and the cause "just" are best addressed in an institute's proper law or left to the prudent judgment of the competent superior. Where proper law provides such criteria, however, care should be taken not to be overly restrictive. These are areas where flexibility and the ability to respond to unforeseen circumstances are significant values and proper law should not unnecessarily curtail the discretion of superiors in this regard.

One frequently encountered situation that can justify a lengthy absence is the need for a member to be absent to care for a seriously ill or infirm parent or other close relative. The need for time apart to discern one's vocation is another just cause that not infrequently arises and can justify a more prolonged absence. One year, however, is the maximum allowed by the law for such absences. An extension of the absence beyond one year, unless for a reason governed by the three criteria described below, requires either a dispensation from the Holy See or an indult of exclaustration.

An absence of more than one year is permissible for any of three, but only three, reasons enumerated in canon 665 §1: health, studies, and apostolic works undertaken in the name of the institute. The list is taxative. The reasons, especially apostolic work undertaken in the name of the institute, are often the justification for variations in living arrangements encountered fairly often today and discussed above in the section dealing with common life. However, the health of a member, physical or emotional, can also justify an absence of longer than one year. So too can studies authorized or required by the religious institute. Significantly, no time limits are placed on absences justified and approved under any of these three criteria. As a practical matter, however, studies and apostolic works undertaken in the name of the community should not ordinarily extend indefinitely. Health, on the other hand, both physical and mental, could well require an absence from traditional community life for an indefinite period. This is a determination left to the prudent judgment of the major superior and his or her council.

When a member is allowed to be absent for more than a year for apostolic reasons, care should be taken to assure that the ministry involved is consistent with the nature and charism of the community and is not simply a private preference of the member. Not infrequently the personal preference of a member is used to justify an open-ended absence from communal life, or perhaps reflects his or her geographic priorities rather than the best interests of the group at large. Moreover, in such cases it is not uncommon for the ministry involved to be out of harmony with the apostolic priorities and needs of the institute itself, or even its charism. Granting permission for the pursuit of members' personal preferences can easily begin to distort the apostolate of the institute and sow confusion regarding its nature and charism. Other members have a right that their fellow members devote themselves fully to the apostolate and charism of the institute, and for this reason alone superiors ought to resist the temptation to grant absences that are not truly undertaken to advance the purposes of the institute.

It is highly recommended that whenever a member is permitted to live outside a house of the institute, either for a just cause or for reasons of health, studies or an apostolate for more than a year, an agreement be entered into between the member and the major superior and council governing the terms and conditions of the authorized absence.

Such agreements should include provisions addressing at least the following:

- The purpose and length of the absence.
- The financial responsibilities of both the member and the institute during the absence, including disposition of income, budgetary guidelines or requirements, and insurance coverage.
- The living arrangements agreed to and authorized.
- Where applicable, an understanding regarding the use, support, and insurance of an automobile.
- The expected participation in the activities of the institute and required contact with superiors and members of the institute.
- Any reporting requirements prescribed by the major superior and council.
- Provisions for periodic review of the viability of the member's continued absence and the terms governing it.

Formation and *Support of Members*

The institute must respect and cultivate the gifts of its individual members and foster their apostolic and spiritual growth. To this end, it is incumbent on the leadership of the institute to make adequate provision of time and resources to assure that all members have the opportunity to grow spiritually and professionally and to deepen their vocational commitment.

Canon 670 is the foundational norm governing this requirement. It obligates the institute to provide whatever is necessary under the constitutions to ensure that a meaningful vowed life in the institute can be achieved by its members. Since many canons focus on the responsibilities and obligations of members, this norm provides an important balance by clearly emphasizing the reciprocal obligation of the institute and its leadership to provide for the needs of its members, particularly what is required for vocational fulfillment. This obligation is very pointedly grounded in the requirements of proper law. In other words, the requirement that an institute provide what is necessary for the achievement of a member's vocational commitment finds its concrete meaning in the charism and proper law of the institute. For example, if an institute is dedicated to the teaching apostolate, and that focus is clearly reflected in the charism and proper law of the institute, a member would not be justified in relying on canon 670 as a basis for asserting a right to community support to pursue other apostolic or personal priorities. A religious is entitled to receive spiritual and professional training to enable him or her to share meaningfully on an ongoing basis in the apostolate of the institute. While this would include reasonable and regular updating in the skills required to participate in the apostolate of the institute, it would not provide carte blanche entitlement justifying a member to pursue any personal or individual interest he or she might desire.

Other needs within the scope of canon 670, while more generic, are no less important. It goes without saying that all religious are entitled to the necessities of life, including not only food, shelter and clothing but also health care and adequate provision for care in one's senior years. Equally important is reasonable access to the time and resources necessary to foster one's spiritual life. The requirements of proper law should spell out what is required in these regards, but it would typically include, at a minimum, in accord with the exhortations contained in canon 663, the opportunity, resources, and time needed for a well-integrated personal spiritual life, including an annual retreat.

Proper law should also provide clear guidance to members on the availability of resources to provide for personal care such as spiritual direction and, where warranted or indicated, personal counselling. Additionally, in keeping with the spirit of canon 670 superiors should regard it as their duty to intervene and require appropriate treatment when a member gives clear evidence of self-destructive behaviors or emotional problems. In these times when the value of psychology is widely recognized, such assistance, even when resisted, should be seen as part of an institute's obligation to provide its members with what is necessary for the fulfillment of the individual member's vocation.[10]

Many believe that policies should be in place in all religious institutes to enable members to assist close relatives in times of need, as this is integral to supporting the well-being and vocation of the member himself or herself. To be meaningful, this should include the possibility of time off from the apostolate and, depending on the financial situation of the family and the institute, the availability of some appropriate level of financial assistance.[11] The need for such a policy is particularly important when a religious is the only family member available to be of help to a needy relative, especially a parent or a sibling. It is argued that the ability to be of such help and the peace of mind it affords the concerned religious is a vocational necessity in the spirit of canon 670.

At a minimum, however, a policy should be in place in every institute that gives members clear guidelines on these matters, not least of all in order to deal with all members equitably. While individual personal needs, issues, and problems inevitably differ and often require individual care and attention, there is a serious responsibility on the part of leadership to give all members (as much as possible) equal access to the assistance and support of the community. Written policies governing the institute's interpretation of the overall requirements of canon 670 are, therefore, an important part of assuring that all members can avail themselves of the community's resources on an equitable and consistent basis.

Another very important area concerns ongoing formation. Canon 661 complements the norm of canon 670. It places a responsibility on the individual religious to make a lifelong commitment to his or her own ongoing formation. It also gives superiors a direct mandate to assure that individual religious have both the resources and time to fulfill this requirement. The obligation to pursue ongoing formation applies to all perpetually professed members and is not reserved to a select few. Moreover, it is not something to be regarded as an option, exceptional or extraordinary. It is intended to be an integral part of every member's religious life. That is not to say that the opportunities and programs made available need to be identical for all members. For example, while sabbaticals have become a significant dimension of ongoing formation in many communities, any number of

---

10 Superiors may not mandate psychological testing or therapy, nor require members to share their medical records, however. See later discussion in this chapter on privacy rights.

11 David F. O'Connor, "Obligations and Rights," in *A Handbook on Canons 573-746*, eds. Jordan Hite, Sharon Holland and Daniel Ward (Collegeville, Minnesota: The Liturgical Press, 1985) 169-186, 189.

factors can and probably should limit their availability. Community priorities, time, resources, and the availability of a suitable opportunity will not normally permit all members to avail themselves of this experience during their years in the community. As long as all can apply and be considered, according to known and equitable criteria, the obligation to deal evenly and fairly with all would seem to be satisfied.

At the same time, it is clear that careful planning and budgeting are required to assure that the overall responsibilities of ongoing formation in the community are properly discharged. Superiors cannot be passive with respect to this obligation. Ongoing training in the spiritual life and the teachings of the Church, as well as in areas of professional competence needed in the apostolate, cannot be successfully provided without a clear-cut plan of action. Each community, therefore, should have an individual responsible for this activity and his or her efforts should be supported with sufficient resources to assure that all members are provided with the opportunities needed to update themselves in their apostolic work and energize their spiritual life on a periodic basis.

In 1990 the Holy See issued norms governing this requirement, providing considerable guidance about the expected dimensions of ongoing formation.[12] Among other things, these norms stress the need in each institute for internal programs and structures to afford members the opportunity to receive ongoing formation. They stress that the responsibility for ongoing formation cannot be fulfilled by relying only on outside resources. The vocational health and vitality of individual members depends on the availability of these resources and programs, but so too does the future of the institute and its mission. It would be very appropriate, therefore, if the proper law of each institute were to set forth expectations and requirements regarding ongoing formation. The implementation of these norms should be supported and enforced by provincial guidelines. Members should be apprised of the opportunities the community is providing for ongoing formation and expectations regarding participation. The leadership of the community should also publicize and disseminate information to the members about ongoing formation opportunities within the structures and institutions of the community, as well as about the availability of and access to outside resources.

Restricted Activities and *Activities Inconsistent with Membership*

In enumerating the obligations and rights of members of religious institutes, the 1983 Code of Canon Law lists clear restrictions on activities in

---

12 Congregation for Institutes of Consecrated Life and for Societies of Apostolic Life, instruction *Potissimum institute*, February 2, 1990: *AAS* 82 (1990) 470-532; *Origins* 19 (1988-1989) 677-699.

canons 671 and 672. Both canons are applicable to religious institutes, while the first does not apply to secular institutes or to societies of apostolic life.

Canon 671 stipulates that members of religious institutes need permission from the "legitimate superior" before she or he may accept "duties or offices outside the institute." Elements forming the foundation of such a restriction include the nature of the religious commitment, the reality of the vow of obedience, and the obligation and right each religious has to minister according to the mission and charism of his or her particular institute. There is also an unspoken presumption that members of religious institutes work in institute-sponsored apostolates. Given that today the number of community sponsored apostolates is declining, requests for permission to accept duties or offices outside the institute have become more common. Through personnel boards or other structures, such requests are carefully evaluated in light of the needs of the community and purpose of the restriction, which is to preserve the nature of the religious commitment, the reality of the vows, and the nature and mission of the institute itself.

According to canon 672, non-clerical members of religious institutes are obliged to observe the same restrictions on activity expected of diocesan clerics—namely, canons 277, 285, 286, 287, and 289. Although the motivation for holding clerical religious to these restrictions can be attributed to their commonly held clerical status, the motivation for holding non-clerical religious to the restrictions is not as clear. There is no explanation in any of the source documents for this and related canons, but one can assume it is related to the nature of the religious commitment which, as with priesthood, involves public ecclesial ministry. The canons which women and men in religious institutes are to observe are found in the section of the code dealing with the obligations and rights of clerics.

- Canon 277 §1 requires the observance of "perfect and perpetual continence," which is already accepted by religious as part of the evangelical counsels. The second paragraph enjoins religious to "prudence" in the company they keep, lest the obligation to continence be endangered or scandal be given to the people. Although the words here are simple, the issues can be very complex. Individual religious are very different, and their ability to tolerate varying circumstances differs. Also, the possibility for scandal or misunderstanding among the people in a specific locale varies according to circumstances and many other factors. It is impossible to set clear rules about which situations are acceptable and which are not. Decisions must be made based on the intent of the law, which is to safeguard continence, and on the fact that members of religious institutes are public ministers in the Church who have certain obligations to their vocation and to the people they serve.

- Canon 285 has four paragraphs, each stipulating a restriction on activity. The first paragraph obliges religious, in accord with particular law, to refrain "from those things unbecoming to their state" (c. 285 §1). The "state" of a religious within the Church is understood to be as an individual in public vows, in public witness to the Church and to the mission and charism of the institute. In the historical milieu, "unbecoming activities" were those which offended against the dignity of the clerical state. Traditional canonical commentators defined unbecoming professions as those held by the "lower classes" of society: actor, innkeeper, gambler, etc. The specific occupations are certainly conditioned by time and circumstance, but the guiding principle was the dignity of the clerical state. Those activities deemed to be beneath its dignity were unbecoming.[13] The difficulty in applying this canon to members of religious institutes is, of course, that what is considered unbecoming in some way to the clerical state might not be at all unbecoming to the religious state. A determination as to whether certain occupations offend against the religious vocation must be made on a case-by-case basis. For some religious, in keeping with their charism and their commitment to the poor, menial occupations are preferred, while those with the traditional image of "dignity" are unbecoming. For instance, working as a waiter or waitress in a restaurant might be unbecoming for a religious, but not those same positions in a soup kitchen or homeless shelter. In dealing with this restriction, it is best to say that those activities are unbecoming to the religious state which cloud or detract from the public commitment an individual has made within the Church to the mission and charism of the institute. Unless one considers these elements of the commitment, it is impossible to make a determination about a specific activity.

- Canon 285 §2 enjoins the avoidance of those things which "although not unbecoming are nonetheless alien" to the religious state. In traditional commentaries on the clerical state the distinction was routinely made between unbecoming and alien activities. While the former offended against dignity, the latter were simply incompatible, diverting the

---

13 See for instance, T. Bouscaren and A. Ellis, *Canon Law: A Text and Commentary* (Milwaukee: Bruce Publishing, 1946) 115-116; see also, John E. Lynch, "Inappropriate Clerical Activity," in *New Commentary on the Code of Canon Law,* eds. John Beal, et al (New York/Mahwah, NJ: Paulist Press, 2000) 373-374, 374.

individual from clerical ministry. Applying this principle to religious life, alien activities are those which divert the individual from public witness and the mission and charism of the institute.

Some activities that are traditionally named by commentators as "alien" activities are treated and explained in canons 285 §§3-4, 286, 287, and 289.

- Canon 285 §3 forbids the undertaking of any public office which involves the exercise of civil power. This prohibition has a long history in the Church and has at times been hotly debated.[14] According to the provisions of canon 87, a dispensation from this disciplinary law is possible, but the individual religious and his or her superiors must take into account the very strong statements in favor of the prohibition made by Pope John Paul II.[15]

However one understands the words "unbecoming" and "alien," and however they are applied to specific situations, the overriding principle in making decisions is the value being upheld by the law: members of religious institutes are called to live lives that are consistent with their vocation both in word and action; the energies of all the members are focused on and contribute to the clarity of their public profession and the fulfillment of the institute's mission and charism.

- Canon 285 §4 prevents religious from undertaking on their own initiative any financial responsibilities, accounting, or debts on behalf of another. Clerical religious must seek permission, as the canon states, from their ordinary. Canon 672 directs members of lay institutes of pontifical right to seek this permission from the proper major superior. The most obvious motivation for this restriction is safeguarding the freedom of the individual religious who, before perpetual profession of vows, according to proper law, either gave up ownership or ceded administration of property and possessions to others. To then take on those same responsibilities for others without permission or approval defeats the role the vow of poverty plays in freeing the religious to focus on ministry and mission.

It must be emphasized that accepting financial liability for others, although alien to the religious state, is not completely forbidden; rather, the requirement is for proper permission. For instance, a religious who must assist aging parents or other relatives by taking over their financial affairs may seek the required

---

14 See John E. Lynch, commentary on canon 285 §3, in *New Commentary on the Code of Canon Law*, 377.

15 Ibid.

permission. Those designated to give permission must understand the details of the situation, ensuring that the individual has access to the necessary information and resources to undertake the task successfully and that the institute is protected from any mismanagement or other unforeseen events. In other words, permission to accept financial liability for others should not be given lightly, nor should it be routinely withheld.

These same principles apply when religious are asked to act as executors of wills or estates or as guardians for children or disabled adults. In such delicate and sometimes emotionally charged situations, open communication, and dialogue between the individual religious and the superior designated to give the required permission contributes greatly to a decision which is mutually understood and accepted.

- Canon 285 §4 also includes a prohibition against clerics assuming "secular offices which entail an obligation to render accounts." There are differing interpretations on the meaning of "secular offices," but whatever meaning is adopted, such offices may be assumed by religious only when the requisite permission has been obtained.[16] As in the previous situation, both the superior and the individual religious must understand the extent of the responsibility being undertaken and evaluate, within the context of open and honest dialogue, the ability of the individual and the degree of liability, if any, which falls to the institute in case of mismanagement.
- Canon 286 treats of another "alien" activity. Religious must not engage in "business or trade either for their own benefit or that of others" without permission from the appropriate superior. For diocesan clerics, the issue of business or trade for personal profit has a long and interesting history.[17] For religious the issue is not as complex since the vow of poverty already excludes any possibility of amassing personal wealth.
- In canon 287 §1 religious are obliged to "foster that peace and harmony based on justice" which is sought by all people.
- In canon 287 §2 religious are enjoined not to be active in political parties or labor unions unless "legitimate ecclesiastical authority" (which is in

16 For instance, Lynch alludes to "secular offices for which they are legally accountable, such as an official in a savings bank, a cooperative, or a charitable association," *New Commentary on the Code of Canon Law*, 378; cf. commentary on c. 286, *The Canon Law: Letter and Spirit,* 164, which defines "secular office" as any non-ecclesiastical office.

17 See commentary on c. 186, *New Commentary on the Code of Canon Law*, 378-379.

this instance the proper religious superior) judges that such involvement will protect the rights of the church or promote the common good. Taken as a whole, this canon presents a consistent and understandable principle: religious, committed as they are to the service of all the people, work for justice in a manner that is not fractured or partisan. Political parties or labor unions might be partisan, so such activity is appropriate for religious only when partisan politics is not present.

- Canon 289 §1 addresses the last activity considered alien to the clerical state and to religious: volunteering for military service without permission from the appropriate superior. As with the preceding canons, the history of this canon is caught up in the history of diocesan clergy. The canon pronounces military service "hardly consistent with the clerical state." Its inconsistency with the religious state is easily understood.
- Canon 289 §2 directs religious to make use of any available exemptions from "exercising duties and public service offices" which are "alien" to the religious state, whether these exemptions come by law, agreements, or customs with respect to the civil authority. For instance, if religious profession is accepted in a certain locality as a reason to excuse an individual from jury service, this exemption should be utilized.

In all these instances of restricted activities or activities inconsistent with membership in a religious institute, the guiding principles are always (1) the primary importance of public commitment in the Church, and (2) the protection of the mission and charism of the institute. All decisions, determinations and dispensations concerning these activities must be grounded in these values.

Separation from the Institute: Departure, Transfer and Dismissal

Members of religious institutes become separated from the institute in one of three ways: exclaustration, transfer, and dismissal. Exclaustration has more to do with the processes involved in living apart from the community, which can be for several different reasons (personal or family needs; ongoing education; discernment). It is only exclaustration with a view toward possible separation from membership in the community that strictly speaking concerns exclaustration in relation to separation, but the process is essentially the same as with regard to the other reasons for exclaustration addressed above. All three of these methods of separation are discussed more fully in chapter seven of this handbook.

General Norms Supporting the Consecrated Life of Members of Secular Institutes

In this section, norms on the following topics will be discussed briefly as they relate to secular institutes:

- Secularity/Secular lifestyle
- Incardination of clerics
- Participation in the life of the institute
- Preservation of communion
- Governance
- Relationship to authority
- Administration of goods
- Spiritual duties
- Formation and support of members
- Departure
- Dismissal
- Transfer

Secularity/Secular Lifestyle

Secular institutes differ from religious institutes in that members live "in the world" (c. 710), as opposed to "separated from the world," the ideal for members of religious institutes. They strive for the perfection of charity and to contribute to the sanctification of the world in that context and especially from within the world. As do members of religious institutes, members of secular institutes make a commitment to live by the evangelical counsels of poverty, chastity and obedience. This does not change a member's proper canonical condition among the people of God, whether lay or clerical, however, even while respecting the prescripts of the law referring to institutes of consecrated life (c. 711). While the constitutions of secular institutes are to establish the sacred bonds by which members assume the evangelical counsels, the proper secularity of the institute is always to be preserved in its way of life (c. 712). The obligation to maintain the secular nature of the institute gives rise to a broad right of the members that the institute must always preserve.

Incardination of Clerics

Clerical members of secular institutes incardinated in a diocese are subject to the diocesan bishop without prejudice to those matters that pertain to consecrated life in their own institute (c. 715 §1). If the institute provides for clerics to be incardinated in the institute itself, according to the norm of canon

266 §3, they are subject to the bishop in the same way that religious are when appointed to works of the institute or governance of the institute (c. 715 §2).

Participation in the Life of the Institute

More like societies of apostolic life than religious institutes, members of secular institutes express and exercise their consecration in apostolic activity so as to imbue all things with the spirit of the gospel for the strengthening and growth of the Body of Christ (c. 713). Thus, a significant difference between secular and religious institutes, which contextualizes the possession and exercise of their obligations and rights as members, is that they exercise their consecration principally through apostolic activity in the world rather than through common life separated from the world. In today's world the distinction between these two forms of consecrated life may not seem as sharp as would have been the case in past ages when those in vowed life in a religious institute were not engaged in apostolic works outside the monastery to the extent that they are today. The difference may therefore seem subtle, but it is no less real in terms of the norms of the law.

Members of secular institutes pursue their own perfection in charity and sanctification, and the sanctification of the world, through life and activity "in the world," that is through a secular lifestyle. As such, members of secular institutes can expect—and in fact have a canonical right—that the secularity of their institute and the nature of their own secular lives always be preserved and safeguarded by the institute. Members are therefore to lead their lives in the ordinary conditions of the world according to the norm of the constitutions, whether alone, or in their own families, or in a group living as brothers or sisters (c. 714).

Preservation of Communion

Members of secular institutes have a canonical duty to preserve communion among themselves, to care for one another (c. 716 §2), and, of course, to preserve full communion with the Apostolic See and the Church as a whole (c. 592). Life in common is normative for religious and integral to the nature of virtually all religious communities. The opposite is true for secular institutes. While a form of common life exists in some secular institutes, it does so only by way of exception. The vast majority of members of secular institutes live apart from one another and quite independent of any form of common life.

Canon 714, however, clearly recognizes that in some cases, where proper law provides or permits, one residential option for the members of some secular institutes is a shared living arrangement with other members of the same institute. In those cases, however, it has been clear since the recognition and authorization of secular institutes in 1947 that shared life for members of secular institutes does not include the normative communal practices of religious or their holding of goods in common, typical of traditional religious institutes. Nonetheless, practical necessity suggests that all secular institutes be permitted the option of maintaining one or more communal residences. The need to bring leadership together for extended periods, as well as the need to provide for members who are incapable of caring for themselves, might well justify the creation of such communities. Also, the need for periods together for those in formation or those on retreat would justify the creation and maintenance of facilities for appropriate communal life. Their use, however, would typically be by way of exception and only for specified purposes authorized in proper law.

Governance and *Relationship to Authority*

Members of secular institutes have a right that their institutes be governed in accordance with the provisions of the Code of Canon Law and the proper law of the institute. No one may be designated as supreme moderator who has not been definitively incorporated in the institute, and the highest duty of those in charge of the governance of the institute is to take care to preserve the unity of spirit of the institute and to promote the active participation of the members (c. 717).

Administration of Goods

The goods of an institute are to be administered in accordance with book V of the code (*The Temporal Goods of the Church*) in ways that express and foster evangelical poverty. Furthermore, the proper law of the institute is to define the obligations of the institute towards members who work for it, especially financial obligations towards them (c. 718).

Spiritual Duties

The code identifies certain spiritual duties members are required to abide by. They are to devote themselves diligently to prayer, give themselves in a fitting way to the reading of sacred scripture, observe an annual retreat, and perform other spiritual exercises according to proper law. Daily celebration of the Eucharist is expected, if possible, and members are to freely approach the sacrament of penance frequently; they are also directed to freely obtain necessary direction of their consciences and to seek such counsel, even from moderators if they wish (c. 719).

Formation and Support of Members

Admission to a secular institute, either for probation or for the assumption of sacred bonds (whether temporarily or definitively and perpetually) is for the major moderators to determine according to the norm of the constitutions (c. 720). Canon 721 identifies additional impediments that stand in the way of valid admission and authorizes such further impediments as the proper law of the institute might establish. Canon 723 outlines the stages candidates are to pass through prior to definitive incorporation, which must always include assuming the three evangelical counsels. First incorporation is to be temporary and may not be less than five years. If a candidate is judged suitable for definitive membership, he or she is to repeat his or her commitment to the sacred bonds assumed to live according to the evangelical counsels. Definitive incorporation is equivalent to perpetual incorporation with regard to its juridic effects as established in the constitutions (c. 723). As with religious institutes and societies of apostolic life, full rights and obligations according to the Code of Canon Law and the constitutions and proper law of the institute accrue to definitively incorporated members.

Similar to members of religious institutes, formation is to continue throughout one's membership, starting with the probationary period, which implies a duty on the part of the institutes to provide meaningful opportunities for continuing formation, and on the part of members to take advantage of those opportunities and continue life-long formation. The obligation of members of secular institutes is more limited and focused than for religious: "Formation . . . is to be continued . . . according to the constitutions" (c. 724 §1). The central and determinative role of proper law is again highlighted by this requirement.

Paragraph 2 of canon 724 helps clarify this obligation by explicitly requiring that the "moderators of the institute are to have a serious concern for the continued spiritual formation of the members." This mandate is clearly in the spirit of the canons regarding religious institutes. Like them, it makes clear that the law of the Church is concerned that those who commit their lives to the service of the Church and the People of God by entering into some form of consecrated life are entitled to the help and support of their sponsoring communities in the realization of their vocational goals. These requirements, of course, differ according to the nature of the commitment made and the nature and proper law of the community in which it is made.

Departure, Dismissal, and Transfer

Temporary members can depart from the institute with relative ease at the end of temporary incorporation. During the time period of temporary membership this should be sought only for a grave cause by way of a freely submitted petition to the supreme moderator who can grant the request with the consent of his or her council (c. 726 §§ 1 and 2). Perpetually incorporated members must seek an indult of departure from the Apostolic See through the supreme moderator if the institute is of pontifical right, or from the diocesan bishop for diocesan right institutes, in accordance with the constitutions (c.727 §1).

If it concerns a cleric incardinated in the institute, the prescript of canon 693 must be observed. The juridic effect of an indult of departure from a secular institute is that all rights and obligations deriving from incorporation cease (c. 729).

Members can be dismissed in accord with the prescripts of canons 694 and 695. The constitutions are to prescribe the causes for which a member can be dismissed—provided the reasons are proportionately grave, external, imputable, and juridically proven—and that the manner of proceeding is consistent with canons 697-700, the precept of canon 701.

Members of secular institutes can transfer to another secular institute following the prescripts of canon 684 §§1, 2, 4 and canon 685, but to transfer to a religious institute or society of apostolic life the permission of the Apostolic See is required, along with observance of any of its mandates in connection with the transfer (c. 730). All three of these methods of separation are discussed in chapter seven of this handbook.

General Norms Supporting the Apostolic Purpose of Societies of Apostolic Life

In this section, norms concerning the following topics will be discussed briefly as they relate to societies of apostolic life:

- The evangelical counsels
- Governance
- Incardination
- Relationship to authority
- Common life
- Ongoing formation
- Fostering of spirituality, professional competence, and religious vocation
- Living outside the society
- Departure
- Transfer
- Dismissal

The Evangelical Counsels

The Code of Canon law states that societies of apostolic life "resemble" institutes of consecrated life. Their members, while in principle not taking religious vows, pursue the apostolic purpose proper to the society. Members live some form of life in common as brothers or sisters "according to their proper manner of life," and they "strive for the perfection of charity through the observance of their constitutions" (c. 731 §1). However, the code admits of societies in which the members *do* assume the evangelical counsels by some bond defined in the constitutions (which could be, but is not necessarily, the profession of vows) (c. 731 §2).

Many of the norms that apply to religious institutes are explicitly made to apply to societies of apostolic life (c. 732)—namely, canons 578-597 and canon 606, without prejudice, however, to the nature of each society. Moreover, canons 598-602 also apply to societies in which the members assume the evangelical counsels by some bond defined in the constitutions (c. 732). Thus, with respect to these norms, unless obviously inapplicable due to the nature of a particular society, societies resemble religious institutes in a number of concrete respects. The norms for admission are not unlike those for religious and secular institutes, calling for a period of probation and incorporation in stages in accordance with a process outlined in the constitutions (c. 735).

Governance, Incardination, and *Relationship to Authority*

The law requires that clerics who belong to clerical societies be incardinated in the society unless the constitutions specifically provide otherwise. For instance, in the Society of Saint Sulpice, a clerical society of secular priests, the constitutions provide that members remain incardinated in the diocese from which they join, although they come under the authority of the superiors of the society, not the diocesan bishop, as long as they remain members[18] (c. 736). The norms for the program of studies and reception of orders of secular clerics are to be observed with respect to clerical members of societies of apostolic life (c. 736). Importantly, canon 737 states explicitly that the obligations and rights of members of societies of apostolic life are to be defined in the constitutions, making the constitutions all-important with respect to members understanding and fulfilling their rights and obligations, and to superiors' supervision of members and enforcement of those rights and obligations.

According to canon 739, all members of societies of apostolic life are "bound by the common obligations of clerics, unless something else is evident

18 Article 55, Constitutions of the Priests of Saint Sulpice.

from the nature of the matter." Commentators differ on whether this statement refers only to clerical societies or to all societies.[19] In any event the canon provides sufficient latitude for each society to make its own determinations, based on its charism, mission and particular law.

Common Life

The law provides that members of these societies are to live in a house legitimately established by the community, observing common life according to the norm of proper law (which is also to govern absences from the house or community) (c. 740). The requirement and experience of common life among members of societies of apostolic life often closely mirrors the common life of religious. However, the constitutions of societies generally allow for more variation and flexibility than is typically true of those of religious institutes, providing more leeway both in the obligation to live a common life and in the style of common life that is permitted. Nevertheless, life in common is considered the norm and, indeed, an essential element of the vocation to a society (cc. 731 §1 and 740). But it must be kept in mind that members of societies of apostolic life are not religious; they do not ordinarily make a public profession of the evangelical counsels. As non-religious, the holding of all things in common, a key aspect of the life in common characteristic of religious, is inapplicable to them and their communities. Moreover, many of the obligations and rights of religious generally (for instance cc. 662-665) do not apply to members of these societies. Furthermore, the code provides greater freedom to societies in the structuring of their common life. For example, unlike religious who are normally required to reside in a house of their institute (c. 665 §1), the norm for members of societies of apostolic life is to live in a house of the institute "or a local community established by competent authority" (c. 733 §1). This flexibility was seen historically as necessary to permit these societies to better achieve their apostolic purposes. The end result is a style of life which, while it may on the surface closely resemble religious life, betrays important and fundamental differences which set it apart.

Ongoing Formation and the *Fostering of Spirituality, Professional Competence and Religious Vocation*

---

19 Sharon L. Holland, IHM, for instance, contends that these obligations apply only to clerical members of societies, not lay members or religious who are not clerics; see commentary on c. 739, *New Commentary on the Code of Canon Law,* 899. O'Connor applies the canon to all members of Societies of Apostolic Life, clerical or lay. "Obligations and Rights," 300.

The obligation to provide members with what is required for vocational fulfillment, although stated with less specificity, is also found in the norms governing societies of apostolic life. Canon 737 provides that incorporation in a society of apostolic life entails reciprocal rights and obligations on the part of the member and the society, according to the constitutions. The society has the obligation "to lead the members to the end of their particular vocation." This responsibility is the functional equivalent of canon 670 and, like that canon, expresses the obligation in terms of the requirements of proper law. Therefore, just as religious must be provided with all that is needed, so too members of societies of apostolic life are entitled to the active support of their society in the realization of their vocational commitment. By analogy, this requirement should be seen as extending to the society's obligation to provide for and encourage the ongoing formation of its members. As we have seen, canon 661 makes this obligation quite explicit on the part of religious institutes, although it is less pointedly stated in the canons governing societies of apostolic life. Nonetheless, canon 735 §3 requires that proper law should provide for suitable formation for the members of a society of apostolic life "in such a way that the members, recognizing their divine vocation, may be fittingly prepared for the mission and life of the society."

The spirit of canon 735 §3 clearly points to the need to provide for more than initial formation; otherwise, the ongoing spiritual and apostolic needs of the society and its members would be neglected. To be suitably trained and prepared for the "mission and life of the society" is, by its very terms, the agenda of a lifetime and as such requires the nourishment and support of an ongoing formation program. Therefore, while the language of canon 735 §3 is clearly a much less pointed and specific requirement than that articulated in canon 661, the spirit of the two norms would seem to require an equivalent effort to assure the ongoing vocational development of their members.

Living outside the Society

Shorter term absences from a house or community, and therefore from the prescribed common life, is to be regulated by proper law (c. 740). This allows each society to craft criteria that best reflect its origins and mission. The end result is the possibility of a more flexible and discretionary set of norms governing life in common and absences from the community than are typical of a religious institute. The rather specific and detailed criteria applicable to absences for members of religious institutes (c. 665 §1) have no parallel in the canons applying to societies of apostolic life (cc. 731-746). Moreover, it is telling that, unlike other provisions in the code governing the lives of members of societies of apostolic life, the law governing religious on this topic is nowhere cited as a guideline to be followed by societies of apostolic life.

For longer term absences a process parallel to exclaustration (c. 686) is provided for in canon 745. In this instance, the absence of a definitively incorporated member must be granted by the supreme moderator with the consent of the counsel and may not be for more than three years. Rights and obligations of the member which cannot be reconciled with the condition of the member under such circumstances are suspended, although the member remains under the care of the moderators. However, if it concerns a cleric, the consent of the ordinary where he is to reside must be obtained, under whose care and dependence he also remains (c. 745).

In light of the basic principle of common life as the norm for members of societies of apostolic life, any significant time away from the community should be regulated by an agreement between the member and the major superior. The principles governing such an arrangement in the case of a religious, as discussed above, should be applied here as well.

Departure, Transfer, and Dismissal

Canon 742 dictates that departure and dismissal of a temporarily incorporated member must be handled according to the constitutions of the society. Canon 743 gives the supreme moderator the authority to grant an indult of departure, with consent of the council, unless it is reserved to the Holy See by the constitutions. Transfer is covered in canon 744 and is granted by the supreme moderator if the transfer is to another society of apostolic life. If transfer involves an institute of consecrated life, permission must be sought from the Holy See (c. 744 §2). Dismissal of a member must follow the same norms that apply to religious (cc. 694-704), with appropriate adaptations (c. 746).

Important Rights Common to Institutes and Societies

- Right to privacy
- Right to a good reputation

Right to Privacy

Any claim a religious might make to a right to privacy within the structure of religious life is not rooted in his or her status as a religious, but in the obligations and rights of all the Christian faithful (see c. 220). Just as a religious does not relinquish basic civil rights upon entering a religious institute, the religious, cleric or lay, does not relinquish her or his claim to the obligations and rights of all the faithful. Consequently, what follows concerning privacy applies to all individuals in religious institutes, societies of apostolic life, or secular institutes.

Within the context of this handbook, the right to privacy might best be discussed in terms of "confidentiality."[20] For instance, an individual has the right to expect confidentiality in relationships with medical or mental health professionals. Information from these professionals concerning individual religious may be given to superiors only with permission. This permission from the individual religious is usually given in writing and for a specific purpose. The requirement of permission for information to be shared by medical, psychological, or psychiatric professionals is highly regulated by civil law in all jurisdictions, including the federal government in the United States today (e.g., *Health Insurance Portability and Accountability Act of 1996*: HIPAA). Religious superiors must therefore be scrupulous in complying with all civil law requirements and members should be made aware of their rights in this regard. Furthermore, superiors must be conscious of the delicate relationship between considerations of internal and external forum in relation to contacts with any professional dealing with the psychological or psychiatric needs of a member. Anything that might appear to be an attempt to coerce a manifestation of conscience should be scrupulously avoided.

Before giving permission, the religious should be told how and with whom the confidential information is shared. There should be clear limits on how long such information is kept in one's personnel file, what the disposition of such information is once the leadership personnel for whom it was intended leave office, or when the purpose for which the information was released is no longer pertinent. For instance, if confidential information is released in order that a psychiatrist or psychologist might issue an evaluation on the suitability of a religious for a particular assignment, policies should be clear on the destruction of the confidential materials once the assignment question is resolved.

Right to a Good Reputation

A right of all the faithful which is related to confidentiality is the right to one's good name (see c. 220). Considering the issue in this light, an individual can expect privacy concerning personnel records and letters of recommendation. Institutes are well advised to have policies on how long sensitive or incriminating materials are retained in files and who oversees their removal and destruction. For instance, if a religious had a substance abuse or mental health

---

20 See Elissa Rinere, CP, "The Individual's Right to Confidentiality," *Bulletin on Issues of Religious Law* 11 (Washington, DC: LCWR, 1995).

problem in his or her past, but successfully underwent treatment and rehabilitation, stated policies providing for the removal of all mention of this history from the files ensure freedom and privacy for the individual.

As is true with all rights in the Church, there are limits. Difficult decisions must be made when the rights of the individual come into conflict with the common good, either of the institute or the larger society. In certain circumstances, because an individual might present a danger to others, sensitive or confidential material that could affect the good name of a member might have to be shared. These situations must be evaluated on a case-by-case basis, and the rights of all parties must be carefully considered and respected. A religious with an active substance abuse problem or uncontrolled and debilitating psychiatric problems cannot demand a right to privacy and good name at the expense of unsuspecting people who are potential victims.

In 1993 a document was published by the NCCB outlining a recommended process utilizing silence—that is, lack of comment or disclosure—as a means of trying to protect privacy as well as the common good.[21] Of course, this whole area has also been impacted enormously by the clergy sex abuse scandals of recent times, the *Charter for the Protection of Children and Young People* of the USCCB,[22] and the *Essential Norms for Diocesan/Eparchial Policies Dealing with Allegations of Sexual Abuse of Minors by Priests or Deacons.*[23] Both superiors and members should take pains to be familiar with the *Charter* and *Essential Norms* and to be prepared to seek out competent canonical advice should a situation arise with implications for their possible applicability.

The right to confidentiality is sometimes seriously transgressed in religious life not maliciously but out of a lack of awareness of what this right entails. It is best respected in situations where personal and institutional boundaries are clear and relationships between members and leaders mature and honest. Many situations arise today where the right to privacy and the right to a good

---

21 USCCB, "Proposed Guidelines on the Assessment of Clergy and Religious for Assignment" (1993). A sample letter of recommendation is included as part of the text, although it is noted: "Failure to provide such a statement is sufficient reason for delaying or denying the appointment to the candidate" (Guideline 4, page 2). The document is available at http://www.usccb.org/issues-and-action/child-and-youth-protection/resources/upload/1993-SuitabilityGuidelines.pdf. It has now been superseded by the *Charter for the Protection of Children and Young People*, available at https://www.usccb.org/offices/child-and-youth-protection/charter-protection-children-and-young-people.

22 See https://www.usccb.org/test/upload/Charter-for-the-Protection-of-Children-and-Young-People-2018-final(1).pdf.

23 See https://www.usccb.org/resources/essential-norms-diocesaneparchial-policies-dealing-allegations-sexual-abuse-minors.

reputation must be considered in relation to the good of the faithful and vulnerable persons. Superiors in particular, therefore, should devote the necessary time and effort to understanding the meaning and implications of the rights of members and seek to protect those rights assiduously, while also understanding the boundary lines between protecting individual rights and the need to act on behalf of the well-being of the community and the Church as a whole. Awareness has grown of the paramount importance today of acting in the best interests and wellbeing of those who might be victims of misconduct. These persons may face very serious life consequences if misconduct is not dealt with appropriately and the necessary means made available to assist those who may have been harmed.

Conclusion

The manner in which the Code of Canon Law protects the rights and identifies the obligations of fully incorporated members of religious institutes, secular institutes, and societies of apostolic life begins with a number of canonical norms that apply to those institutes in common. The applicable norms begin with those that protect the rights and set forth the obligations of every member of the Christian faithful acquired through baptism. More specific rights and obligations attach to an individual through the particular status he or she may have in the Church under canon law (lay or religious; cleric or non-cleric; those that pertain to particular officeholders, etc.). The more general rights and obligations of members of the Christian faithful may, however, be qualified, restricted or expanded in virtue of some more particular status of the person as determined by the Code of Canon Law, by the sacred power conferred sacramentally through ordination, or by the acquisition of some particular office to which special rights and obligations apply. Likewise, the particular canonical rights and obligations that pertain to a given person may be the result of membership in one of the intentional communities that have been considered in this chapter, that is religious institutes, secular institutes and societies of apostolic life, as determined by the constitutions or other particular law of the institute or society to which she or he belongs.

As noted at the outset, we have been concerned in this chapter only with the rights and obligations of fully incorporated members of these communities. While there are rights and obligations that the three types of communities we have been considering are bound by in common, the particular rights and obligations members have that differ from members of the other types of communities relate most importantly to the nature of these three kinds of communities. The three distinguishing and differentiating characteristics of these three kinds of communities are: (1) for religious institutes, life lived in close community, members having taken vows professing the evangelical counsels through which they strive for the perfection of charity separate from the world; (2) for secular institutes, a secular lifestyle lived in the world, not generally in close community, members striving for the perfection of charity through profession of the evangelical counsels, and devotion to living a spiritual life and transforming the secular world "from within," that is living in the secular world; and (3) for societies of apostolic life, the apostolic mission of the society carried out by its members through life in some form of community with or without vows (though generally without), striving for the perfection of charity by faithfully carrying out of the apostolic mission of the society according to the constitutions.

Because of the historical predominance of religious institutes, certainly prior to the eighteenth century, the large core of common rights and obligations among the three communities derive from norms applicable to religious institutes. They are the historical "template" for the structure of rights and obligations that pertain to members of more particular canonically recognized intentional communities in the Church. Thus, many of the rights and obligations of fully incorporated members of all three of these kinds of communities are found in the common norms set forth in the section of the Code of Canon Law that pertains to religious institutes. These exist, of course, against the backdrop of the rights and obligations that pertain to all members of the Christian faithful.

The Code of Canon Law affords wide latitude to the communities themselves to fashion laws and policies, and to define rights and obligations that suit the particular nature of their own particular kind of community, and indeed of their own community itself. Thus, any examination of the rights and obligations of fully incorporated members of religious should begin with the rights and obligations of all members of the Christian faithful, continue with norms common to the three types of communities we are concerned with, and then zero in on the specific rights and obligations of the members of *this* religious institute, secular institute or society of apostolic life as determined by the code and as identified and specified in the constitutions and other particular law of the institute or society.

It is only through such a comprehensive approach that one can be confident of ascertaining the rights and obligations of fully incorporated members in order to vindicate those rights and assure fulfillment of those obligations in ways that will do justice, assure equity, and demonstrate compassion in light of the specific circumstances.

CHAPTER SEVEN

SEPARATION OF MEMBERS FROM THE INSTITUTE

Therese Guerin Sullivan, SP[1]

Members separate from an institute or society in one of two ways: (1) departure, either by transfer or "secularization," or (2) dismissal, either *ipso facto*, mandatory, or discretionary. Although not technically separation, this chapter also treats exclaustration. Each type of separation is unique with the various subsidiary issues. The following material attempts to highlight the essential elements of each type.

Transfer

Definition

Transfer is the change of a perpetually professed member of a religious institute of consecrated life to another religious institute of consecrated life. Usually, the permission to transfer can be given by the supreme moderator and the council. However, the permission of the Apostolic See is required when the transfer involves a member moving from one of the three committed life forms (religious institute, secular institute, or a society of apostolic life) to one of the other forms. The pertinent canons in these situations are 684 and 685 (religious institutes); 730 (secular institutes); and 744 §2 (societies of apostolic life).

Mutual Obligations

As with all requests, the petitioner must provide the reasons for a transfer (e.g., the desire for greater perfection, spiritual welfare, etc.). Permission of the supreme moderators of both institutes, with the consent of each of the respective general councils, is to be obtained (c. 684 §1). In cases of transfers between centralized institutes and monasteries, normally the major superior of the

1 Therese Guerin Sullivan, SP, was the original author and the editor for the revised chapter. David M. Hynous, OP, Patrick T. Shea, OFM, and Madeline Welch, OSU, contributed to the writing of the original chapter.

monastery can act as there is no general superior (c. 684 §3). Proper law is to be observed.

The transfer of a perpetually or temporary professed religious to another institute is a process that requires a timetable and a clear understanding of responsibilities between the two institutes. When the formal period of probation begins, the transferring member assumes to live the obligations of the second institute (c. 684 §2). Salary and expenses then belong to the second institute. During this period, ultimate financial responsibility and accountability remain with the first institute, although an agreement about room and board, medical insurance, etc., will need to be formulated.

If the member decides to end the transfer process, he/she returns to the first institute. The text of the canon states that returning to the first institute is a duty and a right (c. 684 §2).

> It is a right because the superiors of the original institute cannot refuse to take the member back for having tried to transfer to another institute pursuant to Church rules. And it is also a duty because the religious must return "unless an indult of secularization has been obtained" that is, an indult to leave the institute . . . .[2]

During the period of probation, any patrimony being administered by the first institute remains there.

Time Periods

The transferring member will have a period of probation in which to acquire experiential knowledge of the second institute and to evaluate the decision to transfer to another institute. The minimum for this period of probation is three years. Proper law may require a lengthier time.

The transfer is granted according to the norm of law; definitive incorporation into the second institute takes place when the member professes vows in the receiving institute. All obligations and duties of the first institute come to an end. Any patrimony or dowry is transferred to the second institute. At the time of transfer a new act of cession of patrimony and dowry are needed.

Procedures

The procedure found in canon 684 §§1 and 2 are to be followed.

---

2 See Francisco J. Ramos, *Exegetical Commentary on the Code of Canon Law,* II/2 (Chicago: Wilson & Lafleur and Montreal, Canada: Midwest Theological Forum, 2004) 1835.

Note that the transfer of temporary professed members is limited to the monasteries mentioned in canon 684 §3.

SAMPLE DOCUMENT 1
PETITION FOR AND APPROVAL OF TRANSFER

To: Supreme Moderator (of petitioner's own institute)

and

To: Supreme Moderator (of institute to which petitioner requests to transfer)

I, (first and last names of the petitioner; place, day, month and year of birth; place, day, month and year of both temporary and perpetual profession) a perpetually professed member of the (Institute name) of (Place) request permission to transfer from the said Congregation to the (Name of institute going to) ________________ of (Place) __________. The transfer will be effective upon completion of the requirements of canon law and proper law.

My reasons for requesting a transfer are: (e.g. the desire for greater perfection, spiritual welfare, etc.).

I understand the transfer is granted according to the norm of law and definitive incorporation in the Institute must be preceded by a period of probation according to the norm of the particular law of that Institute, observing the prescriptions of canon 685, §1. I understand that throughout the period during which the proposed transfer will be discerned I am subject to the Constitution of (Name of institute going to). I further understand that I must return to the Congregation/Order if I do not make profession in that Institute (c. 684, §2).

Signature of Petitioner: ____

Date: ____

This request is approved and formalized as of the date below and by the signatures of the Supreme Moderators of the releasing and receiving religious institutes having the previous consent of their Councils.

Signature: ____
(Supreme Moderator of releasing institute)

Dated: ________________________________

Signature: ____
(Supreme Moderator of receiving institute)

Exclaustration

Definition

Exclaustration consists in a member of a religious institute living outside a religious institute for a definite or indefinite period of time, with permission granted by legitimate authority, during which time the exclaustrated religious remains a member of the institute but with some alteration of the canonical relationship between the individual religious and the religious institute. This involves a relaxation of some obligations of religious life. The word exclaustration derives from two Latin words, *ex* and *claustrum* and means outside the enclosure.

> This canonical process is limited to members in perpetual vows.
>
> For those in professed temporary vows, there is no need for an indult of exclaustration because the period of temporary vows is a time in which the religious and the institute must discern the religious' vocation to live that life. The indult of exclaustration would defeat the purpose of this stage.[3]

There are several types of exclaustration, two of which are delineated in the code and at least two others that have developed in the practice of the Congregation for Institutes of Consecrated Life and for Societies of Apostolic Life (CICLSAL).

- *Voluntary (or ordinary or simple).* This type of exclaustration is described in canon 686 §1.[4] It may be granted for a grave cause upon the petition of a religious to the supreme moderator of his or her religious institute. Consent of the council is required. Only the Holy See can grant an indult of exclaustration for nuns (c. 686 §2).

- *Involuntary (or imposed).* This type of exclaustration is described in canon 686 §3. It may be imposed upon a religious by means of a petition of the religious institute's supreme moderator made to the Holy See, or to the diocesan bishop in the case of an institute of diocesan right. The supreme moderator can request exclaustration for grave causes, and "equity and charity" are to be observed. "The seriousness of the consequences of imposed exclaustration demand that the measure be

---

3 *Exegetical Commentary* II/2, 1841.

4 Canon 745 provides for a parallel to exclaustration for societies of apostolic life, although it is not termed "exclaustration" but rather "an indult to live outside the society." There is no similar provision regarding exclaustration for members of secular institutes— voluntary or imposed.

taken only for the common good and only after the causes are proved, the incorrigibility is continuous, and the individual is given a chance to defend himself."[5]

- *Qualified Exclaustration.* This is a type of exclaustration given to religious priests who are considering laicization to allow them an environment for discernment in the hopes that they will not seek laicization. Observance of the vows, except the vow of chastity, is suspended as are other obligations of the priesthood; also suspended are certain obligations or rights such as exercise of an apostolate, wearing clerical garb. A priest under such exclaustration is to receive the sacraments like a lay person. Qualified exclaustration has been likened to a temporary lay state. Only the Holy See can grant this type of exclaustration, which does not happen frequently.

- *Ad Experimentum.* This type of exclaustration is granted by the Holy See if a religious priest wants to leave his institute to become a diocesan priest and has found a diocesan bishop willing to receive him on a trial basis.[6]

- *Exclaustration durante necessitate.* It is not clear if this should be a separate type since it is a form of voluntary exclaustration, but it can only be granted by the Apostolic See (or a diocesan bishop in the case of an institute of diocesan right) since its term is indefinite, lasting as long as the reason for which the exclaustration was granted lasts.

Mutual Obligations (Effect of Exclaustration)

Exclaustration involves a freedom for exclaustrated religious from obligations incompatible with their new condition of life. At the same time the religious remains dependent upon and subject to his or her superiors (c. 687). The effects may vary somewhat with the type of exclaustration and the reason for exclaustration. What this means is not always clear. Canon 687 only specifically deals with two effects or rights and obligations: *religious habit* and *active and passive voice.* An exclaustrated member can wear the habit unless the indult of exclaustration provides otherwise. Exclaustrated members lack active and passive voice.

---

5 *Exegetical Commentary* II/2, 1842.

6 In the past, the Congregation for Institutes of Consecrated Life and Societies of Apostolic Life (CICLSAL) granted exclaustration with specific time limits to religious who wished to found new institutes or sought to become virgins or hermits; therefore, the condition of these would not properly be *ad experimentum.*

There are additional items that also require consideration.

- *Poverty*. Exclaustrated religious are freed from many obligations of the evangelical counsel of poverty inconsistent with community life, especially the need to request certain permissions for ordinary expenses and turn over income. The exclaustrated religious is still expected to request permission for extraordinary or very large expenses. The exclaustrated religious is expected to live a simple lifestyle.

- *Financial needs*. Exclaustrated religious are expected to obtain employment, and they may keep the income for support. Whether a religious can obtain employment may be a factor in determining whether he or she can be granted exclaustration. Since involuntary exclaustration is often imposed on a religious for the benefit of the institute and since the religious on whom it is imposed may have problems that make employment unlikely, an institute may have a higher level of obligation to provide support for such a religious. In any event, if a religious on exclaustration is in need, the institute has an obligation to provide support.

  Financial needs can cover many matters. Institutes should consider whether it should provide for: simply a cash gift; continuation on health insurance; an automobile or expenses therefor; and/or a loan. This will be discussed in more detail below.

- *Obedience*. Exclaustrated religious are freed from many obligations of obedience inconsistent with community life, so they need not ask many of the permissions that they have to request if they were living in community. The religious would still have to request permissions or dispensations that have nothing to do with community life and/or which cover important matters (e.g., publishing, travel). Other obligations of the institute and individual religious that should be considered are: updates or reports by the religious on progress or situations or changes of address; receipt of community mailings; visits to the community; and use of a contact person within the institute.

- *Relationship with local ordinary*. Exclaustrated religious remain dependent upon and subject to their superiors and to the local ordinary, especially if the exclaustrated religious is a priest. Moreover, in the granting of simple exclaustration of a cleric, the local ordinary where the cleric is to reside must first give consent. This covers a variety of possible situations that can include a religious priest exercising ministry under the general supervision of the diocesan bishop. It would at least seem to involve in the case of a non-ordained religious, advising the local ordinary of the presence of the exclaustrated religious in the diocese.

- *Chastity*. The obligation of chastity is unaffected by exclaustration.

Time Periods

The time periods vary according to the type of exclaustration. There is a limitation on how long a religious institute can grant exclaustration.

With regard to voluntary or simple exclaustration, canon 686 provides that the religious institute can grant exclaustration for a period not exceeding three years. The canon further says that extending the indult or granting it for more than three years is reserved to the Holy See, or the diocesan bishop in the case of institutes of diocesan right. It is not clear whether institutes can grant extensions in situations in which the institute made the initial grant for less than three years and the extension and the initial grant will not exceed three years; commentators have interpreted this provision both ways and a number of institutes follow the practice of granting exclaustration in periods of less than three years, as long as the total grants do not exceed three years. The indult can provide another limitation on the term; it could state that the indult lasts for a certain time period but only as long as the motivating cause for the exclaustration lasts.

In cases of involuntary exclaustration, the exclaustration lasts as long as the situation that requires the imposition of exclaustration lasts. Thus, the term is indefinite.

Qualified exclaustration has a term of only one or two years, and this is not commonly extended.

In cases of exclaustration *durante necessitate* or any exclaustration that is granted for as long as a condition exists, this must be granted by the Holy See or the diocesan bishop, even if it is likely that it will last less than three years, since it could last longer than three years. Ordinarily this type of exclaustration is granted only after a religious institute has granted exclaustration for as long a period as it could do so.

Voluntary (Ordinary) Exclaustration

Procedures for Petition

- Formalities:

  First and last names of petitioner;

  Place, day, month and year of birth;

  Place, day, month and year of temporary and solemn profession;

  Whether petitioner is a cleric or lay religious;

  If Petitioner is a cleric, place, day, month and year of priestly (or diaconal) ordination;

  Principal ministries of petitioner or his curriculum vitae in the apostolate;

  Petition signed by religious and the essential part of request in his or her handwriting.

- Purpose or reason:

  Written request by petitioner giving reason;

  The reason must be a grave or serious reason. Such reasons could include: vocational discernment, support or care of aged or infirm parents,[7] personal health problems, engagement in pastoral or diocesan work, or business ventures. It is noted that some of these matters could also be handled under permission to be absent from the community (c. 665, §1).

- Permission of local ordinary, if petitioner is a cleric;

  A document from some local ordinary is needed in which the bishop agrees to accept the religious cleric during the period of exclaustration.

- The length of time for which exclaustration is sought (i.e., one year, two years, three years, or as long as the need exists);

- Information and a *votum* from the major superior and the council according to the proper law of the institute or its practices or procedure.

Granting Authority

- Supreme moderator of the institute with the consent of the council, if exclaustration is for three years or less;

---

7 This need for separation may have begun when a member requested permission for an absence from observing common life in accordance with canon 665 and the proper law of the institute. However, the member is now requesting a much lengthier absence which goes beyond the proper law of the institute.

- Diocesan bishop, if it involves an institute of diocesan right and if the term of exclaustration exceeds three years, is an extension beyond three years or is indefinite;
- Holy See, i.e., Congregation for Institutes of Consecrated Life and for Societies of Apostolic Life, if it involves an institute of pontifical right and if the term of exclaustration exceeds three years, is an extension beyond three years, or is indefinite.

Indult

- Formalities: in the form of a decree, signature of the supreme moderator and general secretary at the bottom, date and place of execution, stamp or seal of the institute;
- The day on which exclaustration takes effect and the date on which exclaustration ceases;
- The fact that the member requested exclaustration;
- The serious reason(s) for granting exclaustration;
- A recitation that the supreme moderator and the council consented to the exclaustration;
- If the member is a cleric, a recitation that the consent of the named local ordinary has been obtained;
- The means by which the local ordinary of the place of residence of the member has been or will be informed of the presence and status of the exclaustrated member;
- That the exclaustrated member will not have active or passive voice in the institute during exclaustration;
- Whether the exclaustrated member may wear the habit of the institute or any other insignia or otherwise identify himself or herself as a member of the institute;
- The ways in which the member will be dependent upon the institute during the time of exclaustration: e.g., use of a contact person, frequency and type of contact, etc.;
- The duty of the exclaustrated member to return to the institute immediately if the superior recalls him or her during exclaustration;
- The right and duty of the member to return to the institute if the reason for which exclaustration was granted should cease;
- Whether the member during the time of exclaustration may visit house(s) of the institute, and if so, the member's duty of informing the major superior or other contact person before so visiting.

Involuntary Exclaustration

Procedure

The code provides no procedure, but the Congregation for Institutes of Consecrated Life and for Societies of Apostolic Life (CICLSAL) has indicated that the procedure for dismissal should be followed but with less rigor. This involves the competent authority:

- collecting or completing the proofs;
- warning the religious once in writing or in the presence of two witnesses about the behavior in question, delineating the expected conduct or modification of conduct and the possibility of imposed exclaustration; there must be at least fifteen (15) days between the warnings;
- permitting the religious ample opportunity to respond to the warnings and to defend himself or herself;
- obtaining the consent of the council with regard to requesting imposed exclaustration after fifteen (15) days from the last warning; and
- advising the religious of the request for imposed exclaustration and his or her right to present a defense to the Supreme Moderator.

Petition or Request for Imposed Exclaustration

- Formalities:
    - first and last names of religious
    - place, day and month of birth
    - place, day and month of temporary and perpetual profession
    - religious is a cleric
    - if a cleric, place, day and month of priestly or diaconal ordination
    - principal ministries or curriculum vitae of ministries
- explanation in detail of the situation composed by the competent authority delineating the serious reason(s).

  This type of exclaustration is ordinarily used in the case of a religious who is troubling or has serious problems living in community and a recitation that the competent authority advised the religious of the request for imposed exclaustration and his or her right to provide a defense for himself to the supreme moderator.

- if the case involves a religious cleric, the statement of some local ordinary in which he states that he will accept the religious during the period of exclaustration;
- a request for any special provisions to be placed in the decree of imposed exclaustration, with regard to habit, return to a religious house during the time of exclaustration, etc.

Granting Authority

- Diocesan bishop, if it involves an institute of diocesan right;
- Holy See, i.e., Congregation for Institutes of Consecrated Life and for Societies of Apostolic Life (CICLSAL), if it involves an institute of pontifical right.

Termination of the Decree and Return to the Institute

Since imposed exclaustration is at the discretion (*ad nutum*) of the Holy See or the diocesan bishop, then a petition must be made to the Holy See or diocesan bishop to end the exclaustration because the reason for which exclaustration is imposed is no longer applicable. It is not enough that the exclaustrated religious and the institute agree that the exclaustration should end.

Some Civil Law Considerations

The status of exclaustration raises some civil law concerns. The institute will wish to maintain some ties and give some assistance to the religious departing on exclaustration. On the other hand, since the institute has less control over the religious, it may wish to decrease the likelihood that the institute will be responsible for the debts of the religious or be liable in tort for the misconduct of the religious. There is no sure way to avoid liability. Essentially the more ties that the religious has to the institute, the more likely that a court could find that the exclaustrated religious is an agent or employee of the institute; the less ties that an institute retains, the less it fulfills its assistance to a religious who may have served the institute for many years, and the more likely that the exclaustration will turn into a more permanent departure. There is no definite test for liability, there is no limitation on the number of factors (e.g., five out of ten factors); the test will be a rather subjective balancing test.

- *Agency.* There should be a provision in the indult and in any accompanying agreement that the exclaustrated religious is not an agent and has no power to bind the institute and the institute is not responsible for the actions of the exclaustrated religious.

- *Debts and Obligations.* There should be a statement in the indult and in any accompanying agreement that the institute is not liable for the debts or obligations of the exclaustrated religious unless it has accepted liability in writing.
- *Credit Cards.* If exclaustrated members have credit cards of the institute, they may be perceived as agents of the institute with regard to the use of the card; thus, the religious departing upon exclaustration should surrender institute credit cards to the institute. If the institute helped a religious to obtain a credit card by giving the issuer some sort of guaranty of payment, then the institute should advise the issuer that it no longer makes any such guaranty for the member departing on exclaustration. An institute may also wish to advise any merchant that has regularly extended credit to members that the institute is no longer responsible for credit extended to that member.
- *Automobiles.* Provision of an institute owned automobile to the exclaustrated religious makes the religious seem like an agent, especially when driving. An exclaustrated religious should usually obtain his or her own automobile, or the vehicle should be titled in the name of the religious. If an exclaustrated religious has an institute car, then the accompanying agreement should make it clear that car insurance must be provided and who will provide the insurance.
- *Health Insurance.* Health insurance is a necessity. The institute is obliged to help an exclaustrated religious in case of need, and a major illness could constitute such a need. On the other hand, such insurance is usually provided by employers, and, if at all possible, an exclaustrated religious should find employment that provides this benefit. Provision of this insurance can be construed as evidence of an employer-employee relationship between the institute and the exclaustrated member.
- *Retirement.* This is another benefit that employers usually offer to employees. Some institutes may have formal plans that will determine eligibility and so reference should be made to that in any agreement. Other institutes may have a more informal fund for the care of elderly or infirm members, such that there is no right to accrued benefits. It should be discussed by the member and leadership whether there is a need for the institute to make contributions for an exclaustrated member since the member makes no financial or apostolic contributions to the institute. If there is a decision not to make such contributions, that should be stated in any agreement. The ultimate decision may depend upon whether the exclaustrated member is likely to return and live out retirement in the

institute; there may also be reason to make such contributions where the religious is on imposed or indefinite exclaustration since that religious may not have a job and may be more dependent on the institute during retirement.

- *Social Security.* Some religious institutes have elected Social Security coverage for all members; other institutes consider members who work outside the community and have funds withheld by their employers as not being part of this specially elected coverage since they are employees of their outside employers rather than fictional employees of the religious institute. The institute should treat religious on exclaustration as it would any member working outside the institute.[8] The case may be different, however, for religious on imposed or indefinite exclaustration since it is possible that they do not have employment and they may be more dependent upon the institute.
- *Income Tax.* Since religious on exclaustration have control over their income, the IRS considers them liable for income tax.[9] Moreover, exclaustrated religious are less likely to work for a Catholic organization.
- *Professional Counseling.* The institute paying for counseling of an exclaustrated religious may be another tie to the institute suggestive of benefits supplied to an employee or agent. Yet there may be good reason to do this, especially in the case of members on imposed or indefinite exclaustration, where a psychological condition is part of the reason for exclaustration.
- *Liability Insurance.* If an exclaustrated religious is involved in a business venture or if he or she is earning money as a professional, the institute should advise him/her to obtain the appropriate liability or malpractice insurance.
- *Release of Claims.* Religious institutes should be concerned not only about civil-law claims brought by third parties but also lawsuits by the exclaustrated or departed members for past services, for other obligations allegedly owed them, or for personal property that the institute retains. The institute may wish to insert in any agreement a provision that the religious departing on exclaustration acknowledges that they have in possession all their personal property and effects and

8 The income earned by a member on exclaustration is subject to income tax withholding under federal law and thus state law in turn. Employers are required to withhold FICA tax as well.

9 See IRS Revenue Ruling 77-290 (1977) and IRS PLR 7008310550A (1970).

they release the institute and all organizations affiliated with it from any claims against the institute and affiliated organizations for all claims that they may have against the institute and affiliated organizations, especially for compensation for services.

- *Enforceability of Accompanying Agreement.* Any agreement between the institute and the religious departing on exclaustration will not bind a third party who did not sign the agreement. An agreement is a helpful description of the relationship set out before any litigation arises.

The foregoing checklist is meant as helpful instrument, but it is not exhaustive, nor can it cover every unique situation. Checklists and sample forms are no substitute for the advice of knowledgeable civil and canon lawyers.

SAMPLE DOCUMENT 2 INDULT OF EXCLAUSTRATION
In accord with canon 686, §1 of the Code of Canon Law and in response to his (her) written request, and after having obtained the consent of my council, [and after having obtained the consent of the local ordinary where he will reside (in the case of a cleric)] I, the Supreme Moderator of the _____ Religious Institute (hereinafter "Institute"), hereby grant an indult of exclaustration to ____(name) (hereinafter "Religious") for the period of __(number)__ of year(s) [months] effective from the time of his (her) acceptance of this indult (or effective on the day of______, 199_ and expires on the _day of________________, 199_). This indult is granted for the following serious reason(s): In accord with canon 687, during this period of exclaustration, Religious is free from those obligations incompatible with his (her) new condition of life except that he (she) shall remain bound to chastity and shall ultimately be responsible to the supreme moderator (provincial). The right of the Religious to active and passive voice is suspended. Moreover, he (she) may not wear the habit of the Institute, or other identifying insignia or identify himself (herself) as a member of the Institute. Religious may not act as an official agent of the Institute apostolically or contract debts or obligations on behalf of the Institute. Religious shall keep the Supreme Moderator (Provincial) informed of his (her) residence and telephone number (both home and work) and contact the Supreme Moderator (Provincial) (named contact person) at least every ___ months. Religious is responsible for his (her) own finances according to the attached agreement; Religious can, in his (her) own name: work, earn, retain and dispense funds necessary to provide for his (her) personal needs. The religious understands that he (she) shall be required to comply with all civil laws common to all persons who are not

members of a religious institute, which include but are not limited to federal and state income tax laws.

The Institute will inform the local ordinary where Religious is to reside of the granting of this indult, will send Religious the regular Institute communications, and will fulfill the financial obligations of initial assistance and the like, according to the agreement attached.

For the duration of this indult, Religious may not return to the Institute without first consulting Supreme Moderator (Provincial). This indult may be revoked by the Supreme Moderator for a just cause. This indult will also terminate if the serious reason for which it was given ceases. At least ___days prior to the expiration of this indult, Religious shall advise the Supreme Moderator (Provincial) of his (her) intention either to return to the Institute or to seek an extension of this indult or an indult of departure. At the expiration of this Indult, Religious must return to the Institute, unless further arrangements have been made in accord with canon law.

Granted on this _day of _________, 20_ at the General Curia of the Institute in the City of ______, State of ______.

Signature: ____
Supreme Moderator

Attest: ____

Signature: ____
Secretary

I, ___(name)_______, understand and accept the terms, requirements, conditions, and consequences of the indult of exclaustration which I have accepted. I also understand and accept the terms, requirements, conditions and consequences of the financial agreement which I have entered into with the Institute and which is attached hereto as "Exhibit A" and made a part hereof as though fully set forth herein.

Date of Profession: ____________________________________

Signature: ____

Religious Legal Name, if necessary ______________________

Date of Profession: ____________________________________

Witnesses:____

____

Definitive Departure: "Secularization"

Individuals are free to depart an institute at the completion of the time of temporary vows. Such a departure is legitimate and would qualify for readmission according to canon 690. All rights and obligations entailed by profession cease. Wills, cession of administrative documents and dowry if there is any are returned to the person departing. The one departing may not claim remuneration for any work done while a member of the institute. The institute must observe equity and charity in dealing with the former member.

Temporary Professed Member

- At expiration of vows (c. 688, §1)

  The expiration of vows is at the time of the anniversary of the profession of vows. The individual is free to leave the institute. The request should be in writing and is actually a statement of intent. No further action is required. The departure is legitimate and would qualify for readmission according to canon 690.

- During temporary vows (c. 688 §2)

  If the person departing wishes to leave the institute during the period of temporary vows, the norms of canon 688 §2 are to be followed. The request for an indult to leave the institute should be in writing stating the reasons for it. The departure is legitimate and would qualify for readmission according to canon 690.

  The supreme moderator must act upon the request with the consent of his or her council. In the case of institutes of pontifical right, no further action is required. In cases of institutes of diocesan right and in monasteries mentioned in canon 615, the indult must be submitted to the diocesan bishop of the place where the religious is assigned for his confirmation. Without the confirmation of the diocesan bishop the act is invalid.

  The indult of departure mentioned in canon 692 consists of the request with the affirmative response or the request with affirmative response and the required confirmation. It is subject to the specifications and effects of that norm.

- Exclusion from subsequent profession (c. 689)

  The major superior competent to admit to profession should be indicated in the proper law of the institute. Canon 689 §1 states that the competent major superior is to act after hearing his or her council. Hearing the council constitutes a consultative vote. That section also states that just causes are required for exclusion from subsequent profession. The canon seeks to ensure charity and justice by requiring the opinion of an expert to evaluate the person's suitability for the life of the institute. An exclusion based on health should include the opinion of an expert (c. 689 §2).

"[K]eep in mind that to accept a candidate who is not apt for religious life results in damage to the institute and to the person himself, such that, though seemingly severe, it is in the end truly just."[10]

Perpetually Professed Member

The seriousness of the departure from the institute of a person perpetually professed is emphasized by the wording of canon 691 which states the perpetually professed is not to seek an indult to depart without very grave reasons weighed before the Lord.

The petition for an indult is to be submitted to the supreme moderator who is to transmit it with a personal opinion and that of the council to the competent authority. For institutes of pontifical right the Apostolic See reserves the right to grant the indult. In institutes of diocesan right the diocesan bishop of house of assignment can grant the indult.

The request or petition for an indult of departure should contain: a brief statement of the concrete reasons for the request; specific resources which were used in the attempt to resolve the difficulties mentioned in the request including spiritual, psychological and medical resources; and a curriculum vitae of the person involved. The opinion of the supreme moderator and the council should be objective and should state their approval or disapproval.

---

10 *Exegetical Commentary* II/2, 1851.

SAMPLE DOCUMENT 3
LETTER OF CLERIC SEEKING TO LEAVE WITHOUT LAICIZATION FOLLOWING PERPETUAL VOWS

Dear ____________________:

I am writing to seek your assistance in obtaining my voluntary departure from the Congregation/Order of ____________________.

As you know, I have not been functioning as a priest now for several years. I do not intend to function as a priest in the future. At one time, I had been on exclaustration, but that has also come to a close, and I do not intend to return to the Congregation/Order.

Thus, I am writing to request an indult to leave the Congregation/Order. I am not requesting a dispensation for priestly celibacy. However, I do wish to clarify my relationship with the Congregation/Order, to make it clear that I am not a member of the Order, and to indicate that I will not be functioning as a priest.

At present there is no bishop ready to accept me for priestly service into a diocese. Nor am I actively seeking such a bishop at this time. At present, I simply wish that my separation from the Congregation/Order might be permanent. While separated from the Congregation/Order, and without a bishop, I have no intention of functioning as a priest.

I would appreciate it if you could send this letter with any such information that would be necessary to the proper authorities in order to facilitate my voluntary departure. Thank you very much for your assistance.

Sincerely yours,

Date: ______________________________

[NOTE: *The signed letter, together with a letter from the major superior supporting the petition is sent to the Congregation for Institutes of Consecrated Life and Societies of Apostolic Life.*]

SAMPLE DOCUMENT 4
LETTER FROM SUPERIOR SUSPENDING FACULTIES

Having received the petition of (Name) _____________, a religious priest of (Congregation/Order), to initiate the case for his laicization and dispensation from priestly celibacy, considering the content of the Instruction *Per Litteras* of the Congregation for the Doctrine of the Faith, of October 14, 1980, and the procedural norms contained therein (Art. 4); by this document and in virtue of my office, I prohibit *ad cautelam* (Name) _____________ the exercise of all ministerial activities corresponding to his priestly state, while he is awaiting final resolution of his case. This prohibition, nonetheless, according to the norms of canon 1335, is suspended as often as it is necessary to care for the faithful in danger of death.

Given in (City, State) in (Place), under the seal of the Congregation/Order, (Date).

(Name): ____
Supreme Moderator/ Provincial

(Name): ____
Secretary

Dismissal

Definition

Dismissal of a member from an institute is an action taken by the competent authority which imposes on a professed member permanent departure from the institute. See canons 701 (religious institutes), 729 (secular institutes), and 746 (societies of apostolic life). All rights and obligations arising from profession are dispensed.

There are three types of dismissal:

1) *ipso facto* dismissal is dismissal from the institute of a member who has notoriously abandoned the Catholic faith, a member who has contracted marriage or has attempted it, even only civilly, or certain members who have been illegitimately absent from the institute for a period of at least twelve consecutive months;[11]

2) mandatory dismissal is dismissal for the offenses listed in canons 1397, 1398 and 1395 when those offenses are proved and the member has been given the opportunity of self-defense;

3) discretionary dismissal is the dismissal of a member for other causes, provided they are grave, external, imputable and juridically proven.

Mutual Obligations

Dismissal procedures are subject to strict interpretation according to the norms of canon law because they are connected to penal legislation. The rights of the individual member as well as those of the institute are to be protected.

Proof of grave, external, imputable offenses toward the church or religious community are to be documented.

Time Periods

The competent superior first needs to determine whether any delicts have been committed. The process for making this determination is in Book VI of the code.[12] Since those procedures are beyond the scope of this present work, the superior must consult a canonist for instruction on how to proceed.

---

11 In March of 2019 Pope Francis issued the apostolic letter *Communis vita*, which added the third reason—twelve consecutive months of absence—to canon 694 §1 as a cause of *ipso facto* dismissal.

12 Note that Pope Francis promulgated an entirely new content of Book VI on June 1, 2021, and the norms are effective as of December 8, 2021.

If a delict has been committed, and upon consideration to begin the process for dismissal, the competent superior is to write a letter to the member informing him or her of this process. The letter should indicate the member has the right to defend himself or herself. A time limit is set in which the defense is to be given in writing. After this initial indication of intention, the superior enters into the formal process presented below.

Upon the advice of his or her council, the superior then sends the member the two canonical warnings mentioned in canon 697 at least fifteen days apart. These are sent certified mail with a request for a return receipt. Essential contents of both warning letters are: (1) an explicit threat of subsequent dismissal unless the member reforms, (2) a clear indication of the cause of the dismissal, and (3) notice that the member has the full opportunity of self-defense.

Upon the completed time for the warnings, the decree of dismissal is completed by the council. The acts of the case with two signatures are sent to the supreme moderator with the following: curriculum vitae, report of misdeeds, attempts by major superiors, two canonical warnings, proof of reception of these warnings, defenses given by the religious, acts from the council meeting wherein the dismissal was decided, and a summary and review of the case by the major superior.

It is only after the collegial vote that the supreme moderator issues the decree. The lower council does not actually decide the dismissal. It is to be noted that the diocesan bishop makes the decision in the case of canon 615 monasteries.

Procedures

For *validity*, there must be a council of four in addition to the supreme moderator. The decree itself is an act of the superior, but the decision is made by secret collegial vote. Either the decree, or the cover letter or an excerpt from the council minutes should make clear that the required number were present and whether the vote was unanimous.

For *validity* the decree must contain a summary of the cause of dismissal:

- in fact—the actions of the religious, and
- in law—showing that the violations were contrary to universal and proper law and are of a type and gravity considered in law grounds for dismissal.

For *validity*, the decree must contain notice that the religious has ten (10) days from the receipt of notification within which to appeal. The notification is not communicated to the individual before it has been confirmed.

Particular Types of Dismissal

Ipso Facto

The automatic penalty described in this canon is applied in the case of a member who publicly abandons the Catholic faith, attempts to contract marriage, or has been illegitimately absent from the institute for a period of at least twelve consecutive months and cannot be located (c. 694 §1). The use of this penalty is to protect the institute from the action of a member whose behavior is directly and publicly contrary to the nature of consecrated life.

The behavior of the member effects the penalty. The canon directs the competent superior to collect the proofs and issue a declaration of the fact so that the dismissal is established juridically. Standard rules for proofs apply here. The superior must obtain either documentation; e.g., a certified marriage certificate or testimony from reliable witnesses.

Mandatory

The competent superior must judge the facts and the imputability of the matter and collect proofs of both the facts and the imputability. The accusation and the evidence must be made known to the member, and the member must be given the opportunity of self-defense.

The competent superior is the major superior, such as a provincial if there is one at a lower level than the general superior.

Because of the seriousness of the matter and the complex nature of penal law, qualified experts should be consulted before using the provision of this canon. If the case involves the causes in canon 695, there are no canonical warnings, but rather an emphasis on proofs of fact and imputability.

Discretionary

The other causes mentioned in canon 696 for which a member may be dismissed from the institute are to be grave, external, imputable and juridically proven. These reasons for dismissal can be related to the fundamental obligations of consecrated life. They need not be specified in the proper law of the institute but should constitute repeated behavior on the part of the member.

All prescriptions of the process of dismissal must be observed including the right to self-defense and to recourse. If all procedures are not carefully carried out the dismissal process may be nullified for lack of proper procedure. The decree of dismissal does not take effect until confirmed by the Holy See to whom all the acts of the case must be sent. In the case of diocesan institutes, the confirmation is by the diocesan bishop of the house of assignment.

Competent Dicasteries

A brief mention is in order here about which congregations of the Holy See are competent to hear a given case. Competency depends in part on whether it is the cleric or the superior who is initiating the request; whether the request is for an indult of departure or for dismissal from the institute or society; whether it is part of a penal process; whether laicization is being requested (voluntary or involuntary); and/or whether dispensation from the obligation of celibacy is involved. Some cases (in whole or in part) fall under the jurisdiction of the Congregation for the Doctrine of the Faith, some will belong to the Congregation for Divine Worship and Discipline of the Sacraments, and still others fall to the Congregation for Institutes of Consecrated Life and Societies of Apostolic Life.[13]

SAMPLE DOCUMENT 5 PROCEDURES FOR DISMISSAL
• Consult with council about feasibility of beginning dismissal procedures • Initial warning to member that dismissal procedures are likely to begin • First formal warning in writing by certified mail or with two witnesses after consulting council • Second formal warning after fifteen days in writing by certified mail or with two witnesses • After fifteen days, council votes on forwarding acts of dismissal to superior general • General council votes on dismissal • Member notified of dismissal

13 On April 18, 2009, Pope Benedict XVI granted the Congregation for Clergy three special faculties for dismissal of clerics from the clerical state and the obligations of celibacy in certain circumstances. On March 17, 2010, the Congregation for Clergy issued procedural guidelines for the instruction of cases in which the special faculties apply. The text of the procedural guidelines can be found at Congregation for the Clergy, "Special Faculties: Procedural Guidelines," March 17, 2010, *Roman Replies and CLSA Advisory Opinions* (Washington, DC: Canon Law Society of America, 2010) 41-51. Note that, when requesting application of the special faculties in a given case, superiors of institutes of consecrated life and of societies of apostolic life who are not ordinaries according to the meaning of canon 134 §1 must refer to the competent local ordinary.

SAMPLE DOCUMENT 6
DECLARATION OF DISMISSAL *IPSO FACTO*

We, the undersigned Supreme Moderator and members of the Council of the (Name of institute) ________________ with headquarters in (Place) ______________, (number of) ____ in number, duly assembled at (Place) _______, on the (date) have thoroughly reviewed the proofs and have determined that (NAME), a perpetually professed member of this institute, has attempted civil marriage. We, therefore, declare that the above-mentioned member is automatically dismissed from the Congregation in accordance with can. 694 §§1-2.

An authentic copy of this declaration is being sent to the same member on (DATE).

The documentation pertinent to this case is appended.

Councilor: (Name) ____

Councilor: (Name) ____

Councilor: (Name) ____

Councilor: (Name) ____

Supreme Moderator: (Name) _________________________________

[SEAL]

Secretary: (Name) ____

Note that canon 694 §3 provides that in cases of dismissal for illegitimate absence, "in order to be established juridically, this statement must be confirmed by the Holy See; for institutes of diocesan right the confirmation rests with the bishop of the principal seat."

SAMPLE DOCUMENT 7
FIRST CANONICAL WARNING

TO: (Name) ____

FROM: (Name of Supreme Moderator or Provincial) __________________

You will recall that on (dates) _________, ___________, and ____________, I wrote to you inviting you to return to fraternal life within the (name of province or local house) ____________. This followed oral invitations for you to come back to our community. While you have written me and talked with me on the telephone about some of the issues you have been dealing with in your life at the present time, and you have assured me that you have been meeting periodically with (name of contact person for the institute) _________, the time for your official leave of absence has expired with no indication of your intention to return to our community life. In that sense, you have neither responded to nor complied with my pastoral invitations.

Now therefore in accord with canon law and the law of our Congregation/Order, you are hereby given the first canonical warning required by canon 697 §2 and article (cite number) _______ of our Constitutions prior to being dismissed from the (name of institute) ________________________.

You have been unlawfully absent from the Congregation/Order and community life for more than six (6) months. As noted above, you have failed to respond to various invitations to return and again take up religious life.

I must advise you that your unlawful absence from the institute for more than six (6) months is an imputable offense which subjects you to dismissal from the Congregation/Order under canon 696, 1° and article (cite number) _______ of our Constitutions.

Having heard the advice of my Council, I hereby declare that you will be dismissed from the Congregation/Order unless you:

> return to the (place) ________________________ within fifteen (15) days of receipt of this first canonical warning to take up immediately religious life as a member of the Congregation/Order.

If you fail to comply within fifteen (15) days of receipt of this first canonical warning, I will issue a second canonical warning. If you fail to respond to a second canonical warning, and I with my Council determine that your actions demonstrate incorrigibility and that you have offered an insufficient defense, I will proceed with dismissal by submitting evidence to the Supreme

Moderator and his/her Council, who will decide the case and submit it to the Apostolic See.

You have a right under canon law and the law of order to self-defense, including a canonical counsel in this matter at all stages. You have the right to present your defense to me, in person or in writing against this first canonical warning and proposed dismissal within fifteen days of receipt of this warning and proposed dismissal within fifteen days of receipt if the warning. You also have the right to communicate with and offer a defense directly to the Supreme Moderator.

Please be advised of the seriousness of this matter.

GIVEN AT: (place) ___________________________

Signed: (Supreme Moderator) ___________________________

Signed: (Secretary) ___________________________

CERTIFIED MAIL – RETURN RECEIPT REQUESTED

SAMPLE DOCUMENT 8
SECOND CANONICAL WARNING

TO: (Name) ___________________________

FROM: (Name of Supreme Moderator or Provincial) ___________

You will recall that on (date) _______________ and _____________, I wrote you inviting you to return to community life within the (name of province or local house) _____________. On (date) _______ I issued you a First Canonical Warning. You have neither responded to nor complied with my pastoral invitation or my more formal canonical warning.

Now therefore in accord with canon law and the law of our Congregation/Order, you are hereby given the second canonical warning required by canon 697, 2° and article (cite article number) ___________ of our Constitutions prior to being dismissed from the (name of institute) _______________________.

You have been unlawfully absent from the Congregation/Order and community life for more than six (6) months. As noted above, you have failed to respond to various invitations to return and again take up religious life.

I must advise you that your unlawful absence from the institute for more than six (6) months is an imputable offense which subjects you to dismissal from the Congregation/Order under canon 696, 1° and article (cite number) ____ of our Constitutions/Statutes prior to being dismissed from the Congregation/Order.

You have been unlawfully absent from the Congregation/Order and community life for more than six (6) months. As noted above, you have failed to respond to various invitations and a canonical warning to return and again take up religious life.

I must advise you that your unlawful absence from the Congregation/Order for more than six (6) months is an imputable offense which subjects you to dismissal from the Congregation/Order under canon 696, 1° and article (cite number) ____ of our Constitutions/Statutes.

Having heard the advice of my Council, I hereby declare that you will be dismissed from the Congregation/Order unless you:

> return to the (place) ________________ within fifteen (15) days of receipt of this second canonical warning to take up immediately religious life as a member of the Congregation/Order.

If you fail to comply within fifteen (15) days of receipt of this first canonical warning, I will issue a second canonical warning. If you fail to respond to a second canonical warning, and I with my Council determine that your actions demonstrate incorrigibility and that you have offered an insufficient defense, I will proceed with dismissal by submitting evidence to the Supreme Moderator and the Congregation of _____________ and his/her Council, who will decide the case and submit it to the Apostolic See.

You have a right under canon law and the law of order to self-defense, including a canonical counsel in this matter at all stages. You have the right to present your defense to me, in person or in writing against this second canonical warning and proposed dismissal within fifteen days of receipt of this warning. You also have the right to communicate with and offer a defense directly to the Supreme Moderator at (address, phone number, fax, email).

Please be advised of the seriousness of this matter.

GIVEN AT: (place) ______________________________________

Signed: (Supreme Moderator) ______________________________

Signed: (Secretary) _______________________________________

CERTIFIED MAIL – RETURN RECEIPT REQUESTED

SAMPLE DOCUMENT 9
DECREE OF DISMISSAL

The undersigned General Superior, having proceeded collegially with the General Council on (date) to weigh the proofs, arguments, and defenses in the case, and in the same manner having moved to a decision by secret ballot, decrees that Sister NN, a (perpetually) professed member of the (Congregation) is hereby dismissed, for the following reasons.

According to the proper law of this institute (Constitution numbers) and the law of the Church (canons) religious are obliged to __________. Canon law also recognizes that failure in this matter constitutes a cause for dismissal, stating among other causes "_______________" (c. 696 §1).

In the present case, despite various efforts to correct the situation, including two formal canonical warnings issued (date / date), Sister NN has persisted in the behavior which violates the above religious obligations. (*Brief resume of factual violations which merit dismissal in the case.*)

This decree takes effect following its confirmation by the Holy See. Sister NN then has ten days, following receipt of notification of the confirmed decree, within which she may have recourse to the Holy See.

____

General Superior

Date ________________

[SEAL]

____

General Secretary

SAMPLE DOCUMENT 10
DECREE OF DISMISSAL

(Name) ________________________, a member of our Congregation/Order is dismissed from the Congregation/Order, according to the norm of canon ___ of the Code of Canon Law and of Article (cite number) ____ of the Constitutions/Statutes, because of the delict of unlawful absence from a religious institute.

After having left the religious house lawfully, he remained outside the structures of religious life for more than one year. Numerous informal invitations to return were met with a negative response. Formal canonical admonitions and invitation to return to obedience were sent by the Provincial/Supreme Moderator on ________ and ______. There was no response to either admonition, although certified mail receipts indicate and rove that the admonitions were received.

Therefore, since a year has elapsed since the cessation of his/her permission to live outside the religious house this declaration is authorized, according to which (Name) ______________ is declared lawfully dismissed from the Congregation/Order of __________________.

This declaration is supported by the accompanying copies of letters and admonitions which indicate clearly the reasons for dismissal.

Councilor: (Signed) ____

Councilor: (Signed) ____

Councilor: (Signed) ____

Councilor: (Signed) ____

Councilor: (Signed) ____

Councilor: (Signed) ____

Supreme Moderator: (Signed) ________________________________

Secretary: (signed) ____

Given at (place) ______________________ on (date) ____________

Special Provisions

Readmission to the Same Institute

Canon 690 applies to any religious who has legitimately left after profession. Legitimate departure includes departure:

- at the conclusion of novitiate according to canon 653 §2;
- at the expiration of temporary profession according to canon 688 §1;
- by an indult granted to a religious in temporary profession according to canon 688 §2;
- by exclusion from subsequent profession according to canon 689;
- by an indult granted to a perpetually professed religious according to canon 691; and
- by dismissal according to the various categories and procedures of canons 694-703.

Readmission to the same institute would depend on the present condition of the person involved and the judgment of the competent superior acting with the council and in accordance with the norm of law. The reasons for the departure also need to be evaluated.

> Canon 690 §1. The supreme moderator with the consent of the council can readmit without the burden of repeating the novitiate one who had legitimately left the institute after completing the novitiate or after profession. Moreover, it will be for the same moderator to determine an appropriate probation prior to temporary profession and the time of vows to precede perpetual profession, according to the norm of cann. 655 and 657.
>
> §2. The superior of an autonomous monastery with the consent of the council possesses the same faculty.

Institute's Responsibility for Those Who Have Departed

Canon 702 legally excludes the right of a former member to remuneration for work done while a member of the institute. In a spirit of charity and equity institutes should assess the need of the former member and provide assistance. Institutes that have policies providing for the assistance of former members are in a good position to attend to those people with such charity and equity.

SAMPLE DOCUMENT 11
FORM FOR RELEASE OF MEDICAL RECORDS

AUTHORIZATION FOR RELEASE OF MEDICAL INFORMATION

I, ________________________, do hereby authorize any hospital or doctor from whom I have received medical services or attention to release to ________________________ any and all information from records or personnel which may be in their possession. Such release of medical information shall apply to all organizations and persons who may have medical knowledge concerning my physical and mental health. I further authorize such persons having knowledge about my case to discuss all aspects of m y physical and mental health with any representative of (name institute) ____.

Signed: ____

Dated: ____________

State of ________________________

County of ______________________

Subscribed and acknowledged before me this ____ day of _______, 20__, by (name of member) ________________________________.

____

Notary Public

My commission expires: ____________________________

SEAL

NOTE: Many medical service providers have their own forms for patients to sign when desiring to share medical information with third parties. The blanket form is often considered to be insufficient.

SAMPLE DOCUMENT 12

AGREEMENT FOR ABSENCE FOR HEALTH REASONS

MEMORANDUM OF AGREEMENT FOR HEALTH LEAVE

(Name) _________________________ will begin health leave at (name of medical institution or program) ______________ on (date) __________. This leave for reasons of health will last for (duration) ____________ but may be extended. On successful completion of this program of treatment, (Name) _____ will resume his/her ministry as (cite ministry) _____________ at (place) ______________________.

During this health leave, expenses will be paid by (name of institute, diocese, insurance) ____.

Signed: (Person on leave) ____

Signed: (Superior) ____

Date: ____

SAMPLE DOCUMENT 13
BASIC FACT SHEET

FACT SHEET OF THE CONGREGATION ___(specify name)_________

(To be filled in and transmitted with the other documentation)

Congregation for (Clergy/Divine Worship and Discipline of the Sacraments/ the Doctrine of the Faith/Institutes of Consecrated Life and Societies of Apostolic Life)

ORDER: ______________________________

PROVINCE: ______________________________

First and Family Names of Petitioner: ____________________

Date of Birth:

Place and Country of Birth:

Date of Priestly Ordination/Permanent Profession:

Date of Defection:

Date of Leave/Exclaustration:

Principal ministries exercised by Petitioner:

Studies and degrees competed:

Reasons for petition, existing either before or after ordination/profession:

Juridical status of Petitioner:

If Petitioner has attempted civil or religious marriage, indicate:

Date of marriage:

Status of spouse: (i.e., never married; previously married, divorced; former religious)

Children: (names and ages) ______________________________

Votum of local diocesan ordinary of place where the Petitioner is currently residing, as to absence of scandal if petition is granted:

Votum of Major Superior:

Place: ______________________ Date: __________

Signature (of Instructor of the Case): ____________________

Seal of the Province or Congregation/ Order

SAMPLE DOCUMENT D
BASIC FACT SHEET

CHAPTER EIGHT

THE APOSTOLATE

Brian Austin, FSSP[1]

Introduction

All who have been baptized into Jesus Christ (cf. Rom 6:3; c. 204), the beloved Son "whom the Father consecrated and sent into the world" (Jn 10:36), "are also consecrated and sent into the world to imitate his example and to continue his mission."[2] Members of institutes of consecrated life or societies of apostolic life ("institutes/societies"), however,

> are called to follow Christ more closely, and to make him the "all" of their lives (cf. c. 573). [I]ndeed . . . consecrated life itself is a mission, as was the whole of Jesus' life. . . . It can, therefore, be said that a sense of mission is essential to every institute—not only those dedicated to the active apostolic life, but also those dedicated to the contemplative life.[3]

It must be emphasized that "the apostolate of all religious consists first of all in the witness of their consecrated life, which they are bound to foster by prayer and penance" (c. 673). Institutes entirely dedicated to contemplation "offer an extraordinary sacrifice of praise to God, illumine the people of God with the richest fruits of holiness, move it by their example, and extend it with hidden apostolic fruitfulness" (c. 674). The apostolic action of institutes dedicated to external works of the apostolate "must always proceed from an intimate union with God . . . and is to be carried out in communion with the Church" (c. 675).[4]

---

1 Beverly K. Dunn, SP, was the original author of this chapter. The contributors to that publication were: Sisters Kathleen Ann Bierne, PBVM, Joyce Hoben, SNDN, and Rev. Kevin O'Rourke, OP. Rev. Brian Austin, FSSP, revised this chapter of the *Procedural Handbook*.

2 *VC* 72, at http://w2.vatican.va/content/john-paul-ii/en/apost_exhortations/documents/hf_jp-ii_exh_25031996_vita-consecrata.html.

3 Ibid.

4 The law uses the word "apostolate" to designate the participation of the lay faithful in the mission of the Church, distinguishing it from the term "ministry," which is proper to the clergy.

Although the code addresses the topic of apostolate primarily in terms of an institute's corporate works (cc. 673-683), it also recognizes the apostolate of individual members. All apostolates, however, are exercised in the name of the institute (c. 665 §1) and with the permission of a legitimate superior (c. 671). The proper law of an institute (constitutions, statutes, directories, etc.) can provide more detailed norms than the general ones provided by universal law.

Apostolate of Institutes as Part of the Apostolate of the Church

The code presents the apostolate of institutes as an integral part of institutes and societies and as part of the mission of the Church (c. 675).[5] Although all of them enjoy "a just autonomy of life, especially of governance" (c. 586 §1), matters concerning "the care of souls, the public exercise of divine worship, and other works of the apostolate" (c. 678 §1) are subject to the authority of the diocesan bishop. Although some institutes are "exempt" from the immediate jurisdiction of the bishop for the greater good of the universal Church (c. 591),[6] all of them participate in the apostolate of a particular church in communion with and under the authority of the bishop.

Mutual Relationship between the Bishop and Superiors in the Apostolate[7]

The overlapping authority of bishops and superiors requires them to proceed by means of mutual consultation and acknowledgement of each other's role in organizing works of the apostolate (c. 678 §3; cf. c. 738 §2). The law highlights certain areas requiring particular care in this regard.

Preaching

Members are called to "give witness to the gospel in a special way" (c. 758). At the same time, they are subject to the bishop and to the norms given by the episcopal conference regarding how preaching is to be carried out in a particular diocese. For example, lay persons need permission to preach in churches or oratories (c. 766),[8] and the diocesan bishop can restrict, remove, or restore the right of a particular cleric to preach in his diocese (c. 764).

---

5 Cf. *LG* 12; *PC* 8; *CD* 33-35; *AA* 20d, 23.

6 "At this point in history, exemption is virtually meaningless from a juridical point of view." John M. Huels, "The Demise of Religious Exemption," *The Jurist* 54 (1994) 46.

7 For further reading, see Sacred Congregation for Religious and Secular Institutes and Sacred Congregation for Bishops, instruction regarding the mutual relations between bishops and religious in the Church *Mutuae relationes*, May 14, 1978: *AAS* 70 (1978) 473-506.

8 The complementary norm for the USCCB is at http://www.usccb.org/beliefs-and-teachings/what-we-believe/canon-law/complementary-norms/canon-766-lay-preaching.cfm.

Catechetical and Liturgical Formation

Catechetics, which includes liturgical formation, should play a part in the life of all institutes, according to the character of each institute and the apostolate itself (c. 776). The norms issued by the diocesan bishop for catechetics (c. 775) also bind institutes and societies.

Public Exercise of Divine Worship

The regulation of the sacred liturgy depends on the Holy See and the diocesan bishop (c. 838 §1). Norms issued by the diocesan bishop within the limits of his competence are binding on all (c. 838 §4), including institutes/societies (c. 678 §1; cf. c. 738 §2). Because of the public nature of even private worship (such as devotional practices), these, too, are subject to the bishop (cc. 835 §1; 839 §2).

Catholic Schools and Religious Education

"Institutes whose proper mission is education [are] to strive to devote themselves to Catholic education through their schools, established with the consent of the diocesan bishop" (c. 801). Although it should go without saying, "the instruction and education in a Catholic school must be grounded in the principles of Catholic doctrine. [Moreover,] teachers are to be outstanding in correct doctrine and integrity of life" (c. 803 §2).

It is for the diocesan bishop to regulate and watch over "Catholic religious instruction and education which are imparted in any schools whatsoever or which are provided through the various instruments of social communication" (c. 804 §1). He is to see that teachers of the Catholic religion specifically "are outstanding in correct doctrine, the witness of a Christian life, and pedagogical skill" (c. 804 §2). He also "has the right to appoint or approve teachers of religion and even to remove them or demand that they be removed if a reason of religion or morals requires it" (c. 805). Moreover,

> The diocesan bishop has the right to watch over and visit the Catholic schools in his territory, even those which members of religious institutes have founded or direct. He also issues prescripts which pertain to the general regulation of Catholic schools; these prescripts are valid also for schools which these religious direct, without prejudice, however, to their autonomy regarding the internal direction of their schools (c. 806 §1).

Directors of Catholic schools must also exercise vigilance in these areas, taking care also "that the instruction which is given in them is at least as academically distinguished as that in the other schools of the area" (c. 806 §2).

Media Apostolate

The pastors of the Church are encouraged to make use of the various means of social communication and are also to exercise vigilance over them (cc. 822-832). In general, bishops "have the duty and right to demand that writings to be published by the Christian faithful which touch upon faith or morals be submitted to their judgment and have the duty and right to condemn writings which harm correct faith or good morals" (c. 823 §1). For example, it is necessary to obtain the permission of the local ordinary in order to publish "books of prayers for the public or private use of the faithful" (c. 826 §3) or catechetical works (c. 827 §1). The conference of bishops can establish norms for the participation of both clerics and religious in radio and television programs which deal with questions concerning Catholic teaching or morals (c. 831 §2).[9] "Members of religious institutes also need permission of their major superior according to the norm of the constitutions in order to publish writings dealing with questions of religion or morals" (c. 832). They also need permission of the local ordinary to contribute to publications "which are accustomed to attack openly the Catholic religion or good morals" (c. 831 §1).[10]

Apostolic Works of an Institute

By law, members of institutes/societies are to live in a canonically established house under the authority of a superior (cc. 608; 740). A canonical house differs from a number of members working and living in a local area. It indicates an institute's commitment to a specific mission in a particular place (cf. c. 120 §1). A canonical house may only be established with the previous written permission of the diocesan bishop (cc. 609 §1; 733 §1).

Works Proper to an Institute

Institutes must strive to preserve their spiritual patrimony, including their mission and proper works, according to the norms of proper law (cc. 677 §1; 731 §1). The constitutions refer to the apostolic works proper to each institute (cc. 578; 731 §1); nevertheless, these works are to be prudently adapted in order to meet changed circumstances (c. 677 §1; cf. c. 631 §1). Once an institute establishes a

---

9 The complementary norm for the USCCB is at http://www.usccb.org/beliefs-and-teachings/what-we-believe/canon-law/complementary-norms/canon-831-2-clerics-members-of-religious-institutes-on-radio-television.cfm.

10 For further reading, see Congregation for the Doctrine of the Faith, instruction on some aspects of the use of the instruments of social communication in promoting the doctrine of the faith *The Second Vatican Council*, March 30, 1992, at https://www.vatican.va/roman_curia/congregations/cfaith/documents/rc_con_cfaith_doc_19920330_istruzione-pccs_en.html and in *Origins* 22 (1992) 92-96.

house in a diocese, it has the right to undertake the full range of its proper works, unless the permission of the bishop to found the house restricted them (c. 611, 2°).

The permission to found a house also entitles clerical religious institutes to have a church within which they may conduct sacred ministries (c. 611, 3°), and clerical societies of apostolic life to have at least an oratory (c. 733 §2). Still, the institute must obtain the bishop's permission before building a church (c. 1215 §3) or oratory (c. 1223) in a particular place. Since these churches and oratories are not parish churches *per se*, the clergy assigned to them must respect the rights of the local pastor (*parochus*; cc. 528-531). They must also observe diocesan norms concerning faculties for hearing confessions (cc. 966-976) and assisting at marriages (1109-1112).

Apostolic Works Entrusted to an Institute

The diocesan bishop may entrust apostolic works such as a parish, a school, or a social service agency to an institute (cc. 681 §1; 738 §2; 790). In these cases, the bishop and the competent superior of the institute are to draw up a written agreement which includes, *inter alia*:

- the work to be done;
- the members to be assigned; and
- financial arrangements (c. 681 §2; cf. c. 738 §2).[11]

Entrusting a work to an institute does not *in se* include permission for the institute to engage in its full range of proper works as in canon 611. An apostolate may be entrusted to an individual member, who exercises it in the name and with the permission of the institute (cc. 665 §1; 671) according to the terms of a written agreement.[12] When the work involves the conferral of ecclesiastical office, the diocesan bishop makes the appointment (c. 602).[13]

Such entrusted works are exercised under the authority and direction of the bishop or his delegate (c. 681 §1). For example, the diocesan chancery handles permissions regarding the temporal goods of such a work. This authority of the diocesan bishop over external works, however, does not prejudice the authority of superiors over matters pertaining to the internal governance of an institute's members. Neither does it excuse superiors from the duty to exercise vigilance

11 Cf. Paul VI, apostolic letter *motu proprio* establishing norms for the implementation of certain decrees of the Second Vatican Council, apostolic letter, *Ecclesiae sanctae* I, 30 §1, August 6, 1966: *AAS* 58 (1966) 757-787 (hereafter *ES*).

12 *ES* I, 31.

13 *ES* I, 30 §2.

over the work, lest the institute be held responsible for negligence (cc. 681 §1; 1284; 1287). Thus, superiors may inspect the financial accounts of entrusted works.

If a clerical institute's church is erected by the bishop as a *parish* church, a special written agreement should be made between the diocese and the institute. In this case, the institute maintains ownership of its property, while the property of the juridic person of the parish must be held and administered separately from that of the institute. Such an agreement must carefully spell out the manner of determining the proper recipient of monetary gifts (c. 1267 §1). Additionally, the faithful have a right to know how their offerings are being applied (c. 1267 §3).

Collaboration

"Among the various institutes and also between them and the secular clergy, there is to be fostered an ordered cooperation and a coordination under the direction of the diocesan bishop of all the works and apostolic activities" (c. 680).[14] This collaboration could be fostered by periodic meetings of those responsible for the various apostolates in the diocese in order to promote communication and understanding among them. Individual members of institutes/societies can also participate in diocesan planning processes, such as the diocesan synod (c. 463 §1, 5°), presbyteral council (c. 498 §1, 2°), or pastoral council (c. 512 §1). Coalitions of institutes can pool their resources to initiate new apostolic works in response to new needs.

New Apostolic Works

"Superiors and members are to retain faithfully the mission and works proper to the institute. Nevertheless, attentive to the necessities of times and places, they are to accommodate them prudently, even employing new and opportune means" (c. 677 §1). Any such accommodation must remain consistent with the constitutive elements of an institute's way of life, such as:

- its understanding of its proper works;
- the vowed status of its members, including the obligation to common life;
- discernment of the members' gifts and abilities; and
- the common good of the individual, of the institute, of those served, and of the Church.

---

14 Cf. *CD* 35-36; *AG* 32-33; *ES* I, 28; II, 43; III, 21; *MR* 36, 37, 59.

If an institute decides to begin a new work, it does so with a commitment to that work's future beyond the involvement of its founders. However, that commitment may not guarantee the institute's own members as future staff. Rather, it may entail such resources as governance or association with other established works. Nor must the new work necessarily be one of the institute's proper works. Before instituting a new work, the institute should ask itself some fundamental questions:

- Is this new work in the best interests of those served?
- Does it contribute to the mission and public witness of the institute and of the Church?
- Is it in harmony with the other works of the diocese?
- Is it an appropriate response to people's needs, given the available resources?
- How will the institute and the participating members fulfil their mutual responsibilities of:
    - dependence, limitation of use, disposition of goods?
    - supervision, evaluation, guidance, mutual support?
    - sharing of common life?
    - commitment for the future of this work?

If an institute decides to initiate a new work, it must attend to some practicalities:

- building broad-based support among the members of the institute;
- determining the correct civil and canonical structures;
- developing a strategic plan;
- formulating a written agreement delineating:
    - clear lines of accountability and periodic reviews of the work for the purpose of protecting the mission and assuring proper functioning;
    - financial responsibilities, including liability protection;
    - personnel policies, including qualifications and hiring and firing procedures;
    - means of ending the work and distributing the assets;
- identifying the personnel to staff the new work and the scope of their involvement.

Modifying a Work

During the year dedicated to consecrated life, Pope Francis challenged all institutes to examine their fidelity to their charism and mission, asking themselves "Are our ministries, our works, and our presence consonant with what the Spirit asked of our founders and foundresses? Are they suitable for carrying out today, in society and the Church, those same ministries and works?"[15] The following principles should be kept in mind when seeking to modify an established work.

- Institutes must remain faithful to the mission and works proper to the institute, while continually adapting them to today's needs (c. 677 §1).
- There must be a real "concern to keep alive an authentic fraternal life."[16]
- The bishop coordinates the works of the apostolate in his diocese in mutual consultation with superiors of institutes (cc. 394 §1; 678 §3).
- The consent of the diocesan bishop is required in order to convert the apostolic work for which a canonical house was established to another kind of work (c. 612).

Some changes, such as the addition of new degree programs to a college or university, or the addition of a hospice program to an acute care hospital, indicate growth and development rather than a conversion of purpose. A true conversion would involve a change in the nature of the work itself; e.g., to convert a school to a hospital.

Termination of or Withdrawal from a Work

If circumstances indicate that a particular work has ceased to be viable, an institute may deem it best to terminate or withdraw from it. Major superiors can suppress a proper work of an institute not associated with a legitimately established religious house. But again, they are to do so in consultation with the bishop as coordinator of the apostolate of the diocese. The supreme moderator can suppress a legitimately established house and its associated works after consulting the bishop (c. 616 §1).

---

15 Francis, apostolic letter to consecrated persons on the occasion of the Year of Consecrated Life *Scrivo a voi* I-22, November 1, 2014, *AAS* 106 (2014) 935–947, http://w2.vatican.va/content/francesco/en/apost_letters/documents/papa-francesco_lettera-ap_20141121_lettera-consacrati.html.

16 CICLSAL, instruction regarding fraternal life in community *Congregavit nos in unum Christi amor* 67, February 2, 1994, https://www.vatican.va/roman_curia/congregations/ccscrlife/documents/rc_con_ccscrlife_doc_02021994_fraternal-life-in-community_en.html.

The termination of a work entails the necessity to distribute its assets. If the work is owned by an entity of the religious institute, the assets revert to the next highest structural level. For example, the assets of a suppressed house of a province revert to the province, without prejudice to the proper law of the institute and the intentions of the founders or donors (cc. 123; 616 §1). If the work was civilly incorporated (cf. c. 1274 §5), then the distribution of its assets is also governed by civil law and the articles of incorporation (cf. cc. 22; 1284 §2, 3°).

In other cases, a work may be viable, but the institute may determine that withdrawing its personnel and resources for distribution elsewhere would better serve the needs of people. As part of the withdrawal process, the institute needs to help the new directors of the work make the transition by answering some fundamental questions:

- Will the work remain part of the Church's mission?
- If so, who is responsible for ensuring fidelity to that mission?
- What civil and canonical structures correspond best to the new nature of the work?

In the case of withdrawal from a work rather than termination, the institute usually can claim only those assets for which it can prove prior claim, such as unpaid salaries, loans, etc. The institute needs to attend as well to the transfer of ownership through the sale of the work if this action was not taken previously.

Apostolate and Individual Members

"The tendency, in some institutes, to emphasise mission over community, and to favour diversity over unity, has had a profound impact on fraternal life in common, to the point that this has become, at times, almost an option rather than an integral part of religious life."[17] While there are a number of legitimate exceptions to the general rule, "the norm is that religious live in fraternal communities: the individual is consecrated in this common life and it is in this form of life that such men and women normally undertake their apostolate."[18] This applies also to members of societies of apostolic life.

Ecclesiastical Offices Entrusted to Individual Members

Canon 145 §1 defines an ecclesiastical office as "any function constituted in a stable manner by divine or ecclesiastical law to be exercised for a spiritual purpose." A bishop may entrust an ecclesiastical office to an individual member

17 CICLSAL, instruction regarding fraternal life in community, 59e.
18 CICLSAL, instruction regarding fraternal life in community, 65.

(c. 682; cf. c. 738 §2), or he may entrust to an institute a work which by definition includes an ecclesiastical office (e.g., a parish). The code identifies a number of offices reserved to priests, such as vicar general, pastor, and parochial vicar. Other offices, such as judge, chancellor, and finance officer, are not so reserved. A bishop may also establish ecclesiastical offices for his diocese by decree and may entrust these offices to individual members.

Canons 145-196 in general and canon 682 in particular govern the manner in which members of institutes/societies are appointed to or removed from diocesan ecclesiastical offices.

- The diocesan bishop appoints the member, "with the competent superior making the presentation, or at least assenting to the appointment" (c. 682 §1). For example, the superior does not appoint the pastor of a parish; rather, upon presentation of a suitable candidate by the superior, the bishop makes the appointment.
- Most dioceses require testimonials from major superiors concerning a candidate's suitability and moral character before an office is conferred. Background checks and safe environment policies must be scrupulously followed.[19]
- Either the bishop or the superior may remove a member from office. Each must notify the other, but neither requires the other's consent (c. 682 §2).
- Financial obligations may not necessarily cease with removal from office (cf. c. 195).

To remove a member from office requires "a just cause" (c. 193 §3). Before issuing a decree of removal, the superior is "to hear those whose rights can be injured" (c. 50). If the superior decides to remove a member, the decree of removal "is to be issued in writing, with the reasons [for it] at least summarily expressed" (c. 51; cf. c. 193 §4). A member who considers the removal to be unjust may take recourse according to the norm of canons 1732-1739.[20]

Provision of ecclesiastical offices is also governed by the following norms:

---

19 See USCCB, *Charter for the Protection of Children and Young People*, 14 June 2018, 3rd rev. ed. (Washington, DC: USCCB, 2018), at https://www.usccb.org/issues-and-action/child-and-youth-protection/upload/Charter-for-the-Protection-of-Children-and-Young-People-2018-final.pdf.

20 The administrative procedure for the removal or transfer of a pastor (cc. 1740–1752) does not apply to members of institutes/societies (cf. cc. 682 §2; 738 §2).

- The candidate must be in communion with the Church and qualified (c. 149 §1).
- Offices entailing the full care of souls or the exercise of the priestly order can only be conferred validly upon priests (c. 150).
- An office which is not vacant cannot be conferred validly on another (c. 153 §1).
- A promise of an office, no matter by whom it is made, has no juridic effect (c. 153 §3).
- The provision (c. 156) or loss (cf. cc. 186; 193 §4) of any office is to be made in writing.

A number of roles are considered administrative positions rather than ecclesiastical offices (e.g., secretarial staff). Diocesan personnel policies may address such positions, or the provisions of the code can be applied by way of analogy. At the same time, the Church, as an employer, must also observe the civil laws pertaining to labor as well as Catholic social teaching (c. 1286, 1°). This includes paying "a just and decent wage" (c. 1286, 2°).

Individual Member Proposing a New Work

An individual member may propose a new apostolic work. In this case, the member and the major superior should consider the following questions:

- Is the proposed work an authentic expression of the institute's mission and apostolate?
- Does it foster the individual member's gifts and talents?
- Is it in harmony with the apostolate of the diocese?
- Is it economically feasible?
- How will the member and the institute fulfil their mutual rights and duties, in particular the right/duty of community life?

Once the member and the major superior have formulated an initial proposal, the approval of the diocesan bishop should also be sought (cc. 394 §1; 678 §3; 738 §2). Finally, a written agreement among the relevant parties ought to be drawn up concerning:

- the work to be accomplished (cf. c. 681 §2);
- clear lines of accountability and periodic reviews of the work for purposes of protecting the mission;

- financial and legal matters, such as sources of income, insurance, taxes, liabilities, agency, licenses, supervision, relationship with the institute's civil corporation(s);
- civil contracts which ensure an arm's-length relationship between the institute and the new work.

The major superior, who has discerned that the new work corresponds to the institute's mission, gives the mandate to the individual member.

Governance of External Apostolic Works

External apostolic works of institutes/societies are part of the apostolate of the local Church. As such, their governance falls under the authority of both the diocesan bishop and the superiors of the institute (cc. 394 §1; 678; 738).

The Responsibility of the Bishop

Fostering and Coordinating the Apostolate

The bishop fosters and coordinates the various forms of the apostolate in his diocese (c. 394). ICLSALs are to contribute to the apostolate according to their spiritual patrimony and discipline (cc. 677 §1; 678 §2; 731 §1).

Visitation

The bishop exercises oversight of apostolic works through visitation. At least every five years (cf. c. 399) he is to visit persons and Catholic institutes, including churches, oratories, schools open to the public, and other works of the apostolate (cc. 397 §1; 683 §1; 806 §1).

Correction of Abuses

If the diocesan bishop becomes aware of abuses in the apostolate and has warned the superior in vain, "he himself can make provision on his own authority" (c. 683 §2; cf. c. 392). It should be recalled that, for theological as well as practical reasons, "the diocesan bishop in the diocese entrusted to him has all ordinary, proper, and immediate power which is required for the exercise of his pastoral function" (c. 381 §1), except for cases expressly reserved in law. On the other hand, abuses of episcopal authority can and ought to be denounced; a member or institute aggrieved by any singular administrative act of a bishop has the right to challenge it (cc. 1732-1739).

Forbidding an Individual Member to Reside in a Diocese

"When a most grave cause demands it, a diocesan bishop can prohibit a member of a religious institute from residing in the diocese if his or her major superior, after having been informed, has neglected to make provision; moreover, the matter is to be referred immediately to the Holy See" (c. 679; cf. c. 738 §2). Ordinarily, as soon as the major superior is informed of the situation, he or she will take the appropriate action. In the truly exceptional circumstances of canon 679, the diocesan bishop can and should intervene.

Forbidding an Institute to Conduct an Apostolic Work in the Diocese

The law makes no specific provision allowing a diocesan bishop to forbid an institute to conduct its proper work once a house has been canonically established. Nevertheless, the bishop remains the coordinator of the apostolate of the diocese (c. 394) and can withdraw an entrusted work from an institute according to the norm of law.

The Responsibility of the Religious Superiors

An entire book of the code is devoted to temporal goods and their correct administration (Book V), the prescripts of which are explicitly applied to religious institutes (c. 635 §1), secular institutes (c. 718), and societies of apostolic life (c. 741 §1). Superiors have the right and duty to see that the prescripts of Book V are observed by the institute and the members, according to the specific norms provided both by the code (cc. 634-640; 718; 741 §1) and by proper law.[21]

The governance and oversight of other areas is regulated both by universal law (cc. 617-633; cf. c. 734) as well as proper law (cc. 617; 717 §1; c. 734). In general, members are subject to their proper superiors in the exercise of the apostolate (cc. 678 §1; 738 §2). Chapters also have a governance role to play in apostolic works (cc. 631-633). Taking the mode of governance of a diocese as a model, the following considerations are proposed for proper law.

Superior of Members of the Institute Participating in Its Mission

In exercising oversight over the apostolate, superiors are "to govern their subjects as sons or daughters of God and, promoting the voluntary obedience of their subjects with reverence for the human person, they are to listen to them willingly and foster their common endeavor for the good of the institute and the Church" (c. 618). They are also "to meet the personal needs of the members appropriately, solicitously to care for and visit the sick, to correct the restless, to console the faint of heart, and to be patient toward all" (c. 619). It is in the spirit of these canons that superiors are to:

---

21 See herein chapter nine, "Temporal Goods."

- encourage members to offer their gifts to the apostolate according to their talents and the needs of the time and place;
- assign members to or approve their involvement in a particular work;
- make periodic visits to the apostolates.

Responsible for Oversight and Vigilance

An Apostolic Work

An institute's commitment to an apostolic work brings with it an obligation for its oversight. Failure to exercise adequate oversight can expose an institute to liability for negligence or worse. Some of the means superiors may use for oversight can include:

- assessment of the work's participation in the institute's mission and response to the needs of people;
- use of mandatory reporting processes;
- mandatory approval of some categories of decisions, such as purpose, financial policies, etc.;
- periodic visits.

Correction of Abuses

The obligation for oversight and vigilance over apostolic works and individual members also entails the obligation to correct abuses. Some methods could include:

- reassignment of members;
- granting of a sabbatical for spiritual and professional renewal;
- hiring and firing key personnel in an apostolic work;
- enforcement of policies;
- in clerical institutes/societies of pontifical right, the application of penal remedies or penances (cc. 1339-1340) or even penal sanctions (c. 1312).

In all of these actions, "superiors are to exercise their power, received from God through the ministry of the Church, in a spirit of service" (c. 618), "according to the norm of universal and proper law" (c. 617).

Apostolic Works in Civil Society

Apostolic works are also subject to civil law (cf. c. 22). Particular care must be taken in the areas of finances and liability.

Remuneration

In virtue of the vow of poverty, anything a religious acquires through personal labor or on behalf of the institute by way of gift, offering, stipend, fee, salary, pension, subsidy, insurance settlement, or similar manner, belongs to the religious institute and not the individual religious (c. 668 §3). This includes royalties for published work. Copyrights should be held in the name of the religious institute. If religious are dispensed from their vows and leave religious life, Social Security benefits and the like accompany them and no longer belong to the institute.

Institutes must follow IRS regulations in order to maintain tax-exempt status. This includes: (1) members working in apostolates as mandated by their superiors; and (2) turning control of their income over to the institute.[22] Even though institutes may be tax-exempt, individual members might be subject to paying taxes on their salaries. One should consult a tax attorney.

In light of Catholic social teaching, members have the right to seek a just and decent wage (cf. c. 1286, 2°).

- Members seeking employment should seek a compensation package (e.g., salary) commensurate with their experience, education, and level of responsibility.
- Members seeking employment in positions of direct service to the poor may apply for subsidies or grants from the institute if available.
- Members engaged in individual apostolates should submit at least annual financial reports to the major superior.

If an apostolate is recognized as Catholic by the diocesan bishop, it may be listed in the *Official Catholic Directory* and use the IRS group tax exemption granted to the USCCB.

Liabilities: Institutes and Incorporated Works

Formerly, charitable institutions could not be sued. That protection, however, ended decades ago. Today, many apostolates incorporate civilly as non-profit corporations. Incorporation provides the benefit of civilly separating the assets of the work from those of the institute and thereby limiting the institute's liability. A non-profit corporation possesses a legal identity separate from those who govern it. As a result, governing boards have limited personal liability for the

---

22 Due to the complexity and changeable nature of IRS regulations, they cannot be included here.

corporation's debts, so long as they are acting only in their corporate capacity (as employee, officer, director) without intention to defraud.

Institutes must take care to respect the reality of the separation of the incorporation, lest it be interpreted by a civil judge as a mere formality and the institute lose its protection from liability. An institute can demonstrate the separation through different names, assets, logos, addresses, and boards of directors. An institute can lose its protection if it gains economically from the corporation beyond fees for services rendered or if it exerts undue control over the governance of the corporation. An institute can structure an incorporated work in such a way that those responsible for the institute assure the work's fundamental purposes and integrity.[23] Canonical commentators vary in their opinions about the effect of civil incorporation on the work's canonical status in terms of governance. An institute needs to consult a canonist when structuring a civil corporation for an apostolate.

Institutes and Members

The individual member, the institute, and its civil law corporation(s) are all distinct legal entities. There is nothing intrinsic to the relationship between the individual and the institute that automatically renders the institute liable for all the actions of its members. Membership in an institute of consecrated life or a society of apostolic life creates a *canonical* relationship with *canonical* obligations; as such, being assigned to an apostolate does not necessarily constitute an employee-employer relationship in civil law, nor is the institute always liable for the actions of its members. On the other hand, there are cases in which institutes are liable for the actions of its members, whether vicariously or directly. In such cases, institutes should retain legal counsel.

Membership in an institute/society does not change the *civil* status of a member. Therefore, members have the same civil rights and obligations as other citizens. The major difference lies in the fact that a member of the Catholic Church is subject to two legal systems: canonical and civil. Although members sometimes need permission from canonical superiors in order to exercise their civil rights (cf. c. 639 §2), the validity of such actions in civil law does not depend upon this permission.

---

23 See A.J. Maida and N.P. Cafardi, *Church Property, Church Finances and Church-Related Corporations: A Canon Law Handbook* (St. Louis, MO: The Catholic Health Association, 1984) 189–215.

Sponsored Works

Some apostolates have evolved into large, complex systems (e.g., hospitals) that the institute is no longer able to staff with its own members. This has led to a mode of governance sometimes referred to as "sponsorship," although this is not a canonical term.

Relationship to the Institute

Institutes can participate in a sponsored work in a variety of ways. Three common relationship models are described below.

Governance Relationship

A governance relationship model describes the situation in which an institute retains primary responsibility for the sponsored work's governance. The institute may hold the work as part of its own assets and govern it as part of itself. On the other hand, the work may have received separate incorporation, where the articles of incorporation and the by-laws place the responsibility for its governance ultimately in the hands of the superiors of the institute. Some of the various ways of formulating the civil documents to accomplish this situation could include:

- identifying the major superior and council as the board of directors of the work;
- requiring that the institute's members, appointed or approved by the major superior, comprise a certain percentage of the board of directors;
- using a membership corporation structure, where certain decisions, such as approval of the board of directors, the mission statement, certain financial activities, etc., are reserved to a panel of persons (the members of the corporation) appointed or approved by the institute. The major superior and council or others appointed by them could comprise the panel.

In this category of relationship, the ultimate responsibility for governance rests with the religious institute, which assures the Catholic identity of the work.

An Influence Relationship

An institute may participate in the sponsorship of a work in partnership with others, Catholic or not. The institute enters into such a partnership by means of a formal agreement on the issues of purpose and structure, which cannot violate fundamental Catholic values. If the institute holds a position of major partner, then it can exert considerable influence on the formulation of that agreement and the handling of new issues as they arise. For example, if an institute sponsors a school, a hospital, or a healthcare system and enters into an equal or majority member partnership, the institute can exercise considerable influence over the governance decisions of the new entity. Usually, the greater the holdings of a partner, the greater potential for influence. The resultant new entity may or may not retain a Catholic identity, as determined by the formal agreement and the approval of the bishop.

An Advocacy Relationship

At other times, collaborative agreements may result in an institute sponsoring a minor component of a larger entity. Again, such a partnership requires a formal agreement, which cannot violate fundamental Catholic values. In this case, the institute usually can exercise only a reduced level of authority. Its role becomes one of advocacy. For example, if an institute sponsors a healthcare or social service agency that joins a larger system, the institute may not be able to exercise major influence in governance decisions. However, it can always be a voice for the demands of the Gospel and natural justice in making those decisions. Again, the formal agreement and the approval of the bishop would determine any Catholic identity of the new entity.

Catholic Identity

Sponsorship concerns Catholic identity, among other things. Since the Catholic identity of charitable institutions relates primarily to the mystery of the Church, no single formulation can completely capture its essence. One sample model for a Catholic university formulates it thus:

> By institutional commitment it brings to its task the inspiration and light of the Christian message. Catholic ideals, attitudes and principles penetrate and inform its activities. It operates as an institution in which Catholicism is vitally present and active.[24]

Ecclesiastical Structures

An apostolic work can be structured in a number of different ways.

Juridic Personality

An apostolate can be constituted as a juridic person if it is "ordered for a purpose in keeping with the mission of the Church" (c. 114 §1). Juridic personality functions in canon law similarly to the way articles of incorporation function in civil law. The law itself recognizes some organizations as juridic persons; e.g., dioceses, parishes, seminaries, religious institutes, their provinces and houses. A

---

24 John Paul II, apostolic constitution concerning Catholic universities *Ex corde Ecclesiae* 14, August 15, 1990: *AAS* 82 (1990) 1475–1509.

competent ecclesiastical authority can establish other juridic persons by decree (c. 116).

The law recognizes two kinds of juridic persons: public and private (c. 116). A public juridic person is established for a specific purpose congruent with the mission of the Church and acts in the name of the Church (c. 116 §1). This purpose includes "works of piety, of the apostolate, or of charity, whether spiritual or temporal" (c. 114 §2). The temporal goods of a public juridic person are ecclesiastical goods (c. 1257 §1) and are governed by Book V. A private juridic person acts to further the mission of the Church in its own name. It does not, therefore, act in the name of the Church (c. 116), nor are its goods ecclesiastical goods in the sense of Book V. A private juridic person is less closely governed by a bishop than a public juridic person.

The Congregation for Institutes of Consecrated Life and Societies of Apostolic Life is the ecclesiastical authority competent to grant juridic personality to works of the apostolate which cross diocesan boundaries (e.g., a network of hospitals). Such petitions should briefly summarize the history of the apostolate, the reasons for the request, and the juridic consequences. Petitions regarding an apostolate contained within the boundaries of a single diocese should be directed to the diocesan bishop.

Recognition as Catholic

A bishop, by means of a public document, may recognize an organization or work as Catholic without establishing it as a juridic person (cc. 216; 300; 803 §1; 808). The entity publicly participates in the mission of the Church while it remains a private endeavor under private governance. Since the entity's continued recognition depends on the bishop's ongoing acceptance of it as Catholic, it would be prudent to identify some basic elements for making the grant in writing.[25]

Ecclesial Structures of Sponsored Institutions

There are a variety of forms the structural relationship between sponsored institutions and the sponsoring institute can take.

Institutions with formal juridic bonds to the Church

Institutions with formal juridic bonds to the Church fall into one of three major categories:

---

25 An example of this kind of institution would consist of a school established by private individuals who run it as a Catholic school, have received public recognition of it by the bishop, but who have not sought to receive juridic personality for it.

- Institutions operating under a public juridic bond, either:
  - through participation in a public juridic person, such as a religious institute or a diocese (most Catholic schools and healthcare institutions are in this category);
  - through their own public juridic personality obtained by virtue of their establishment by ecclesiastical authority.[26]
- Institutions operating under a grant of private juridic personality by ecclesiastical authority.
- Institutions recognized by ecclesiastical authority as Catholic.

Catholic entity managed under Catholic auspices, while owned and operated within a larger secular institutional framework

A Catholic campus within a largely secular hospital or school would illustrate this case. Contractual and civil law documents, as well as the local bishop, would specify the extent and manner of the unit's relationship with the Church. A religious institute could contract to manage or to operate the unit.

An institution which operates in the Catholic tradition and which incorporates that commitment into its civil law documents and policies but which does not possess formal juridic bonds to the Church

An institution's articles of incorporation may commit it to teach a Catholic curriculum, follow Catholic healthcare ethical guidelines, or require representation on its board of directors from a religious institute. In this category, the facility would not possess juridic standing in the Church, because it is not a part of a juridic person (such as a religious institute), nor has it received juridic personality from ecclesiastical authority. Such a facility would require the bishop's permission to use the name Catholic (cc. 216; 300; 803 §3; 808). Many Catholic universities and schools in the United States operate under this model. The board of directors could contract with an institute to operate, manage, or govern the institution.

An institution which operates in the Catholic tradition, but which possesses no civil or juridic bonds to the Church

26 For example, CommonSpirit Health, an alignment of Catholic Health Initiatives and Dignity Health, includes healthcare institutions founded by over a dozen religious institutions across the nation. The system has obtained public juridic personality of its own, and the original sponsoring institutes have withdrawn sponsorship from the component institutions. In return, the institutes provide members of the board of directors. See https://commonspirit.org/.

In this category, the institution has not bound itself in either the civil or ecclesiastical sphere as a Catholic institution. The personal commitment of the governing authorities and staff maintains the ecclesial connection. Canon law would not apply to the facility itself. However, Catholics involved would be subject to some canonical regulations, such as the need for the bishop's permission to call the facility Catholic (c. 216). As in the previous example, the institution could make contractual arrangements with a religious institute or individual member for its operation, management or governance.

A secular institution, i.e., non-ecclesiastical institution, under the management of an ecclesiastical entity, such as a religious congregation

A non-ecclesial institution may contract with a religious institute to operate, manage, or govern it. The civil law contract regulates the situation, not canon law. Members of institutes involved in the work are nevertheless bound by the obligation to maintain communion with the Church and to observe both universal and proper canon law. An example of this arrangement could include a contract with a Catholic institution to manage an onsite food service.

Conclusion

> More than in external works, the mission consists in making Christ present to the world through personal witness (cf. c. 673). This is the challenge, this is the primary task of the consecrated life! The more consecrated persons allow themselves to be conformed to Christ, the more Christ is made present and active in the world for the salvation of all. Thus it can be said that consecrated persons are "on mission" by virtue of their very consecration, to which they bear witness in accordance with the charism of their institute.[27]

27 *VC* 72.

SAMPLE LETTER OF SUITABILITY

Date

Major Superior

Dear Bishop N:

I am writing to certify the suitability of ---, a member in good standing in --- Institute.

She/he has permission to serve at (name of apostolic work) from --- to---.

Furthermore, I have carefully reviewed the personnel records which we maintain, and I have consulted with some who served with him (her) in the works assigned under our authority. Based on these inquiries, I testify to the best of my ability that --- is a person of good moral character and reputation and is qualified to serve in an effective and suitable manner in your (arch)diocese. In addition, also based on inquiry and to the best of my knowledge, I assure you that nothing in his/her background would limit or disqualify him (her) from assignment or cause scandal.

I hereby grant him (her) permission to serve in your (arch)diocese under your authorization.

A curriculum vitae including name, date of birth, place and date of profession of vows/ordination, formation/seminary, and previous assignments is enclosed.

Signature

Title

SAMPLE CANONICAL AGREEMENT BETWEEN AN INSTITUTE AND A BISHOP CONCERNING MEMBERS WORKING IN AN (ARCH)DIOCESE

Parties to the Agreement: In accord with c. 681 §2, this agreement is entered into between the ____ Institute and the (Arch)diocese of ____ for the services of the following members of the Institute: (list of members).

Duration of Agreement: The agreement for services shall begin ____ and extend through ______.

Terms of Service: (Listing of mutually agreed upon conditions of service)

Compensation: The (Arch)diocese agrees to remit payment to the Institute as remuneration for services rendered under this agreement by members of the Institute as follows: (terms of agreement).

Termination: This agreement may be terminated or altered by mutual agreement of the parties. Termination can apply to one or more of the members listed or to all members who serve under this agreement. Notification shall be made as follows: (details of notification process)

Signatures of the Contracting Parties

By: ______________________________ for ______________________________
Signature (Arch)diocese

______________ Date ______________________________
Title

By: ______________________________ for ______________________________
Signature Institute/Society

______________________________ Date ______________________________
Title

SAMPLE OUTLINE OF AN INTER-INSTITUTE AGREEMENT TO JOINTLY SPONSOR A WORK

Introduction

- Parties to the Agreement

Provisions

- Statement of Purpose of the Work
- Governing Structure/Officers of the Work
- Funding, Including Contributions by Participating Parties
- Evaluation Structure
- Dissolution Mechanism and Distribution of Assets

Signatures, Titles and Dates

CHAPTER 9

TEMPORAL GOODS

Daniel J. Ward, OSB[1]

Although there is an entire book of the code devoted to the study of "temporal goods," the Code of Canon Law does not define the term. Various commentators hold that temporal goods include ownership of or interest in real property, personal property, and investments. The simplest definition is the term "assets," which is used by the Congregation for Institutes of Consecrated Life and Societies of Apostolic Life.[2] Temporal goods that belong to a public juridic person in the Church are "ecclesiastical goods" and are governed by Book V of the Code of Canon Law.[3]

Religious institutes, secular institutes, societies of apostolic life, or a part of one of these, such as a province,[4] are public juridic persons and thus are governed by Book V on temporal goods. In addition, they are governed by canons 634-640 (in Book II) which are specific to the administration of temporal goods within a religious institute.

The Code of Canon Law

The canons require that a religious institute is to have a finance officer who is distinct from the major superior.[5] There is also to be a financial council or at

---

1 Daniel J. Ward, OSB, was the original author and also revised this chapter. He is grateful for the cooperation, comments and suggestions made by Sister Margaret Modde, OSF, Father Francis Morrisey, OMI, and Father Kevin Seasoltz, OSB, in the writing of the original chapter.

2 See Congregation for Institutes of Consecrated Life and Societies of Apostolic Life, guidelines *Economy at the Service of the Charism and Mission* 15 (Vatican City: Libreria Editrice Vaticana, 2018) (hereafter "*ECSM*") 29.

3 See c. 1257 §1.

4 This chapter will use the term "religious institute" to include not only religious institutes but also secular institutes, societies of apostolic life and parts of them. Province is used to refer to a part of an institute but also includes autonomous houses of monastics and canons regular.

5 See c. 636 §1.

least two financial advisors to assist the finance officer.[6] The finance officer is to give the major superior and others as provided in the proper law, reports on the financial administration of the religious institute. The proper law is to set norms for the financial transactions such as expenditures of monies and conveyance of assets. The norms are to state the financial limits for expenditures and conveyances by the major superior or other administrators that do not require the consent of a council, a chapter, or another designated body (ordinary administration). The norms also are to state the financial amount above which the major superior or other administrators must obtain the consent of a council, a chapter or another designated body (extraordinary administration).[7]

Canon law encourages the use of approved budgets.[8] If a budgetary process is used, it replaces the individual approvals of extraordinary administration since the budget approves and authorizes the expenditures contained in the budget. Expenditures other than those in the budget require additional approvals.

The Practice of the Congregation for Institutes of Consecrated Life and Societies of Apostolic Life

On January 6, 2018, the Congregation for Institutes of Consecrated Life and Societies of Apostolic Life issued the document *Economy at the Service of the Charism and Mission*. Pope Francis approved the document in an audience on December 12, 2017. The document, referred to as "Guidelines," sets a theological framework for administration of temporal goods, and provides norms to be followed in the administration of temporal goods. The norms, based on canons in the Code of Canon Law, explain the applications of the canons and the procedures of the congregation to be followed in the administration of a religious institute. The remainder of this article will summarize the norms and point out where the applications and procedures have changed from past practices.

Stable Patrimony

The norms of canon law govern the stable patrimony of a religious institute.[9] However, "stable patrimony" is not defined in the canons. The Guidelines define stable patrimony as all those assets that ensure the realization of the mission of the religious institute.[10] Stable patrimony may include real

---

6 See c. 1280.
7 See c. 638 §1.
8 See c. 1284 §3.
9 See c. 638 §3.
10 See *ECSM* 40; cf. also *ECSM* 72.

estate, investments, historical and artistic pieces of cultural heritage, and security funds. The Guidelines recommend that the designation of assets as stable patrimony should be regularly evaluated to determine if changing circumstances requires some assets to no longer be included in stable patrimony and others to now be included.

The proper law or another similar document is to include the following regarding stable patrimony:

> The stable patrimony consists of all immovable and movable property that by means of a specific assignment are destined to guarantee the economic security of the institute. For the goods of the entire institute, the General Chapter or the General Superior with the Consent of his/her Council makes the assignment. For the assets of a province, as well as for the assets of a legitimately established house, the Provincial Chapter or other similar assemblies (cf. can. 632) or the Provincial Superior with the consent of his/her Council and confirmed by the Superior General makes the assignment.[11]

Alienation

Alienation and acts "by which the public juridical person could be damaged"[12] require the permission of the Holy See if the alienation or act exceeds the amount set for an individual region. The permission is to guarantee that the transaction comports with the purposes of patrimony and the good use of the assets.[13]

Contracts

Permission from the Congregation for Institutes of Consecrated Life and Societies of Apostolic Life is required if the value of a *contractual* transaction exceeds the maximum amount set for an individual region *and the contract has a duration of more than six years* in the following transactions:[14]

- loans;
- ceding of land rights;
- giving use,
- providing housing;

---

11 *ECSM* 38; cf. *ECSM* 72.
12 *ECSM* 57; cf. c. 638 §3.
13 See *ECSM* 57.
14 See *ECSM* 78.

- leasing;[15] or
- establishing the right of usufruct.[16]

The above approval is a new requirement since these contractual obligations are not alienation in the traditional sense, which meant the transfer of ownership.[17]

Permission of Congregation for Institutes of Consecrated Life and Societies of Apostolic Life

The sale or donation of properties that exceed the maximum amount also require the permission of the Congregation for Institutes of Consecrated Life and Societies of Apostolic Life. Traditionally this has meant the sale or donation of real property. However, the Guidelines now include not only the sale or donation of real property, but also contracts for the exchange of goods.[18]

---

15 See the USCCB Complementary Norms for additional information on canon 1297 and the leasing of ecclesiastical goods by religious institutes and societies of apostolic life:

> Canon 1297 - Leasing of Church Property
>
> On November 13, 2002, the [USCCB] legitimately approved complementary legislation for the implementation of canon 1297 of the Code of Canon Law for the dioceses of the United States. The action was granted *recognitio* by the Congregation for Bishops . . . dated May 2, 2007. Wherefore, and in accord with the prescripts of canon 1297, the [USCCB] decrees that the following norms shall govern the leasing of Church property:
>
> [. . .]
>
> (4) The valid leasing of ecclesiastical goods owned by a pontifical institute of consecrated life or society of apostolic life requires, in addition to the consent of the competent major superior and council, the *nihil obstat* of the diocesan bishop when the market value of the property to be leased exceeds $1,000,000 or the lease is to be for 3 years or longer.
>
> (5) The valid leasing of ecclesiastical goods by any public juridic person requires the consent of the Holy See when the market value of the goods exceeds $5,000,000.

The full text of the complementary norm is available on the USCCB website at https://www.usccb.org/committees/canonical-affairs-church-governance/complementary-norms#tab--canon-1297-leasing-of-church-property.

16 "Usufruct" is the temporary right of a person or entity to use the property of another and can include the right to derive income from the property.

17 See, e.g., Francis Morrisey, commentary to canon 1291 in *The Canon Law Letter and Spirit* (Collegeville, MN: The Liturgical Press, 1995) 732, para. 2572.

18 See *ECSM* 81.

Approval is required whether or not the property is designated as stable patrimony.[19]

The request for approval by the congregation must include the following:[20]

- a stated just cause;
- the use of the proceeds;
- a professional assessment;[21]
- for institutes of pontifical right the *opinion* of the local ordinary of the place where the property is located;
- for institutes of diocesan right and monasteries *sui iuris* the *consent* of the local ordinary of the place where the property is located;[22] and
- if the property is divisible, the indication of properties which have possibly already been alienated. This requirement is *for validity*.

If the reason for the alienation is because the proceeds from the alienation are needed to subsidize financial difficulties, the request must contain the following additional information:[23]

a. If the sale is to subsidize immediate financial needs, the request must provide information regarding the causes of financial need and present clear proposals for solving the financial situation.

b. If the sale is absolutely necessary to pay debts incurred in carrying out its apostolic works, the request must include a plan rectifying the financial situation.

---

19 Canon 1291 of book V only requires approval "for the valid alienation of goods which constitute by legitimate designation the stable patrimony of a juridic person." However, canon 638, specifically governing religious institutes, has no clause limiting the requirement of permission to assets designated as patrimony. See also the interpretation given by the Pontifical Council on Legislative Text (PCLT), "Canons 638 §§3, 4; 1293 Interpretation of Guidelines on Temporal Goods for Institutes of Consecrated Life and Societies of Apostolic Life," in *Roman Replies and CLSA Advisory Opinions* 2019, ed. Sharon Euart (Washington, DC: CLSA, 2019) 11.

20 See *ECSM* 81.

21 Canon 1293 §§1-2 uses the word "experts," which has been interpreted as *two* assessments. However, in the Guidelines, the singular is used, calling for "a professional assessment." *ECSM* 81.

22 Cf. *ECSM* 94.

23 See *ECSM* 81.

Sale of Apostolic Works

There are now specific requirements for the sale of apostolic works. The procedures are the same as for the sale of real property.[24]

Financial Transactions

In cases of financing transactions that incur debts, the authorization of the Congregation is required if the financing exceeds the amount set for a region. The request is to include:[25]

a. the reasons;

b. the over-all debt situation; and

c. an amortization plan.

Since the authorization to incur debt is based on a financial transaction that could worsen the patrimonial condition,[26] it is important to analyze the transaction. For instance, the refinancing of an existing debt is usually done for the purpose of obtaining more favorable terms. It does not impair but improves the patrimonial condition and thus authorization would not be required except the authorizations internal to the institute. The same is true when it is financially advisable to secure outside financing, such as a bond issue, rather than use the institute's own assets when the interest on the outside financing is less than the interest made on investments.

Financial Transactions and Apostolic Ministries

In many instances, when a religious institute separately incorporates an apostolic work, the institute retains sufficient control, usually through reserved powers, so that the work is not canonically alienated. In the past, when assets were transferred to the corporation of the work and the assets exceeded the value requiring approval of the Congregation for Institutes of Consecrated Life and Societies of Apostolic Life, authorization was not sought from the congregation since there was no canonical alienation. While the assets were civilly transferred from the corporation of the religious institute to the corporation of the apostolic work, there was not canonical transfer (alienation) because the apostolic work and the assets remained part of the public juridic person of the institute.

---

24 See *ECSM* 86.
25 See *ECSM* 88.
26 See c. 638 §1.

The Guidelines seem to change the above position.[27] They speak of "associated civil entities" which are defined as civil entities "linked to the canonical juridical person"[28] or "connected to the institute."[29] If assets are transferred to an associated civil entity and the value of the assets exceed the maximum amount set for the region, the permission of the congregation is required. The procedures to be followed are those cited above for alienation of property and transfer of works.[30] Such approval could be quite costly based on the tax charged by the congregation.[31] The tax is charged even if the transfer involves no financial remuneration. In such cases it is advisable to request no tax or a reduced tax.

Conclusion

The Guidelines provide many suggestions about the proper administration of temporal goods and finances such as planning,[32] transparency,[33] accounting,[34] financial statements,[35] record keeping,[36] administrative procedural manual,[37] and internal controls.[38]

The overall emphasis of the Guidelines is to assist religious institutes in "*Rethinking economic matters in a manner faithful to the charism.*"[39]

Finally, it should be remembered that the Guidelines contain the requirements for submission to the Congregation for Institutes of Consecrated Life and Societies of Apostolic Life when requesting approval for an alienation or other financial transactions.

---

27 Cf. PCLT, "Canons 638 §§3, 4; 1293."
28 *ECSM* 89.
29 *ECSM* 90.
30 See *ECSM* 81 and 86.
31 In 2020 the tax charged was $1,000 per $1,000,000 of the selling price or, if there is no financial remuneration, the value of the asset itself.
32 See *ECSM* 26.
33 See *ECSM* 41.
34 See *ECSM* 43.
35 See *ECSM* 43.
36 See *ECSM* 44; cf. also *ECSM* 93.
37 See *ECSM* 62.
38 See *ECSM* 67.
39 *ECSM* 3 (emphasis in original).

PROCEDURES WHEN SUBMITTING REQUESTS FOR APPROVAL TO THE CONGREGATION FOR INSTITUTES OF CONSECRATED LIFE AND SOCIETIES OF APOSTOLIC LIFE

Alienation of Real Property by an Institute of Pontifical Right

The Acts to be sent to the Congregation for Institutes of Consecrated Life and Societies of Apostolic Life ("the Congregation") require:

- A petition addressed to the Congregation and signed by the competent superior;
- The petition must include:
  1. The request for approval to alienate a described parcel of real property;
  2. The reason for the alienation;
  3. If the property is being sold, the use of the proceeds;
  4. If the property is being sold for less than estimated evaluation of the property, the reason why;
  5. If the property is being conveyed without compensation, the reason why;
  6. If the property is divisible, the portions or parcels that have already been alienated; and
  7. A statement of the consent of the council/chapter consent.
- Excerpts from the minutes of the council/chapter signed by the secretary;
- The professional valuations;
- The opinion of the diocesan bishop of the place where the property is located; and
- Other requirements of the proper law.

Note: If a provincial is submitting the request, it is sent to the general superior who, with the consent of the council, submits to the Congregation the materials submitted by the provincial accompanied by a letter of the general superior stating that he/she and the general council approve the request.

Alienation of Real Property by an Institute of Diocesan Right

The Acts to be sent to the Congregation require:

- A petition addressed to the Congregation and signed by the competent superior.

- The petition must include:
    1. The request for approval to alienate a described parcel of real property;
    2. The reason for the alienation;
    3. If the property is being sold, the use of the proceeds;
    4. If the property is being sold for less than estimated evaluation of the property, the reason why;
    5. If the property is being conveyed without compensation, the reason why;
    6. If the property is divisible, the portions or parcels that have already been alienated; and
    7. A statement of the consent of the council/chapter.
- Excerpts from the minutes of the council/chapter signed by the secretary;
- The professional valuations;
- The written consent of the diocesan bishop of the place where the property is located;
- Other requirements of the proper law.

Alienation of Real Property to Subsidize Financial Difficulties

The Acts to be sent to the Congregation are the same as above for the Alienation of Real Property except the following two additional items must be included in the petition:

- Cause of the financial difficulty and
- A plan for rectifying the financial situation.

The Sale of Works

The requirements are the same as established for the Alienation of Real Property.

Financial Transactions (Indebtedness)

The Acts to be sent to the Congregation require:

- A petition addressed to the Congregation and signed by the competent superior;
- The petition must include:
    1. The request for approval of the transaction;
    2. The amount of the transaction, e.g., the amount of the debt;
    3. The reason for the transaction;

4. The over-all indebtedness of the religious institute;
5. The amortization plan;
6. Statement of the consent of the council/chapter;

- Excerpts from the minutes of the council/chapter signed by the secretary;
- Other requirements of the proper law.

Leases, Loans and Other Similar Contracts

The Acts to be sent to the Congregation must include:

- A petition that includes:
  1. The request;
  2. Statement of the consent of the council/chapter; and
  3. If required by the USCCB complementary norm on leasing for canon 1297, norm (4), the *nihil obstat* of the diocesan bishop.
- Draft of the contract; and
- Excerpt from the minutes of the council/chapter signed by the secretary.

SENDING MATERIALS TO DICASTERIES IN ROME

OPTION 1

Transmittal to Apostolic See through the Apostolic Nunciature

(A) When a religious institute/monastery transmits material directly to a dicastery (congregation) at the Apostolic See, leaders may send the written materials through the courtesy of the Apostolic Nunciature in Washington, D.C.

(B) The procedure to follow is:

1. Place the written material in an unsealed envelope addressed to the dicastery.
2. Address a letter to the Nuncio requesting that the enclosed envelope be sent by diplomatic pouch to the dicastery. In the letter indicate the nature of the materials.
3. Place the letter and the unsealed envelope addressed to the dicastery in another envelope addressed to:

   Apostolic Nunciature
   3339 Massachusetts Avenue, N.W.
   Washington, D.C. 20008

There is no charge by the Nunciature for the use of the diplomatic pouch.

OPTION 2

Transmittal to Apostolic See through
Use of a Procurator or Person Living in Rome

(A) A religious institute may have a procurator general in Rome who personally takes materials to a dicastery. This is the practice of men's religious institutes with a generalate or house in Rome. Women's institutes of the same family often use the procurator general of the men's institute.

A religious institute or its canonical advisor may have a contact in Rome who personally will bring materials to a dicastery.

The advantage of having materials personally brought to a dicastery is that there is assurance that the materials were delivered. Moreover, the procurator/person living in Rome can also shepherd the materials through the dicastery especially if there is a problem or a delay.

A stipend is usually offered to the person delivering the materials to a dicastery.

(B) This method is particularly useful if the request is urgent such as a request for approval of an alienation or the incurring of a debt. The procurator/person living in Rome can receive the document from the dicastery and immediately fax a copy to the appropriate leadership personnel and later send the original (although at times the dicastery will send the original by diplomatic pouch).

(C) If this method is used, the materials should be sent to the procurator/person living in Rome using an international delivery service such as FedEx, DHL or UPS. The materials should never be sent by regular international mail (USPS).

CHAPTER TEN

JUDICIAL AND EXTRAJUDICIAL PROCESSES

Victoria Vondenberger, RSM[1]

Resolution of Disputes about Rights

Boards of Reconciliation

In the church and within religious communities and societies of apostolic life, persons have rights which must be protected. It is helpful if a congregation has some kind of reconciliation or appeal process in which members' rights—including due process rights—are safeguarded. In such a process, conflicts of interest (even when rights are not involved) could be resolved, and conflicts of rights could be conciliated, mediated and/or arbitrated. Such a process is designed to facilitate better relationships among members of a community. A reconciliation or appeal process is a way to deal with situations when religious need assistance in their interactions with each other, perhaps when personality differences interfere with conflict resolution as well as the perceived violation of rights. It is assumed that healthy adult relationships are both the goal for religious communities and the basis for such reconciliation procedures.

Credibility of witness to the Gospel demands fidelity to justice among religious themselves (Mt. 18: 15-17). A reconciliation process exists to defend *human rights* based on the dignity of the human person, *ecclesial rights* from baptism as Christians, and *ecclesiastical rights* related to rights of office when other appeal processes are not in place for those. Any reconciliation process must recognize the limitations on the independent exercise of power by persons in authority. Far from undermining authority, this limitation does much to win respect for it and thus to enable persons to govern more effectively.

---

1 Victoria Vondenberger, RSM, was the original author and also revised this chapter. She is grateful to Paulissa Jirik, SSND, and David M. O'Connell, CM, for their contributions to the original version of this chapter.

There are many and varied models for the resolution of disputes about rights.[2] A generic plan is presented here to help communities develop protocols to fit their specific resources and needs. Such procedures are not part of the Code of Canon Law but become part of the particular law of institutes and societies when properly established by them.

Any professed religious may refer a matter to the reconciliation process. The matter referred must be a perceived injustice (not merely a breach of charity), the violation of a right generally accepted as granted by membership, or an instance where human dignity has been violated.

Both parties to the dispute must agree to participate in the process. Good will on the part of all those involved is essential if the process is to be efficacious.

A violation of confidentiality in the process is a serious failure of trust and immediately terminates the process. Discretionary consultation among the members of the board of reconciliation is not a violation of confidentiality.

In the preliminary step, a religious contacts a member of the board of reconciliation for informal, preliminary counsel about the process. The board member helps the religious determine whether the matter is proper for the process and explains the options the person has.

Step One: Conciliation

Conciliation is a process of compromise between disputing parties to settle a controversy. The board of reconciliation member is an objective listener to each party. The goal is to assist both parties in understanding the issue, to clarify perceptions and feelings, and to bring about resolution or reconciliation.

The initiator contacts a member of the board by phone, mail or email and requests that person serve as the conciliator. The initiator provides a written and signed statement describing the nature of the difficulty.

The conciliator sends a copy of the initiator's statement to the other party

---

2 In 1991, the CLSA published a short booklet titled *Protection of Rights of Persons in the Church: Revised Report of the Canon Law Society of America on the Subject of Due Process* (Washington, DC: Canon Law Society of America, 1991). It contained suggested processes for conciliation and arbitration. Because the suggested procedures were directed toward the resolution of diocesan and parochial disputes, the text specifically says that "disputes involving religious in their strictly internal affairs . . . are not subject to settlement under [the suggested conciliation or arbitration procedures]" (pages 13 and 18). Still, the publication can be helpful for institutes and societies that are seeking to develop a model for use within their own communities.

involved requesting the other party's written and signed statement (usually within two weeks). The process is considered terminated unless the conciliator has written and signed statements from both parties.

The conciliator meets with each party separately to provide an opportunity to express feelings and clarify concerns and expectations concerning the outcomes of the conciliation procedures. Such a meeting is held in a place of privacy and usually limited to no more than one hour.

Within two weeks the conciliator prepares a written summary of his/her observations for both parties and encourages them toward reconciliation or reminds them about further options in the appeal process.

Records of the conciliation process are signed and sealed by the conciliator and kept in a confidential file in the province (regional, area) offices of the community, open to further steps of the process (mediation or arbitration) *only* with the written consent of *both* parties and destroyed after a period of three years. No one else has access.

Step Two: Mediation

In mediation, the board of reconciliation member is a facilitator for a meeting of the parties pursuing reconciliation. The goal is to bring the parties together with a third person to facilitate settlement of the issue in a simple, informal manner.

Either party may pursue mediation usually within two weeks of the end of conciliation procedures. This is an option only when level one (conciliation) is completed and found to be inadequate. The second level initiator selects a member of the board of reconciliation as a mediator. Both parties must agree to mediation and to the mediator. This could be the same person who handled the conciliation for these parties. If the parties cannot agree on a mediator, the process cannot go forward and so it is terminated.

The mediator arranges a meeting with both parties in a private setting with a usual time limit of one hour. Each has the other's written statement of the issues. The mediator first checks for any needed clarification about the content of the statements. The mediator might request access to the conciliation file.

The mediator facilitates both parties speaking in the first person and taking responsibility for their own actions, feelings, etc. as well as helping each party understand the actions and feelings of the other. Gently but firmly, the mediator tries to move both parties toward decision or action explaining the options of giving/receiving forgiveness, requiring a second session with the mediator rather than unduly prolonging the first, seeking professional assistance for the issue/interaction, or pursuing arbitration (reviewing those procedures). The mediator assists both parties to communicate with each other.

The mediator prepares a summary report giving copies to both parties and placing a copy in the confidential file with the same restrictions about access *only* with the written consent of *both* parties and only for possible arbitration, as well as destruction after three years.

Step Three: Arbitration

Arbitration is a last resort designed to resolve a controversy through voluntary agreement of those concerned to abide by the decision made by a panel of three impartial parties. Three members of the board of reconciliation function as objective evaluators whose majority decision will settle the dispute. The goal is to bring the dispute to settlement.

This is an option only if steps one (conciliation) and two (mediation) have been completed with the issue still unresolved. One must be sure the matter is appropriate for arbitration and both parties must consent or the process is terminated. This is a formal process and it is important that all steps be followed carefully.

A panel of three persons from the board of reconciliation serve as evaluators. Each party selects one arbitrator from the board of reconciliation and those two choose a third board member who serves as chairperson. It is highly recommended that the third panel member be acceptable to both parties.

Both parties agree to accept the judgment of the panel before the arbitration process begins or the process is terminated. The panel chairperson arranges a meeting of the three arbitrators and the parties. Each party has one half hour to present each position. Panel members ask questions for clarification. The panel may choose to have one or more meetings with the parties. Within two weeks of the final meeting the chairperson delivers the decision. A written summary prepared by the chairperson is given to both parties and placed in the confidential file, dated, and sealed, to be destroyed after three years.

Further appeal is possible to a central or general board of appeal for larger institutes and always to the institute's major superior. If an institute has, for example, seven units such as provinces, each unit will have a reconciliation board and each unit will select a certain number of members for a central or general board of reconciliation, especially for issues in which those concerned are from different units or provinces. Such a board will be approached if both parties seek further review, if there is not a unit board in place for some reason, if the process was terminated for a reason other than that the initiator's willingness to cooperate, if unit directives refer the issue to the central board, or if the religious involved in the dispute are not members of the same unit.

The general administration of the institute designates one member of the central board as the facilitator for the board. This person selects three persons acceptable to both parties. A hearing is held within thirty days of selection and acceptance of the panel. Prior to the hearing the central panel, arbitrators review all materials from the unit (province, region, area) process released by signatures of both parties. Within ten days of the hearing, both parties are notified of the panel's decision. All maintain professional confidentiality. By mutual written agreement of the parties involved, opinions reached as a result of the central appeal process may be communicated to appropriate persons or made public. Records are kept in the central administrative offices and destroyed after three years.

Board members number at least ten with three alternates available to replace a member or complete an unfinished term. These religious are nominated by all the religious they could serve and elected from a slate of those willing to accept the role. The term of service is whatever time period parallels the chapter or elected leaders' term. No members of the province (regional, area, institute) administration may be members of the board. At least once in every term of leadership there should be an evaluation of the processes and pertinent recommendations.

Matter appropriate for appeal through the reconciliation board would include perceived injustice involving two members of a unit (province, region, area), a member and a group of members such as a local community (represented by a designated spokesperson unless the issue is within the group when all would participate in the process) or a decision of unit (province, regional, area) administration. There is no appeal for a disagreement of a member with a decision of community authority where there is not a perceived injustice except through the usual appeal to a major superior. Inappropriate matters are those which involve institutions (sponsored or not), parishes, schools, staffs, dioceses who may employ religious (the member should use the channels of due process of the place of employment), decisions about admission of members to stages of incorporation or decisions about religious in perpetual profession for which canon law or particular law makes provision such as imposed exclaustration or dismissal.

Rights of the Parties Involved

In recognizing the right to due process, the church says explicitly that people have the right to be informed of proposed actions which affect their rights, the right to be heard in defense of their rights, the right in the face of accusation to confront their accusers, and the right not to be judged by their accusers.[3]

A religious brought to a process of conciliation, mediation or arbitration as well as a canonical trial certainly has at least the rights which church law affords a respondent in a marriage case. These include the following:

- The right to appoint an advocate and procurator (cc. 1477, 1481);
- The right to be summoned (cc. 1507 § 1, 1686);
- The right to know the allegation(s) (c. 1508);
- The right to name witnesses (c. 1551);
- The right to know the other witnesses usually before they are heard (c. 1554);
- The right to inspect the acts of the case, all documents and testimony, with careful safeguarding of the right to defense even in matters which concern the public good where some part of the evidence may be shown to no one (c. 1598 §1);
- The right to propose new evidence and proofs after reviewing the acts (c. 1598 §2);
- The right to reply to any further statements or pleas of the other party (c. 1602);
- The right to know the contents of the decision (c. 1614);
- The right to appeal (cc. 1628, 1689) or propose a plea of nullity (c. 1626).

If a penalty is imposed as a result of a process of reconciliation, more rights need to be safeguarded. A main underpinning of penal law is canon 18, which insists on the very strict following of procedures with regard to penalties and penal trials. Penalties must be a last resort for handling problems (cc. 1317, 1341) and should be designed to restore justice, repair scandal, or reform the accused. No one is to be punished through church procedures except strictly according to law (c. 221 §3).

The code presents three distinct levels or stages which should be pursued before any penalties are imposed:

1. The preliminary investigation (cc. 1717-1719) focuses on the imputability of the one accused of misconduct to determine if an offense truly occurred and if the accused can be held responsible for that

---

3 See generally *Protection of Rights of Persons in the Church.*

offense. Care must be taken to protect the good names of those involved. There must be the highest degree of confidentiality.[4]

2. In the penal process (cc. 1720-1728), the accused must be fully informed and have the opportunity to respond to the allegations.[5] There can be a canonical trial only for offenses listed in canons 1364-1398 or in the particular law (cc. 1315-1320). The accused must have a capable advocate and must be given the right to write or speak last in the process. The accused is never bound to confess and cannot be administered an oath (c. 1728 §2).
3. The victim has the right to seek repair of damages (cc. 1729-1731) sustained due to an offense.

Canon law has a history of concern for the guaranteeing of rights and has affirmed the availability of a judicial remedy for the protection of rights (cc. 1732-1739). This process is called hierarchical recourse.

A religious also would have the right to defend legitimate canonical rights through a church court (c. 221). Such rights as presented elsewhere in this book would include the following:

- The rights of all Christians (cc. 208-223);
- The rights and obligations of laity (cc. 224-231) or of clergy (cc. 273-289);
- The specific rights of religious (cc. 662-672);
- Various other rights gleaned from canons 598, 607, 618, 620, 627, 631, 635, 643, 653, 654, 656, 657, 659, 660, 661, 675, 676, 678, 680, 681, 682, 683, 684-704, 737, 738, and 739.

Penal Procedures

Dismissal of a Member

The rights and obligations of a member of a religious institute or a society of apostolic life cease when membership is terminated either voluntarily through legitimate departure or transfer, or involuntarily through a process of dismissal initiated by legitimate authorities with ultimate confirmation by the Holy See (or the diocesan bishop where he is the proper authority).

---

4 The CLSA produced a four-part Penal Law Webinar Series in 2020 addressing the penal process. Part 2 addresses the preliminary investigation. This series is available to CLSA members through the CLSA's website at clsa.org.

5 See, e.g., CLSA Penal Law Webinar Series Part 3.

Dismissal is a serious action taken by competent ecclesiastical authority through which permanent departure is imposed on a member with resulting dispensation from vows and from all rights and obligations arising from profession or incorporation. This juridic procedure is initiated by legitimate authority only for the most grave causes which must be external, imputable and juridically proven. What applies to institutes of consecrated life also applies to societies of apostolic life unless otherwise noted in the appropriate universal or particular law (c. 746).

Dismissal is a penal procedure, and so it is subject to strict legal interpretation regarding exact procedures according to canon 18 as has been repeatedly demonstrated by the Congregation for Institutes of Consecrated Life and for Societies of Apostolic Life.

The rights and obligations of a member of an institute or society cease when membership is terminated by:

- legitimate (involuntary) dismissal (c. 701);
- departure, which is a voluntary choice of the individual with approval from competent ecclesiastical authority (cc. 686-693), or
- proper canonical transfer (cc. 684-685).

For dismissal, a careful process must be observed (cc. 697-699) and confirmed by the Holy See (c. 700), except for an institute of diocesan right, where the confirmation belongs to the bishop of the diocese. The member has the right of self-defense throughout the process (c. 695 §2).

There are three types of dismissal described in the Code of Canon Law: automatic (c. 694), compulsory (c. 695), and facultative (c. 696). Automatic (*ipso facto*) dismissal occurs when a member either has notoriously abandoned the Catholic faith, has contracted or attempted marriage, even only civilly, or has been illegitimately absent for twelve consecutive months (c. 694 §1). The major superior with the council is to collect proofs and issue a declaration of the fact so that the dismissal is established juridically.

Notorious rejection of the Catholic faith must be an irrefutable, public act as in the case of heresy, apostasy, or schism (c. 751) and not merely a matter of personal or private disagreement with the church and its teachings. In addition to automatic dismissal, such rejection warrants automatic excommunication (c. 1364). Attempted marriage by a member, whether a cleric (c. 1087) or not, is also cause for automatic dismissal and for other appropriate canonical penalties (c. 1394 §1, 2°). Illegitimate absence of a member for twelve consecutive months is still a relatively new reason for dismissal. [6] The major superior and council should seek advice from a competent canonical advisor to make sure that the proper canonical warnings were issued and that other criteria are met before declaring the factors for imposition of automatic dismissal to have been met. Otherwise, the Holy See (for institutes of pontifical right) or the diocesan bishop (for institutes of diocesan right) may refuse to confirm the declared dismissal, thereby keeping it from being juridically constituted (c. 694 §3).

Compulsory dismissal (c. 695) results from kidnaping, homicide, mutilation, and serious wounding of a person (c. 1397), from procurement of an abortion (c. 1398), and from external violations of the sixth commandment (c. 1395), unless the major superior determines otherwise with regard to delicts mentioned in canon 1395 §2. In the case of external sexual misconduct, obviously incompatible with religious life and its obligations, the major superior must carefully balance the harm done to the victim, the rights of the accused, and the good of the church seeking Gospel justice. There may also be civil and other canonical consequences of these actions.

Facultative dismissal (c. 696) includes grave, external, imputable and juridically proven offenses such as habitual neglect of serious obligations associated with religious life, repeated violations of sacred vows or bonds, grave disobedience of lawful prescriptions of superiors in serious matters, grave scandal from culpable behavior, holding or spreading doctrines condemned by the magisterium of the church as well as adherence to ideologies infected by materialism or atheism, unlawful absence (c. 665) from the institute or society lasting six months and other similar serious causes.

The habitual neglect of serious religious obligations includes neglect of the observance of the Gospel, of the law of the church, or of the institute or society (cc. 662-672, 573). There must be genuine evidence of these offenses and not mere accusation or presumption. If there is a question of disobedience, it must be demonstrable, stubborn rejection of serious matters prescribed by a lawful superior. If there is a question of other culpable behavior, it must be the occasion of scandal, leading another to evil or sin (*Catechism of the Catholic Church*, 1994).

---

6 For more on dismissal for illegitimate absence, see Francis, motu proprio *Communis vita*, March 19, 2019: *L'Osservatore Romano* (March 27, 2019); see also Michael Joyce, CM, "Missing in Action: Absent Member in Institutes of Consecrated Life and Societies of Apostolic Life," CLSA *Proceedings* 2020 (Washington, DC: CLSA, 2021) 200-212.

As causes for dismissal, adherence to teachings condemned by the magisterium or to materialistic, atheistic ideologies must be pertinacious and unyielding on the part of the offending member. Regardless of the canonical category in which a cause for dismissal is classified, the process of dismissal itself requires the most careful discretion and observance on the part of ecclesiastical authorities concerned (c. 696 §2).

Dismissal may be initiated by the legitimate major superior (c. 697) after having heard the council. Consent of the council is not required but consultation is necessary (c. 127) and the superior should not act contrary to a consensus of the council unless there be an overriding reason. The major superior must: collect proofs and inform the member; warn the member explicitly either in writing or in the presence of two witnesses regarding the consequences of the action and of the dismissal process; give the member the opportunity for an appropriate self-defense and for reform and, if needed, provide a second warning in the same manner as the first. Fifteen working days must elapse between the initial warning and the second (c. 201). Another fifteen working days must pass before the major superior must transmit all acts of the dismissal process signed by a notary, along with the signed response of the member, to the supreme moderator (c. 697). Throughout the process, the major superior must inform the member of the right to communicate with and offer a defense directly to the supreme moderator (c. 698). If the member is a cleric, the notary in this process must be a priest (c. 483 §2).

Once the acts of the case are transmitted to the supreme moderator, she or he must proceed collegially with at least four councilors for validity, weighing the proofs and defenses presented. A secret ballot yielding an absolute majority decision precedes the drafting of a decree of dismissal by the supreme moderator which must express the motives for dismissal in law and fact for validity (c. 699). In the case of autonomous monasteries (c. 614), the diocesan bishop fulfills the role of major superior.

The decree of dismissal for members of pontifical institutes or societies does not take effect until it is confirmed by the Holy See, having received all the acts of the case. If the institute concerned is of diocesan right, the diocesan bishop of the house to which the member is assigned issues this confirmation. For validity, this decree must indicate the member's right of recourse to the Congregation for Institutes of Consecrated Life and Societies of Apostolic Life. This recourse has a suspensive effect upon the decree and must be exercised within ten working days of the notification (c. 700).

Once ultimately confirmed by the congregation of the Holy See or the diocesan bishop, the decree of dismissal communicated to the member terminates the member's vows, rights, and obligations as a member of the institute or society (c. 701). She or he can request nothing from the institute or society for past service although the code encourages the institute to observe charity and equity toward the dismissed member (c. 702). If the member is a priest, the exercise of sacred orders is prohibited until he is received for priestly service by a diocesan bishop.

The identification of dismissed members is to be included in reports sent by the supreme moderator to the Holy See (c. 704).

Specific Rights of the Accused in a Penal Process

All the rights and obligations which a member of a religious institute or society of apostolic life ordinarily possesses remain intact during a penal process unless otherwise specified in the universal or particular law. The same is true for a member involved in the process of mediation, conciliation or arbitration mentioned above. The following rights should be specifically protected by all concerned with the penal process:

- The right to a good reputation and to privacy (c. 220);
- The right to vindicate and defend ecclesial rights in an appropriate ecclesiastical forum in accord with the norm of law applied with equity and the right to not be punished except in accord with the norm of law (c. 221);
- The right to know the offense, the accusation, and the proofs (cc. 694, 695);
- The right to formal notifications and warnings (cc. 695, 697);
- The right to know the offense and the effects of the action contemplated (c. 697);
- The right to self-defense and to reform (cc. 695, 697, 698);
- The right to confidentiality (cc. 1361 §3, and 1455);
- The right to contact the supreme moderator directly throughout the process (c. 698);
- The right to recourse with suspensive effect on the action contemplated (c. 700);
- The right to strict interpretation of penalties and careful observance of all dimensions of the penal process and any restriction of rights (c. 18).

The penal law of the church affecting a member of a religious institute or a society of apostolic life goes to great lengths to protect the rights of the accused in a penal process while balancing those rights with the rights and obligations of others in the church. Major superiors are encouraged to consult with a canonist prior to and throughout any penal process to ensure these rights and this balance are maintained for the protection of all concerned and for the good of the church.

CHAPTER ELEVEN

THE SACRAMENT OF ORDER

Michael P. Joyce, CM[1]

Initial Formation for the Sacrament of Order

Admission into Candidacy

This rite is mandated for those seeking the diaconate, either transitionally or permanently. Canon 1034 §2 exempts permanently vowed members of clerical institutes of consecrated life and definitively vowed members of societies of apostolic life seeking the ordained priesthood.

Candidates

While the code does not require perpetually vowed members of clerical institutes of consecrated life or societies of apostolic life to celebrate the rite of candidacy before ordination, a close reading of the code makes clear that the rite is obligatory for members of some institutes or societies:[2]

- members of lay institutes of consecrated life (even if bound by vows or promises, etc.). This situation occurs in the case of a brother in such an institute seeking permanent diaconate or priesthood;
- members of clerical societies of apostolic life who do not pronounce vows but make some other form of commitment (oath, promises, etc.);
- members of institutes or societies who have not yet pronounced vows when the institute or society requires them.

Some institutes and societies find it helpful to have candidates participate in the rite. The participation can help the candidate to have a distinct

---

1 Rev. Michael P. Joyce, CM, was the original author and also revised this chapter. He is grateful to Rev. Vincent B. Grogan, OFM, for his contributions to the original version of this chapter.

2 Canon 1034 §2. Note the phrase "A man who has not been admitted through vows to a clerical institute. . ." The term *vows* is not modified by the adjective *religious*. See canon 731 §1, which describes societies of apostolic life.

understanding of the difference between membership in the institute or society and the clerical state. In these situations, it would aid to have a temporal distinction between definitive incorporation into the institute or society and admission into candidacy.

Requirements for Admission into Candidacy

The requirements are:

- a minimum age of twenty and the beginning of theological studies for those aspiring to the transitional diaconate;
- specific qualities expected in the candidate: signs of possessing an authentic vocation, presence of suitable moral characteristics, absence of serious mental and physical deficiencies (i.e. disorders or disabilities that would prove a hindrance to the exercise of the sacrament of order), irregularities, and a desire to dedicate themselves to the service of the church;
- a formal written petition to the major superior in which the person indicates explicitly that he is seeking candidacy freely;[3]
- a formal written acceptance of the petition by the major superior with the prior recommendation of the formation team and the local superior.

Celebration of Admission into Candidacy

The proper minister of the rite in clerical institutes or societies is the major superior (or his delegate). In lay institutes or societies, the bishop of the domicile of the member admits to candidacy at the formal written request of the major superior.

Records

A record of the rite of admission (including the name of the celebrant, the place, and the date) is kept in the person's file. A copy is placed in the archives of the religious house where it was celebrated (or in the diocesan archives when the bishop has presided over the rite). A certificate attesting to admission to candidacy is also presented to the individual admitted.

Canonical Effects

There are no canonical effects that follow from this rite. Therefore, no canonical act is necessary if the person subsequently decides to leave the institute or society.

---

3 See the appendix for a sample petition.

Institution into Ministries

Candidates

The code (c. 1035 §1) prescribes that before ordination to the diaconate, the individual must receive the ministries of lector and acolyte. Either or both of these ministries may be conferred on members of lay institutes of consecrated life of men and on lay members in a clerical institute of consecrated life or a clerical society of apostolic life; that is, these ministries are not restricted to candidates for the sacrament of order (see c. 230 §1).

Requirements for Installation into Ministries

The requirements for candidates to be installed into either ministry of lector or acolyte are:

- minimum age of eighteen;
- suitable preparation and training in the various aspects of the respective ministry;
- a formal letter to one's major superior requesting installation to the specific ministry;
- the member must indicate that he is seeking it freely and of his own will;[4]
- a recommendation from the person(s) responsible for the candidate's formation mentioning that the required training for the ministry has been given if the individual is in formation for either definitive incorporation or ordination;[5]
- formal written approval of the request by the major superior;
- observance of intervals between the installation into each ministry.

Celebration of Institution

The major superior in clerical institutes of consecrated life and societies of apostolic life is authorized to institute his subjects in the ministries. He may also designate another priest to do so.[6] In lay institutes of consecrated life and societies of apostolic life the local ordinary of the individual's residence

---

4 See the appendix for a sample petition.

5 If the individual is not in a formation program (e.g. a perpetually professed brother in an institute of consecrated life or a society of apostolic life), the approval of one's local superior is appropriate. The superior needs to make the recommendation and state that the required training has been given.

6 See circular letter to US bishops by the then general secretary of the then NCCB, April 7, 1976. The clarification had been communicated to the apostolic delegate to the United States by the Congregation for the Sacraments and Divine Worship.

institutes the member into the ministries. The major superior needs to request the local ordinary formally to institute the member in the ministry.

Records

A record of the institution including the name of the one who instituted the person in the ministry and the date and place where the celebration took place is retained in the personal file of the member and in the archives of the house where the institution took place. A record should also be placed in the diocesan archives if the bishop performed the institution. A formal certificate attesting to the institution is also given to the individual.

Canonical Effects

No canonical effects result from institution in the ministries. Therefore, if a member subsequently departs from the institute or society, no canonical act is required. Profession of perpetual vows or promises is not required in order to be instituted in the ministries (as it is for candidacy or ordination). Temporary vows or promises suffice. Novices, postulants, or aspirants may be instituted in the ministries. However, the institute or society may choose to restrict institution in ministries to those related to the institute or society by at least a temporary bond so that the focus of formation in the earlier stages of entrance into consecrated life is not confused with the preparation for ordination. This action may be done in the institute's or society's policies or proper law.

The ministries may be received in either sequence. Institution into the ministry of lector, however, may be more appropriate before the ministry of acolyte, taking into consideration the liturgical focus on word and sacrament. Canon 1035 §2 implies that the ministry of acolyte occurs after the ministry of lector and requires it prior to ordination to the diaconate.

Transitional Diaconate

The code mandates a host of prescriptions, some on the part of the candidate, some on the part of the seminary personnel, some on the part of the major superior that must be fulfilled before ordination to the transitional diaconate.

- Qualifications affecting the candidate
    - profession of perpetual vows (or permanent commitment) in the institute or society;
    - minimum age of twenty-three;
    - completion of third year of theological studies;

- reception of baptism and confirmation;[7]
- institution in the ministries of lector and acolyte;[8]
- admission to candidacy (if applicable; see above, under *Admission to Candidacy*);
- an interval of at least six months from institution in the ministry of acolyte;
- a formal, handwritten letter by the candidate to his major superior in which he requests ordination, indicating both that he is seeking it freely and that he intends to dedicate himself permanently to ecclesiastical ministry as a celibate;
- a profession of faith and oath of fidelity[9] by the candidate in the presence of the major superior or his delegate;
- proper training in the diaconal ministry and knowledge of the obligations inherent in it;
- a retreat of at least five days duration.

- From the rector of the seminary (or director of formation)
  - submission of a report on the suitability of the candidate to the major superior.[10]
- From the major superior
  - formal acceptance of the candidate' s request, communicated to him in writing;
  - some institutes or societies may require in their proper law that he consult with his council or obtain their consent before he accepts the candidate's request for ordination;

---

7 A record of the reception of the sacraments is in the candidate's personal file since proof of reception is necessary for admission to religious life.

8 A record of institution in the ministries is kept in the candidate's file.

9 See Rescript from a papal audience published by the Congregation for the Doctrine of the Faith: "Formula to be used for the profession of faith and for the oath of fidelity to assume an office to be exercised in the name of the Church," July 1, 1988: *AAS* 81 (1989) 1169; https://www.vatican.va/roman_curia/congregations/cfaith/documents/rc_con_cfaith_doc_19880701_professio-fidei_en.html.

10 The report refers to "the sound doctrine of the candidate, his genuine piety, good morals, and aptitude to exercise the ministry, as well as, after a properly executed inquiry, about his state of physical and psychological health" (c. 1051, 1°). Frequently, a vote on the candidate taken by the formation personnel accompanies the report. The major superior can also use other means to ascertain the person's suitability, such as testimonial letters, the publication of ordination banns, etc.

- issuance of dimissorial letters (testifying to the fulfillment of all the requirements) to the ordaining bishop.[11]

- Records

  After the candidate is ordained to the diaconate, the ordaining prelate signs a formal document indicating both the date and place of the ordination. A copy of this document is presented to the individual and a copy is placed in his personal file. A copy likewise is retained in the archives of the diocese where the ordination was celebrated. Notification of diaconal ordination must be sent to the individual's place of baptism or place of reception into full communion.

- Canonical effects

  With ordination to the diaconate comes formal entrance into the clerical state and incardination into the religious institute or society.[12] The deacon may not validly marry.[13] Likewise, he now has the obligation of daily praying the Liturgy of the Hours.

- Irregularities

  Canonical legislation stipulates certain irregularities to ordination. The major superior must ensure and so state in his dimissorial letters that the candidate has not contracted any of these. Here is a listing of the current irregularities (see c. 1041):

  - one who suffers from insanity or from any other psychological disorder, which disorder is judged to render him incapable of

---

11 The letters may be sent to any bishop of the rite to which the member belongs. The author of these dimissorial letters depends on the type of institute or society. The major superior is competent to issue dimissorial letters in clerical institutes of consecrated life of pontifical rite and in clerical societies of apostolic life of pontifical rite. In lay institutes whether pontifical or diocesan and in clerical institutes or societies of diocesan rite, the letters are not issued by the major superior of the institute or society but rather by the bishop of the diocese of domicile of the candidate at the request of the major superior. The diocesan bishop is technically the proper ordaining prelate as well. He issues dimissorial letters to the ordaining prelate only if he will not be the one conferring the sacrament. See cc. 1019, 1016 and 1018. See the appendix for a sample dimissorial letter.

12 The revised rite for the ordination of bishops, presbyters, and deacons requires members of institutes of consecrated life who are to be ordained to the rank of deacon and presbyter to promise obedience to the diocesan bishop as well. See *Rites of Ordination of a Bishop, of Priests, and of Deacons* (United States Conference of Catholic Bishops, Washington, DC) 157.

13 This impediment to marriage for members in perpetual vows already exists. However, the revised rite for the ordination of bishops, presbyters, and deacons requires those who have professed perpetual vows in a religious institute to make the profession of celibacy during the ordination rite. See ibid., 156.

properly exercising the ministry after consulting with experts;[14]

- one who in the past was guilty of formal heresy, schism, or apostasy;
- one who has attempted marriage even civilly either while he himself was prohibited from doing so by an existing marriage bond, by ordination, or by the public and perpetual vow of chastity, or who attempted marriage with a woman validly married or bound by the same vow;
- one who has committed deliberate homicide, or who has actually procured an abortion, or who has positively cooperated in either of these;
- one who has gravely and maliciously mutilated himself or another person, or who has attempted suicide;
- one who has exercised an act of the sacrament of order reserved to those in the episcopal or presbyteral rank while lacking that rank himself or while prohibited from the exercise of the sacrament of order by some canonical penalty either formally declared or imposed.

- Impediments

While the impediments to ordination listed below (see c. 1042) may hardly seem to apply to someone living the consecrated life, it is possible that they may exist. The impediments are:

- a married man, unless he is seeking the permanent diaconate;
- one who exercises an office or administration prohibited to clerics in accordance with canons 285 and 286 for which he must render an account;
- a *neophyte*,[15] unless in the judgment of the major superior, the man has been sufficiently tested (i.e., lived a suitable amount of time as a Catholic).

- Dispensation from irregularities and impediments

If the fact on which an irregularity is based has been brought to the judicial forum, ecclesiastical or civil, the dispensation from the irregularity is reserved to the Holy See. Likewise reserved to the Holy See, if public, are the following irregularities:

---

14 Consultation with experts by the person(s) making the determination is very important. It implies that before the major superior makes such a determination, he should use competent, professional advice.

15 The term *neophyte* in this context applies both to those baptized as an adult as well as to those who entered into full communion with the Church as an adult.

- apostasy, heresy, or schism;
- attempted marriage even civilly when already bound by an existing marriage bond, ordination, or by a public and perpetual vow of chastity; or who has attempted marriage to a woman bound by a marriage bond or by the public and perpetual vow of chastity;
- deliberate commission of homicide or procurement of an abortion or cooperation in either such crime, whether public or occult (see c. 1047 §2, 2 °).

All other irregularities or impediments can be dispensed by the major superior in clerical institutes or societies. The local ordinary can dispense for other institutes or societies.

- Irregularities and impediments after ordination

  The existence of irregularities or impediments render the exercise of the sacrament of order illicit but not invalid. In most aspects the existence of irregularities or impediments mirrors the irregularities for ordination as presented above. Here are the irregularities to the exercise of an order already received:

  - one who while affected by an irregularity for ordination illicitly was ordained;
  - one who is guilty of public apostasy, heresy, or schism;
  - one who attempted marriage either while himself prohibited from marriage by an existing marital bond, ordination, or a public and perpetual vow of chastity; or who attempted marriage with a woman already validly married or bound by the same vow;
  - one who has committed deliberate homicide or procured an abortion or who has positively cooperated in the same;
  - one who has gravely and maliciously mutilated himself or another, or who has attempted suicide;
  - one who has exercised an act of the sacrament of order reserved to those in the ranks of the episcopate or presbyterate while himself either lacking that rank or while barred from its exercise by a canonical penalty, declared or imposed.

  The two categories of men who have impediments to the exercise of orders already received are:

  - one who while hindered by an impediment to ordination was illicitly ordained; and

- a person who has become insane or suffers from some other serious psychological disorder which renders him incapable of fulfilling the order received.[16]

- Dispensation from the above irregularities or impediments to the exercise of an order already received

  If the fact on which an irregularity is based has been brought to an ecclesiastical or civil judicial forum, the dispensation from that irregularity is reserved to the Holy See. Also reserved to the Holy See are:

  - one who has attempted marriage in public cases as described above;[17]
  - one guilty of deliberate homicide or procurement of abortion, or who has positively cooperated in the same, whether public or occult (see c. 1047 §2, 2°).

All other irregularities or impediments to the exercise of an order already received may be dispensed by the major superior in clerical institutes or societies. The local ordinary can dispense in other institutes or societies.

Permanent Diaconate

This order is open to lay members of clerical institutes of consecrated life as well as to lay members of clerical societies of apostolic life and to members of lay institutes and societies. A prerequisite for ordination to the permanent diaconate is the making of a permanent commitment in the institute or society by vows, promises, or other bond.[18]

The fundamental requirements for the transitional diaconate hold as well for the permanent diaconate with the following differences:

- minimum age of twenty-five;

---

16 This impediment involves consultation with experts. The impediment to exercising an order received continues until the major superior—after consulting experts—allows the order to be exercised.

17 The irregularity is public whether it is actually known or there is a strong possibility it will become known.

18 The re-establishment of the permanent diaconate in an institute or society is reserved to the Apostolic See. The institute must develop a program of formation and submit it to the Congregation for Institutes of Consecrated Life and Societies of Apostolic Life. Congregation for Catholic Education, Congregation for the Clergy, *Basic Norms for the Formation of Permanent Deacons, Directory for the Ministry and Life of Permanent Deacons* (Washington, D.C.: United States Conference of Catholic Bishops, 2002) 31-32.

- completion of a three-year preparation program (c. 236);[19]
- dimissorial letters.[20]

All the other requirements (e.g., formal letter requesting ordination, the profession of faith, the report of formation personnel, certification of the completion of the training program, the five-day retreat, the recording of ordination and the notification of the place of baptism) for the transitional diaconate hold also for ordination to the permanent diaconate.

Denying Ordination to the Presbyterate

Canon 1026 forbids coercing a person to be ordained and canon 1038 focuses on the freedom of a transitional deacon to refuse presbyteral ordination and permission to exercise the diaconal ministry with all things being equal. Canon 1030 addresses the issue of a major superior prohibiting presbyteral ordination to a transitional deacon. The superior's prohibition must be founded on a canonical cause or reason and not on his mere whim. Such a cause is found among the irregularities and impediments to receiving orders listed above or in a deficiency of the broad requisites enumerated in canon 1051, 1° noted above or as delineated in canon 1029: an "integral faith . . .right intention, . . . requisite knowledge, . . . a good reputation, . . . integral morals, and proven virtue, . . . and the other physical and psychological qualities in keeping with the order to be received." While it is true that ordination to the transitional diaconate does not confer an automatic right to subsequent presbyteral ordination, it implies that ordination to the presbyterate will follow in due course.

The most commonly occurring basis for denying presbyteral ordination is found in canon 1041, 1° which lists among the irregularities to receiving the sacrament of order: some form of insanity or another psychic defect which renders one unsuitable for properly fulfilling the ministry. Experts must be consulted according to this canon. Ultimately, it is the major superior who makes the decision. Even an occult reason (i.e., one incapable of proof in the external forum) suffices to prohibit ordination. The sacrament of order exists primarily for the good of the Church and not simply for the benefit of the person who is ordained. Therefore, when there is a serious doubt about the suitability of the individual, the benefit of the doubt must be given to the Church community and not the individual. Justice requires the major superior to share the reason for denying ordination with the individual.

---

19 Also see canon 659 §3 on the formation of members preparing to receive holy orders.

20 See footnote 11 above.

A deacon who is refused presbyteral ordination by his major superior retains the right of appeal to the superior general of the institute or society. He has recourse to the Congregation for Institutes of Consecrated Life and Societies of Apostolic Life if the general upholds the denial of ordination. If the denial of priestly ordination is based on evidence of a psychic disorder, it is possible that the disorder can be treated by psychological therapy or controlled by medication. When psychological therapy seems hopeful, the major superior can delay ordination until the therapy is completed. He can do the same if the deacon's behavior has improved or changed due to medication. Then, after consultation with the therapist or expert, the major superior renders a decision on presbyteral ordination. If uncertainties or doubts remain unresolved, the benefit of the doubt goes to the Church, not to the deacon.

The Presbyterate

Basically, the same prerequisites for diaconate ordination hold as well for presbyteral ordination with the following differences:

- minimum age of twenty-five;[21]
- prior reception of the diaconate;
- completion of four years of theological studies and the exercise of diaconal ministry in a pastoral setting for a suitable time period;
- an interval of at least six months from the reception of diaconate;
- the absence of any irregularity or impediment.[22]

All other stipulations for diaconate ordination (i.e., written request of candidate, formal written acceptance by the major superior, testimony on the person's suitability, the issuance of dimissorial letters, a five-day retreat, recording of the ordination and notifying the place of baptism or reception into full communion) are also required for presbyteral ordination.[23]

Faculties

The term *faculties* refers to authorization by a competent superior to allow priests and deacons to perform certain acts of the sacrament of order. The acts for a deacon that require faculties are preaching and officially witnessing the celebration of marriage. In addition to these acts, presbyters also need faculties

---

21 The major superior in clerical institutes or societies may dispense for up to a year's lack of age for both the diaconate and the presbyterate (canon 1031 §4).

22 A profession of faith and oath of fidelity are not required.

23 See footnote 12 above regarding a promise of obedience to the diocesan bishop.

to grant sacramental absolution. The law itself (c. 764) gives presbyters and deacons the faculty to preach everywhere with some possible exceptions.

Clerical religious institutes or societies of pontifical rite

Major superiors in these institutes can usually grant faculties for sacramental absolution to other members of the institute or society. The constitutions and statutes of the institute or society will govern this power and need to be consulted. The faculties do not extend outside of the institute or society. Superiors in these institutes or societies receive their faculties from the universal law.[24]

Outside the institute or society

A religious presbyter receives faculties for granting sacramental absolution from the local ordinary of the diocese in which he has a domicile. Members of religious institutes and societies of apostolic life receive their domicile from the house to which they are attached (c. 103). They do not necessarily need to be living in the house to have their domicile there.

Ordinarily the presbyter's major superior requests faculties from the local ordinary. The current practice in the United States is that the major superior gives a written statement to the local ordinary about the presbyter's good standing.

Faculties to witness marriage usually accompany assignment to a parish. If the presbyter is not assigned to a parish, he receives the faculty to witness the marriage from the pastor of the parish in which the marriage is to be celebrated. There may be ministries other than parochial, such as campus ministry, for which the local ordinary will grant a general faculty to witness marriages.

Departure of an Ordained Member from the Institute or Society[25]

Departure of a Deacon

Other chapters in this handbook treat dismissal and transfer of a member to another religious institute or society of apostolic life. This chapter presents two other means for a deacon to depart from the institute or society. The individual may wish to leave the consecrated life but continue as a diocesan cleric, i.e., to be incardinated into a diocese (c. 693). The procedure is the same for a religious deacon as it is for a religious priest and the canonical process will be treated

---

24 Canon 968 §2. They can also grant to any presbyter whatsoever the faculty to hear the confession of their subjects and of others living day and night in the house (c. 969, §2). This phrase "day and night" can be broadly interpreted to include those who visit the house for one day.

25 See Randolph R. Calvo and Nevin J. Klinger, eds., *Clergy Procedural Handbook*, (Washington, DC: CLSA, 1992) 67-89 and 238-275.

below. When a permanent or transitional deacon seeks incardination into a diocese, the issue of economic support must be addressed beforehand. He can sustain himself by secular employment or he might find full-time employment in an ecclesiastical setting.

Another possibility is that the deacon may wish to both leave religious life and be relieved of the obligations of the diaconate, including that of celibacy. The following are required for the canonical procedure:

- a formal letter of petition offering grave reasons (c. 290 3°);
- results of the evaluation by the seminary or formation faculty of the person prior to his ordination along with any written observations or comments entered in the evaluation process;
- the evaluation of the person's suitability in summary form for religious life and the diaconate given by his formation directors during his period of training for religious life and the diaconate;
- a curriculum vitae which includes his place and date of birth, place, and date of his permanent commitment to the institute, the place and date of his diaconal ordination, and his appointments since ordination;
- a *votum* of the major superior including his judgment of the reasons offered by the person, attempts he made to dissuade the man from seeking the dispensation, and his own opinion about the request;

The documents are transmitted to the general curia of the institute or society. The actual dispensation is granted by the Congregation for the Clergy.

When the dispensation has been received, a copy is sent to the individual along with a statement of notification to be signed by him. The dispensation takes effect when the individual is notified. He does not need to accept the dispensation for it to be effective. The signed document of notification is kept in the individual's personal file and a copy is sent to the general curia. The rescript itself (or a copy) is also retained there. Notification of the dispensation is also sent to his place of baptism or place of reception into full communion.

Departure of a Presbyter from the Institute or Society

Besides dismissal or transfer to another institute or society, three additional possibilities exist:

(1) *Incardination into a diocese as a secular cleric* (cc. 691-693).

When incardination is granted, it in effect dispenses the person from all the obligations of the vows (or promises) and renders him a cleric attached to a local

Church. (The obligation of celibacy remains in effect). The following are required for this procedure:

- a formal letter of petition by the individual to the Holy Father providing serious reasons for the request;
- a formal statement from a local ordinary expressing a willingness to accept the person either immediately or on an experimental basis;[26]
- the *votum* or recommendation of the major superior.

Either the major superior or the receiving diocesan bishop can present the petition. If the major superior presents the request, all the documents are transmitted to the general curia of the institute or society which in turn presents them to the Congregation for Institutes of Consecrated Life and Societies of Apostolic Life (CICLSAL). The actual indult is granted by CICLSAL.

When the indult is received, it is retained in the person's file. A copy is given to the individual along with a formal statement of notification. The priest forwards the signed notification to his major superior to place in his file. A copy is sent to the general curia and likewise, a copy of the indult is sent by the major superior to the bishop who is receiving the man into his diocese. Until the religious is officially incardinated in the diocese, he remains technically a religious or a member of the society. Therefore, he may return to the institute any time prior to the incardination and does not need any approval to return.

(2) *Departure from the institute or society with a dispensation from religious vows or promises and from all the obligations of the clerical state with the obligation of celibacy remaining.*[27]

Essentially the documentation of this process must clearly manifest that the petitioner will remain firm in his intention of maintaining celibacy as a lay person and will not change his mind at some future point in this regard. The latter requirement ordinarily prohibits any priest younger than forty years old ineligible for the dispensation except for cases of most serious sexual misconduct. The required documents for the procedure are:

---

26 If the permission is on an experimental basis, the religious is automatically incardinated after five years unless the bishop at some earlier point formally incardinates him. The priest is bound to return to his institute or society if the diocesan bishop discontinues the permission before the five-year period has expired or at its expiration. Similarly, if the person wishes to return to his institute or society at any point during the five-year probationary period, he may do so.

27 Admittedly, this request rarely comes from a religious cleric. CICLSAL issues such indults and sometimes maintains the obligation of celibacy when it confirms the dismissal of an ordained member from an institute.

- a formal petition in which the person explains in detail his reasons for requesting the dispensation and his assurance of a firm purpose of observing celibacy;
- a curriculum vitae of the petitioner providing his full name, place and date of birth, place, and date of permanent commitment in the institute, place, and date of both his diaconal and presbyteral ordination, and his assignments;
- the evaluation of the man' s suitability for the religious and clerical life given by the formation personnel at the time of his preparation for vows or promises and ordination;
- the results of the evaluation of the individual prior to his making permanent commitment in the institute or society and prior to his diaconal and presbyteral ordinations along with any observations or notations entered in the evaluation report;
- formal *votum* of the major superior referring to attempts he made to dissuade the person from seeking the indult, his assessment of the reasons offered by the petitioner, references to how the man conducted himself in the priestly ministry, his character, and his conduct in general, mention of abandoning the institute or society illegally, if such is the case, and his own opinion about the request.

The documents are forwarded to the general curia of the institute or society. The actual indult is granted by the Congregation for Clergy.[28]

When the indult is received, a copy is sent to the person along with a statement of notification. The individual returns the signed document to the major superior to be kept in the person's file and a copy is sent to the general curia. The original indult, or at least a copy, is also placed in the person's file.

(3) *Departure from the institute or society with both a dispensation from the obligations of the religious vows or promises and the obligations of the clerical state, including that of celibacy.*[29]

The investigation of the request for laicization is to be done either by the major superior or by the local ordinary of the person's actual residence. If the local ordinary conducts the investigation, the *votum* of the person's major superior must be included in the documentation. Three copies of the documentation are sent to the Congregation for the Clergy. Permission must be obtained from the Congregation for the Clergy for an ordinary other than the man's major superior or bishop of his residence to investigate the case.

---

28 On August 1, 2005, competency was changed from the Congregation for Divine Worship and the Discipline of the Sacraments to Congregation for the Clergy.

29 This procedure is commonly called *laicization.*

The documents that must be obtained in the course of the investigation are:

- a table of contents;
- a formal letter to the Holy Father in which the person clearly indicates his wish to be dispensed;[30]
- a curriculum vitae of the petitioner;
- a mandate for a qualified priest to serve as instructor of the case and another priest to be the notary;
- testimony of the petitioning priest covering his early family life, his religious and priestly formation, his presbyteral ministry, and the reason for his departure from active ministry;
- the testimony of several witnesses who know him well;
- the testimony of experts who may have treated him;
- evaluation reports from his religious and priestly formation;
- a summary by the priest-instructor of the case;
- a *votum* by the major superior;
- a *votum* from the petitioner's local ordinary regarding possible scandal;
- a certificate of authenticity by the notary.

The documentation is then sent to the general curia of the institute. The Congregation for Divine Worship and the Discipline of the Sacraments is responsible for issuing the indult. A copy of the indult and a statement of notification is sent to the priest. The dispensation becomes effective when the priest receives it. He returns the signed statement to the major superior who will forward the statement to the general curia. The parish of baptism or reception into full communion is informed of the indult.

Dismissal

Although this topic is presented elsewhere in this handbook, it is presented again in this section because of the civil liability that an institute may face with an ordained member who refuses to seek a dispensation from obligations arising from his ordination or transfer to another institute or to a diocese. The institute's leadership can use the procedure for dismissal of a member. It may want to inform the member prior to initiating the procedure what it intends to do and the rationale for the using this particular procedure.

---

30 Upon receiving this letter, the superior is formally to suspend the priest from the exercise of orders. However, this action is not ordinarily taken because it can cause more harm than good. If the person has already attempted marriage, such a suspension on the part of the superior is unnecessary because the person was *ipso facto* suspended when he attempted marriage (c. 1394 §1).

APPENDIX: SAMPLE DOCUMENTS

SAMPLE PETITION FOR ADMISSION TO CANDIDACY FOR THE DIACONATE AND FOR THE PRIESTHOOD

Current date
The Reverend N.
Provincial Superior (Superior General)
Street address
City, State, Zip Code

Dear Father N.

In accordance and compliance with canon 1034 §1 of the *Code of Canon Law,* I hereby formally petition for admission to candidacy for the orders of the diaconate and the priesthood. In making this request, I declare that I wish to dedicate my life to the service of the Church for the glory of God and the good of souls.

I realize that admission to candidacy for the sacrament of order does not carry with it any of the duties, rights, or privileges of clerics. However, I realize that in virtue of your acceptance of me as a candidate for the orders of diaconate and priesthood, I must care for my vocation in a special way and foster it. I also realize that I acquire the right to the necessary spiritual assistance by which I can develop my vocation and submit unconditionally to the will of God.

In presenting this petition, I solemnly declare that I am not motivated by fear, either physical or moral. In no way am I coerced by parents, relatives, or any other agency whatsoever. Finally, I declare that I am making this request for admission to candidacy for the sacrament of order of my own free will.

Sincerely,
Signature

1. The petition must be handwritten on 8½ x 11 stationery. If it is necessary to go to a second page, write on the back of the paper.
2. The petition is to be addressed to the petitioner's own major superior.
3. The petition is submitted to the formation director to be forwarded to the major superior.

SAMPLE PETITION FOR INSTALLATION INTO THE MINISTRY OF LECTOR

Current date
The Reverend N.
Provincial (Superior General)
Street Address
City, State, Zip Code

Dear Father N.:

In accordance and compliance with canon 1035 §1 of the *Code of Canon Law*, I am petitioning to be installed in the ministry of Lector.

I realize that as lector I am appointed for my own proper function, that of reading the Word of God in the liturgical assembly. In order that I may more fittingly and perfectly fulfill this function, I realize that I should meditate on the Sacred Scripture.

I am aware of the ministry I am undertaking and I shall make every effort and employ suitable means to acquire that love and knowledge of the Scripture that will make me more a disciple of the Lord. I also realize that the conferral of this ministry does not imply the right to sustenance or salary from the Church.

In presenting this petition, I solemnly declare that I am not motivated by fear, either physical or moral. I am not coerced in any way by parent, relative, or any other agency whatsoever. Finally, I declare that I am making this request for installation in the ministry of lector of my own free will.

Sincerely yours,
Signature

1. The petition must be handwritten on 8½ x 11 stationery. If it is necessary to go to a second page, write on the back of the paper.
2. The petition is to be addressed to the petitioner's own major superior.
3. The petition is submitted to the formation director to be forwarded to the major superior.

SAMPLE PETITION FOR INSTALLATION INTO THE MINISTRY OF ACOLYTE

Current date
The Reverend **Name**
Provincial Superior (Superior General)
Street Address
City, State, Zip Code

Dear Father **Name**:

In accordance and compliance with canon 1035 §1 of the *Code of Canon Law,* I am petitioning to be installed in the ministry of Acolyte.

I realize that as an acolyte I am appointed to aid the deacon and to minister to the priest. I understand the corresponding ordinary and extraordinary duties. In order that I may more worthily perform these functions, I realize that I should participate in the Holy Eucharist with increasingly fervent piety, that I should receive nourishment from it, and that I should deepen my knowledge of it.

Destined in a special way for the service of the altar, I realize that I should learn all matters concerning public divine worship and strive to grasp their inner spiritual meaning. In that way I shall be able to offer myself daily entirely to God, be an example to ally by my seriousness and reverence in the sacred building, and have a sincere love for the Mystical Body of Christ, the people of God, especially the weak and the sick.

I realize that the conferral of this ministry does not imply the right to sustenance or salary from the Church.

In presenting this petition to you, I declare that I am not motivated by any fear, either physical or moral. In no way am I coerced by parents, relatives, or any other agency whatsoever. Finally, I declare that I am making this request for installation into the ministry of acolyte of my own free will.

Sincerely yours,
Signature

1. The petition must be handwritten on 8½ x 11 stationery. If it is necessary to go to a second page, write on the back of the paper.
2. The petition is to be addressed to the petitioner's own major superior.
3. The petition is submitted to the formation director to be forwarded to the major superior.

SAMPLE REQUEST TO LOCAL ORDINARY FOR FACULTIES

Date

Name
Title
Address
City, State, Zip Code

Dear **Name**:

Grace and Peace in the Lord Jesus!

I am pleased to present to you the Reverend **Name**, and I ask you to grant him the faculties of your (arch)diocese for the exercise of priestly ministry. Effective **Date**, Fr. **Name** became the **Ministry** at **Institution**. Father resides at our community residence at **Address**.

Attached is the customary attestation of fitness for ministry. It is without hesitation that I present Fr. **Name** to you to grant him faculties.

If you need additional information, please contact me.

Sincerely in Christ,

Name
Provincial

CERTIFICATE OF APTITUDE FOR PRIESTLY MINISTRY

I hereby certify that Rev. **Name**, born **Date of Birth** and ordained **Date of Ordination**, is a priest in good standing in the **Name of Institute Or Society** with the faculties of the same Province for the exercise of his priestly ministry. He is assigned in the **Diocese of Assignment** as of **Effective Date of Assignment**. Father is the **Office** at **Institution**. His canonical house of assignment and residence is **Name of Assigned House, Address, City, State, Zip Code**.

After adequately reviewing his file and checking with those who have lived and worked with him, particularly his own provincial superior, I am able to certify without qualification that Father **Name** has:

1. Never been suspended or otherwise canonically disciplined.
2. Never had criminal charges brought against him.
3. Never manifested moral or other behavioral problems in the past that would indicate he might deal with minors or adults in an inappropriate manner.
4. Never had against him an allegation of sexual abuse of a minor.
5. Never been involved in an incident which called into question his fitness or suitability to fulfill the responsibilities and duties of his priestly ministry due to alcohol, substance abuse, or other causes.
6. No mental or physical attribute, condition and/or past situation which would adversely affect his performance of priestly ministry.

I am able to state without qualification [or "to the best of my knowledge"] that Father **Name** is of good character and reputation and qualified to perform his priestly duties in the **Name of Diocese** for the period of his assignment there. Also, Father is current with our Safe Environment training.

Given at the Provincial Office in **City**, **State**, this **Day** of **Month** in the year of our Lord **Year**.

Signature
Printed Name

Title

DIMISSORIAL LETTER

By virtue of this letter, I grant permission to **Name of the one to be ordained** to receive the Order of **Deacon** or **Presbyter** from the Most Reverend **Name of Diocesan Bishop where ordination is to take place**, or, according to the norm of canon 1021 of the Code of Canon Law, by any other Bishop who is in Communion with the Apostolic See.

By this letter, I affirm that the above-named candidate has complied with the following requirements:

1. he became a permanently professed member of **Name of Institute** on **Date of Permanent Profession**.
2. he has manifested his free intention to receive the Order of **Deacon** or **Presbyter**.
3. he has the required age.
4. he has received approbation from the rector and faculty of the seminary and has completed the required studies.
5. he has been instituted into the required ministries for the Order he is requesting and has observed the prescribed intervals.
6. he has made the Profession of Faith, Declaration of Freedom, and fulfilled his spiritual obligation.
7. he is free of any impediments, irregularities, or censures and his moral character corresponds to the requirement of the Order he is about to receive.

Given at **Place** on this **Day** of **Month, Year**

____

Provincial

____

Provincial Notary

CHAPTER TWELVE

Secular Institutes

Sharon Holland, IHM[1]

Introduction

Although secular institutes have existed in some form in the Church for over two hundred years, their official recognition as a true form of consecrated life dates only from 1947.[2] Vatican Council II clearly recognized them as distinct from religious institutes in *Perfectae caritatis* 11, and the 1983 Code now provides for them, for the first time, in the Church's universal law. Canons 573-606 apply to them as institutes of consecrated life; canons 710-730 address their specificity as secular institutes.

Certain canons of the latter section help to indicate what is characteristic of secular institutes. The member's consecration in a life of the evangelical counsels is lived out in the midst of secular realities. It is within that context that members seek their own growth in charity and work to effect the sanctification of the world from within (c. 710). Consequently, the biblical image of leaven is often used to convey the notion of an individual presence, seeking to bring about the transformation of temporal realities through the power of the Gospel (c. 712).

Members of each institute are urged to a strong sense of communion in a common vocation (c. 602) without, however, the obligation of common life. Of its nature, consecrated secularity calls for the flexibility in living situations provided by canon 714.

While some institutes do have one or more corporate apostolates, it is clear from the canons that such works are not the expectation. Rather the more individual leaven-like presence in one's place of work and the diversity of living situations are characteristic.

---

1 Sharon Holland, IHM, was the original author and also revised this chapter.

2 Pius XII, apostolic constitution *Provida Mater Ecclesia*, February 2, 1947: *AAS* 39 (1947) 114-124; *CLD* 3: 135-146.

Like other institutes of consecrated life, secular institutes can be either clerical or lay (c. 588). The sphere of their apostolic endeavors follows accordingly (cc. 711, 713).

In a 1976 address, Pope Paul VI offered a new image for the role of secular institutes. He saw them as the potential "experimental laboratory" in which the Church could test concrete ways of relating to the world.[3]

The post-synodal apostolic constitution *Vita consecrata* speaks of secular institute members as "a leaven of wisdom and a witness of grace within cultural, economic, and political life."[4]

Erection and Recognition

Secular institutes, in accordance with the norms common to all institutes of consecrated life (cc. 573-606), are erected and recognized as diocesan or pontifical institutes in accordance with the procedures outlined in chapter two of this book. Likewise, their constitutions are approved by the same ecclesiastical authority in accord with canon 587. The provision of *Authenticum charismatis* in November of 2020, which requires a bishop to obtain written permission from the Holy See before erecting an institute, applies equally to secular institutes.

Status of Members

Members of secular institutes are consecrated and remain in the state of life they have as lay persons or clerics (c. 711). Consequently, other parts of canon law apply to them in those respective states while religious law, unless expressly invoked, does not.

In keeping with this fact, a member's way of involvement in service to the ecclesial community will be as an individual lay man or woman or as a diocesan cleric (c. 713). Only if an institute actually has or accepts an institutional apostolate would there be consultations or written agreements between the institutes as such and the bishop.

Beyond their secular occupation, lay members are subject to the diocesan norms for lay participation in the life of the Church. Likewise, the diocesan norms for clerical personnel would be followed for clerics, with the exception of cases mention in canon 715 §2 regarding clerics incardinated in an institute.

---

3 Paul VI, "A Living Presence in the Service of the World and of the Church," in *Secular Institutes, Documents* (Rome: CMIS, 1998) 97.
4 *VC* 10.

Similarly, the living arrangements of members follow from their status as laity or as secular clerics. Canon 714 provides for living alone, with family, or in groups, according to the "ordinary conditions of the world" and to the institute's constitutions.

Incardination

The norm for clerical secular institutes is incardination in the diocese (cc. 715, 266 §3). Studies, admission to orders, apostolic obedience, and the observance of particular law are essentially those of the secular clergy. (See chapter 11 on "The Sacrament of Order.")

As is clear from canon 266 §3, it is reserved to the Apostolic See to permit incardination in a secular institute. If this is granted, it would most probably be at the time of pontifical recognition of the institute. However, it must be noted that major superiors of clerical secular institutes of pontifical right are not ordinaries in the sense of canon 134 §1 and thus do not have the authority to grant dimissorial letters for their members. Rather, the member's ordination will be governed by the law for seculars (c. 1019 §2).

The major superior in such cases would need to provide the necessary information and guarantees of preparation to the member's proper bishop who, according to canon 1018 §1, 1°, may issue the dimissorials if he himself will not be the ordaining bishop.

An ordained member who is incardinated in the institute, according to canon 715 §2, will relate to the diocesan bishop more in the manner of a religious when assigned to proper works of the institute or when exercising governance in the institute.

Should it happen that an institute with diocesan incardination also has some proper work, an agreement would have to be reached with the bishop when initiating its presence in the diocese, including the way in which members would be appointed to that work. Likewise, if a member incardinated in the diocese is elected to a position of internal governance which would significantly affect his commitments in the diocese, an agreement would need to be reached with the bishop. Canon 718 addresses the institute's financial responsibility for such members.

Participation in Life and Governance

Chapters and Assemblies

Although there is no direct reference to a collegial governing body in the canons on secular institutes, canon 596 from the common norms recognizes for both superiors and chapters the authority given them in universal law and constitutions. Further, secular institutes enjoy that just autonomy of life, especially of governance, described in canon 586. In fact, a general chapter or assembly does exist in each institute and must be provided for in the constitutions.[5]

Moderators

Although it is not stated in canon 717, it is common practice that the supreme moderator be elected by the collegial governing body referred to above, following the norms for canonical elections, as presented in the constitutions.

The supreme moderator must be definitively incorporated. The length of a moderator's term of office and the manner of choosing them is to be defined in the constitutions.

In addition to the moderator's role stated in canon 717 §3 of seeking to preserve unity of spirit and to promote the active participation of members (cf. c. 716), other responsibilities of moderators may be gleaned from the canons. These illustrate not only their role but also the necessity of their having a council.

Moderators have a role in the administration of any temporal goods belonging to the institute (c. 718); they are expected to be available to members for spiritual direction and advice (c. 719 §4); major moderators with their councils decide on the admission of candidates to probation and to the assumption of sacred bonds (c. 720) and they handle questions of separation from the institute (cc. 726-727; 729-730).

When canon law—or the constitutions—requires the advice or consent of the major moderator's council, the process is regulated by canon 127 §§1 and 3. For consent it is required that there be a meeting of the council and that the consent of an absolute majority of those present be obtained. In the case of needing the advice (counsel) of the council, there is to be a meeting unless proper law determines otherwise, and the counsel of all who are present must be sought. These elements are necessary for a valid act on the part of the moderator (c. 127 §1). In all cases the members of the council are to give their opinions sincerely and when the matter requires it, they must observe secrecy (c. 127 §3).

---

5 When approving secular institutes, *Provida Mater Ecclesia* (IX) provided for them to adopt office and organs of governance based on those religious societies but with adaptation.

The guidelines for the general moderator's periodic report to the Apostolic See are provided in chapter two.[6]

Administration of Goods

As public juridic persons, secular institutes have a right to acquire, retain, administer, and alienate temporal goods (c. 1255). As institutes which do not, as a rule, have common life or corporate apostolates, their transactions of this kind will be fewer than those of religious institutes or societies of apostolic life.

The norms of Book V of the Code (c. 718) apply and the basic procedures described in chapter nine above would be followed. Proper law must determine when a major moderator with the consent of his or her council may act and when transactions are reserved to the supreme moderator.

Proper law must also establish how it will handle its financial responsibilities toward members who, because of work for the institute, are not earning a living elsewhere. It is common practice that institutes have a system by which members contribute from their earnings to provide funds to cover the expenses of formation and governance. Moderators and formation personnel are not necessarily engaged full-time in internal work; however where these roles or engagement in some corporate work involves a member more fully, provision must be made for their living expenses, insurance, and retirement.

Admission

Canon 720 requires that the constitutions of each institute provide for which major moderator may act, with what role of the council, in admitting candidates to probation (cc. 721-722), to temporary incorporation (c. 723 §§1-2), and to perpetual or definitive incorporation (c. 723 §§3-4).

Canon 721 lists three invalidating impediments to admission to probation in a secular institute. Here the minimum age is majority, age 18 (c. 97 §1). The impediments of marriage bond, sacred bonds, or incorporation in a society of apostolic life may be supplemented by others in the constitutions. In addition, canon 597 from the common norms must be observed, requiring that a candidate must be Catholic, of right intention, possess the necessary qualities, and be free of impediments.

---

6 The 1988 version of these guidelines contained a separate section for moderators general of secular institutes for what their reports should include. The 2008 update, as included in chapter 2, does not distinguish secular institutes from religious institutes, so the report of the moderators general should follow the same guidelines.

Although the canons on secular institutes do not detail all of the same documents and requirements for admission as are given for religious institutes, the procedures discussed in chapter four of this book can be helpful. It must be kept in mind, however, that the absence of a common life as a norm and the life of secular consecration in the ordinary working world can significantly affect the criteria used by an institute in admitting candidates.

If the evaluation of experts is used to judge the maturity of the individual (c. 721 §3), then canon 220 must be observed, protecting the individual's right to his or her good reputation and to privacy. This involves the usual release of information forms and the strictly confidential use of information on the part of those whose authority to admit candidates gives them access to it.

Formation

The canons regulating formation in secular institutes (cc. 722 and 724) leave a great deal to proper law. In keeping with their secular nature, the institutes do not require a common residence in which formation takes place. Rather, it is often carried out through correspondence, individually used courses of study followed in regular contact with a formator, tapes, occasional visits, participation in local gatherings of members, and annual retreats. In some areas, seminary or university courses in spirituality, theology, scripture, liturgy, etc. may be available. Videos, webinars, and workshops also can provide study opportunities and are widely used today. In this way, formation goes forward without professional work being interrupted.

Constitutions must establish the length and method of formation before the first assumption of sacred bonds. However, it cannot be shorter than two years (c. 722 §3). The fact that formation is a life-long project is clear from canon 724, which calls for uninterrupted formation after first incorporation in matters both human and divine. Likewise, moderators must concern themselves with the continuous spiritual formation of members.

From various canons the broad areas of the content of formation can be gleaned:

- candidates must understand the vocation to secular consecration and be formed in the particular spirit and way of life of the institute;
- they must learn to fully translate their life into apostolate which, like leaven, strives to imbue all things with the spirit of the Gospel;
- lay members will be formed to share in the Church's evangelizing tasks using the means which most clearly respond to the purpose, spirit, and character of the institute;

- candidates for ordination will be formed for sacred ministry;
- all, according to their state, will study how to order and inform the temporal order according to the values of the Gospel;
- candidates must be formed as ecclesial men and women who think with the Church;
- All will receive formation for a life of prayer, both personal and liturgical, enabling them to fulfill fruitfully those obligations mentioned in canon 719.

Incorporation

As mentioned above, constitutions must establish which major moderator is to judge the suitability of the candidate for incorporation at the end of initial probation and with what role of the council. Consequently, each institute must also give thought to how they can provide for contact between candidates and major moderators or councilors and for appropriate evaluation from those responsible for formation. Where candidates have the possibility of participating in local groupings of members on a regular basis, those members also might have a role in evaluating the suitability of the potential new member.

The code leaves to the constitutions of each institute the determination of the sacred bonds by which the evangelical counsels will be assumed (c. 712). The bonds, whether vows (cc. 1191-1192), oaths (cc. 1199-1200), acts of consecration binding in conscience, or promises are recognized as sacred, that is, effecting the consecration of the members to God. The constitutions must also provide detail on the obligations which further specify the content of canons 599-601 of the common norms preserving "the proper secularity of the institute" (c. 712). It is also customary for the constitutions to contain the formula used at the time of incorporation.

It is clear from the canons (c. 723 §2) that first incorporation is "temporary," that is, taken for a specified amount of time. While it may not be less than five years, constitutions are to specify whether the original commitment is renewed annually, is made immediately for five years, or is made in some other combination of renewal periods.

Since the code expresses only the minimum and not the maximum time in temporary incorporation, the constitutions should provide (a) after how many years one may be admitted to perpetual incorporation or definitive incorporation, and (b) whether all members are incorporated in the same way or if there is an option between perpetual and definitive incorporation.

The law is silent on the point of a moderator receiving the sacred bonds because that is a characteristic of the public vows of religious which are received in the name of the Church (c. 1192 §1). Proper law, however, should indicate in what setting the sacred bonds are assumed, whether they are witnessed in silence or if they are received on behalf of the institute. Likewise, there should be provision for how they are recorded in the archives of the institute.

Associates

Since their formal recognition by the Church as a form of consecrated life, many secular institutes have also had other persons associated with them. It is clear from the preceding canons that members—in what *Provida Mater* (III, 2) called the "strict sense"—are those who assume the evangelical counsels through sacred bonds, either perpetually or definitively. The fundamental difference between celibate chastity and conjugal chastity most clearly highlights the difference between the two states.

The constitutions of each secular institute with associates must clarify what bond is used to associate a person with the institute (c. 725). Furthermore, proper law or policies should identify (a) the requirements for becoming associated, (b) the rights and obligations which flow from association both on the part of the individual and of the institute, (c) how those associated are formed and assisted in striving for evangelical perfection according to the spirit of the institute, and (d) the way in which those associated may participate in its mission. Only members in the strict sense have the right and duty to participate in the life and governance of the institute in the sense of canons 716 and 717 §3.

Separation of Members

Departure During Temporary Incorporation

Canon 726 envisions three ways in which those in temporary incorporation may leave the institute. The fact that the similar canons of religious law are neither invoked nor fully repeated indicates that they should not be applied in these cases.

- When the time of temporary incorporation elapses, the individual, not having requested renewal or definitive incorporation, is free. The matter should be discussed in advance with the competent moderator and the fact noted in the records of the institute.
- The competent major superior may exclude a member from the renewal of sacred bonds. He or she is required to hear the council first. The just cause which is required must be evaluated in terms of the requirements

of universal law and the proper law of the institute and knowledge of the member during the previous period of temporary incorporation.

- One who feels urged by a grave cause to leave the institute before the time of temporary incorporation has lapsed presents a written request for an indult of departure to the supreme moderator expressing the reasons for the request. Proper law may ask that the petition be channeled through a more immediate major moderator but granting the indult is reserved to the supreme moderator with consent of the council.

The canon makes no distinction between pontifical and diocesan institutes. The effects of the indult are in canon 728: "all the bonds as well as the rights and obligations deriving from incorporation cease."

Departure of the Perpetually Incorporated

For the departure of a perpetually incorporated member, there must be recourse to ecclesiastical authority (c. 727).

- In pontifical institutes, the petition, written after serious prayer, is forwarded to the supreme moderator who sends it to the Apostolic See. While not stated in the canon, it would be appropriate for the supreme moderator to add his or her opinion in the forwarding letter.
- In diocesan institutes the constitutions should provide further precision. The indult could be sought from the Apostolic See or from the diocesan bishop of (a) the principal seat of the institute or (b) the diocese where the member lives and works. It is always channeled through the supreme moderator.
- In the case of a cleric incardinated in the institute, the provisions of canon 693 are invoked, requiring that a benevolent bishop be found before the indult is granted.

In institutes where some or all of the members are definitively rather than perpetually incorporated, constitutions must indicate whether the above or a purely internal procedure is followed in cases of departure.

Effect of the Indult

In any case, the indult of departure takes effect when granted legitimately. The sacred bonds cease to bind and all rights and obligations arising from incorporation cease (c. 728). The normal procedure is that the indult is communicated back to the petitioner using the same channels through which it was submitted to the competent ecclesiastical authority.

For a secular institute cleric incardinated in the diocese, the indult terminates incorporation in the institute leaving him incardinated in the diocese and fully subject to the diocesan bishop.

Dismissal

For cases of dismissal, canon 729 applies a number of canons from religious law to parallel situations in secular institutes. In 2019, the apostolic letter *Communis vita* added illegitimate absence as §3 to canon 694 for religious institutes; however, the section is not applicable to secular institutes since members are not required to live communally. The reader may refer to chapter seven for those dismissal procedures.

- *Ipso facto* dismissal is handled according to canon 694, §§1-2.
- Mandatory dismissal is handled according to canon 695.
- For discretionary dismissal, causes must be established in the constitutions of each secular institute. While they must be proportionately grave, external, imputable, and juridically proven; the causes listed in canon 696 are not repeated here for secular institutes.
- The procedure for discretionary dismissal is that of the religious canons 697-700 with the effects expressed in canon 701.
- Canon 702 is not invoked since it is presumed that secular institute members are self-supporting through their work. However, when proper law does call for some form of community of goods, attention must be given to the equity and evangelical charity due to members separating from the institute (cf. c. 702 §2).

Transfers

In the case of transfers between two secular institutes, the religious canons are again employed, omitting only canon 684 §3 on monasteries (c. 730). The basic principles explained in chapter seven would apply.

If, however, the transfer involves a secular institute and either a religious institute or a society of apostolic life, the written petition and the letters of consent from the supreme moderators given with the consent of their respective councils must be forwarded to the Apostolic See. In granting the permission, certain particular mandates may be added to accommodate differences such as the presence or absence of vows or the mode of incorporation which are not provided for in the canons on transfer between two institutes of the same kind.

CHAPTER THIRTEEN

SOCIETIES OF APOSTOLIC LIFE

Michael P. Joyce, CM[1]

Societies of apostolic life have their origins in the sixteenth and seventeenth centuries with the Oratories of Saint Philip Neri in Rome and Pierre Berulle in Paris, along with the Congregation of the Mission and the Daughters of Charity of Saint Vincent De Paul, and the Society of Saint Sulpice founded by Jean Jacques Olier, and others. The founders did not intend the members to live the religious life for a variety of reasons. However, the lifestyle of these societies approached that of religious institutes in many ways. The 1917 Code of Canon Law called these groups societies of common life without vows. The law for the societies in that code treated them as religious congregations. The commission for revision of the law for institutes of consecrated life gradually accepted the position that societies of apostolic life should not be considered institutes of consecrated life. This position is reflected in the schema of 1980. Since societies of apostolic life are not institutes of consecrated life, they have their own section of law although they share in some ways a law in common with institutes.[2]

Inasmuch as this handbook treats procedures for societies of apostolic life, it is not appropriate to present a history of the societies here. The above paragraph briefly shows the treatment they have received in canon law. The remainder of the chapter will examine the universal law for societies canon by canon. The reader will be referred to previous chapters when appropriate because the canons require societies to follow the law for institutes of consecrated life. This chapter will give specific procedures for societies when the law requires them.

Those who are implementing procedures for societies of apostolic life always need to attend to the proper law of the society (the constitutions, statutes, directories, etc.) because the general law gives precedence to the proper law of the society as the canons indicate. While this principle is effective as well for institutes

---

1 Rev. Michael Joyce, CM, was the original author and also revised this chapter.

2 Cecil L. Parres, CM, "Societies of Apostolic Life" in *A Handbook on Canon 573-746*, Jordan Hite, TOR, Sharon Holland, IHM, Daniel Ward, OSB, eds. (Collegeville, Minnesota: The Liturgical Press, 1985) 289.

of consecrated life, it is particularly pertinent for societies because each society has a unique character which the 1983 Code of Canon Law recognizes.

The Bond with the Society

While there are several notable distinctions between societies of apostolic life and institutes of consecrated life, the most remarkable is that members of societies are not consecrated by religious vows (c. 731 §1). Societies in some respects resemble religious institutes; however, the members do not have public vows as defined by canon 1192 §1.

Some societies do establish the bond between the members and the society through vows. These vows, however, are private as defined in c. 1192 §1. As section 2 of canon 731 notes, there are other ways that societies can establish the bond. The method is described in the constitutions of each society. Likewise, if the society does use vows as a method for creating the bond, the effects of the vows are also determined in the constitutions. Canons 598 to 602 also apply to these societies.

The society needs to determine clearly how the bond is created. Competent superiors and members should sign some form of a document indicating how, when, and where the bond became effective. A copy of the document is placed in the individual's personnel file and notification is sent to the general headquarters of the society. See the appendix to this chapter for a sample form of attestation.

The general law does not legislate the manner in which the common life is experienced. As section 1 of canon 731 states, this matter is treated in the constitutions of the society. Usually, the constitutions will give a general prescription for the observance of the common life. The provincial and local levels of leadership then make more concrete criteria for how it is exercised.

When there is a need for a society or its members to communicate with the Holy See, the proper congregation to contact is the Congregation for Institutes of Consecrated Life and for Societies of Apostolic Life (CICLSAL). The title of the congregation indicates its competency.

General Norms

Rather than repeat principles already enunciated in the code, canon 732 refers members of societies of apostolic life back to canons introducing institutes of consecrated life. The topics those canons cover are the intent of the founder or foundress, establishment of societies by diocesan bishops, aggregation, divisions, and mergers of societies. Subsequent canons address changes subject to the Holy See: suppression, autonomy, and proper law. The introductory canons also describe the various types of institutes, exemption, communication with the Holy See, and relationship to ecclesiastical authority. This section of the law on institutes of consecrated life also explains the authority of superiors and chapters, and general norms for admission. Canon 606 invokes the principle of equal application of the law to societies of men and of women.

While societies of apostolic life are subject to these general norms, the particular character of each society is still respected. The great difference between societies highlights the critical importance of their proper law.

The procedures used in establishing new societies and the aggregation of a society to another society or to an institute of consecrated life are the same as for religious institutes (see c. 579 and c. 580 respectively). The procedures for mergers and union of societies as well as procedures for suppression of a society are the same as those for religious institutes (see c. 582 and c. 584 respectively).

A society of apostolic life needs to look to its proper law for the procedures for dividing into parts, establishing new divisions, joining previously erected ones, or defining the parts in another way. One should consult with the supreme authority of the society for these procedures (c. 581). Suppression of various parts of the society (c. 585) belongs to the competent authority of the society. The supreme authority of the society should be consulted for the proper procedures.

Changes in matters which have been approved by the Apostolic See cannot be made without its permission (c. 583). As mentioned above, the Congregation for Institutes of Consecrated Life and Societies of Apostolic Life (CICLSAL) handles these matters.

While religious institutes have a rightful autonomy of life, and local ordinaries are to safeguard and protect that autonomy (c. 586), there are many instances in which societies and local ordinaries need to cooperate, especially in the apostolate. Societies can follow similar procedures as religious institutes in protecting their self-governance as well because many societies also enjoy the privilege of exemption.

Canon 587 addresses constitutions, statutes, and directories of societies. These documents are of great importance for societies of apostolic life because the common law frequently defers to the proper law of societies of apostolic life in determining what is normative.

Societies of apostolic life can enjoy the privilege of exemption (c. 591) mentioned above as spelled out in their constitutions. At the same time, supreme moderators of societies of apostolic life must give regular reports to the Apostolic See on the status and life of the society. For societies of apostolic life of diocesan right, the diocesan bishop of the principal seat of the institute approves the constitutions and confirms any changes in them (c. 595). He also deals with matters of greater importance which affect the whole institute and are beyond the power of its internal authority. He can also grant dispensations from the constitutions in particular cases. An example of matters of greater importance is alienation of temporal goods.

The law for societies of apostolic life and their members applies equally to either sex (c. 606) unless the context of the wording or the nature of the matter indicates otherwise. The nature of clerical societies of apostolic life requires some differences in applying canon law to the members of the society.

If members of a particular society undertake living the evangelical counsels, they are also bound by canons 598 to 602. Again, the proper law of the society describes in more detail how the counsels are lived by the members. Each of the mentioned canons refers to the proper law of institutes of consecrated life.

Houses and Local Communities

Unlike institutes of consecrated life, societies of apostolic life can establish local communities in addition to erecting houses (c. 733). The erection of houses and the establishment of local communities are done by the competent authority of the society after receiving the written consent of the diocesan bishop. When a house or local community is suppressed, the competent authority must consult the diocesan bishop before the suppression.

The proper law of the society determines the governance, the manner of life in common of the members, and the relationship to other parts of the society for local communities. The general law is silent on these matters. Houses have the right to have at least an oratory in which to celebrate and reserve the Holy Eucharist.

Governance

Governance in societies of apostolic life is determined by the constitutions of the society (c. 734). However, the constitutions must take into consideration canons 617 to 633. Canons 617 to 630 address superiors and their councils. Canon 620 establishes who in societies of apostolic life are major superiors; namely, the general superior of a society, those who govern a province or its equivalent, and their vicars. Canon 621 describes what the universal law considers a province. There are four requirements for a province. It must be (1) a union of several houses, (2) under the same superior, (3) constituting an immediate part of the society, and (4) established by the legitimate authority of the society. One needs to consult the proper law of a society regarding further requirements for establishing a province. Canon 623 requires the proper law to indicate what are the qualifications for valid appointment or election to the office of superior in terms of the length of membership in the society. Furthermore, proper law must determine terms of office and methods for removal or transfer from the office (c. 624).

General superiors of societies of apostolic life are chosen by canonical elections as indicated in their proper constitutions. Diocesan bishops preside at the election of a supreme moderator of societies of diocesan right (c. 635). Superiors, apart from supreme moderators, are instituted according to the constitutions of the society. They have councils to assist them in carrying out their office. The council members must give their consent or counsel for various matters according to universal or proper law (c. 627).

Superiors in societies who are charged with the responsibility of visitation are to fulfill the duty according to the norms of the proper law of the society (c. 628). All superiors of a society have the obligation to reside in their respective houses or local community (c. 629). However, proper law may provide for the use of a regional superior for several houses or local communities within a given area. Superiors are not to hear the confessions of their subjects unless a subject takes the initiative and requests it (c. 630 §4). This norm provides protection for both superiors and subjects in regard to the internal forum. Canon 630 requires ordinary confessors for lay societies in houses of formation and in large communities.

Societies of apostolic life must have a governing structure akin to the general chapter of religious institutes (c. 631). These bodies may have other names in societies to distinguish the society from religious institutes; however, their functions are the same for the society as a general chapter is for a religious institute. Societies may have other organs as well for consultation and participation of members (c. 633). These bodies must be carefully established and regulated.

Admission, Incorporation, and Initial Formation

Each society is allowed to determine in its proper law its own norms for admission, probation, incorporation, and formation of its members (c. 735). However, the society must follow the requirements of canons 642 to 645 for admission. Canon 642 demands that those seeking admission must have the required age, health, character, and maturity that the society requires. Canon 643 lists factors that render admission invalid. One also needs to consult the proper law of the society because it can establish further impediments. If the person seeking admission is a diocesan presbyter or deacon, the superior must consult his local ordinary before admitting the cleric (c. 644). Likewise, the superior is not to admit someone so burdened by debt that the person cannot repay it. Canon 645 indicates what documentation is required for admission.

Although the canons referred to are in the context of a novitiate, societies are not required to have a novitiate. The canons need to be read in the context of the first probationary period of membership in the society.

Incardination

Members of clerical societies of apostolic life are incardinated into the society unless the constitutions provide otherwise (c. 736). One exception is the Society of St. Sulpice in which members are incardinated into their diocese of origin. Initial formation programs for ordination are to follow those for diocesan clergy which can be found in the national *Program for Priestly Formation.*[3]

Societies that have clerical members incardinated into dioceses must clearly define in the constitutions or in a contract the relationship of the member with the diocesan bishop. A diocesan cleric entering into a society maintains incardination in the diocese until he is definitively incorporated into the society unless the constitutions of the society maintain incardination in a diocese (see cc. 268 §2 and 266 §2).

Rights and Obligations of Members

The rights and obligations of members of societies of apostolic life are found in the constitutions of the society (c. 737). Canons 662 to 672 concerning the rights and obligations of members of institutes of consecrated life do not apply to members of societies of apostolic life. Constitutions must attend to the distinction of temporary and definitive incorporation. The rights and obligations of members in temporary incorporation will differ from those belonging to members who are definitively incorporated.

Although members of societies of apostolic life are not bound to the rights and obligations of religious, they are bound to the rights and obligations of clerics (c. 739).[4] These obligations include reverence and obedience to the pope and to their proper ordinary (c. 273), union and cooperation with one another in a mutual

---

3 The latest edition for the United States is United States Conference of Catholic Bishops, *Program of Priestly Formation*, fifth edition (Washington, D.C.: United States Catholic Conference, 2006) available at http://www.usccb.org/beliefs-and-teachings/vocations/priesthood/priestly-formation/index.cfm (accessed on March 2, 2021). It is reported that the sixth edition was approved by the USCCB in 2019, but it has not yet received the *recognitio* from the Congregation for Clergy. Once approved, it will undoubtedly be available on the USCCB website.

4 Commentators disagree on the meaning of canon 739. However, this book addresses procedures rather than commentary, so it is beyond the scope to discuss it here.

and prayerful bond (c. 275), the pursuit of holiness (c. 276), the observance of perfect and perpetual continence and avoidance of activities alien to their state and way of life (c. 277 §§1-2). There are some rights and obligations that do not belong to lay members of societies. The context determines those that require the sacrament of holy orders to exercise them.

Relationship with the Diocesan Bishop

Members of societies of apostolic life are subject to the diocesan bishop in the spheres of public worship, the care of souls, and other works of the apostolate (c. 738). When members of a society are incardinated in a diocese, their relationship with the diocesan bishop is governed by the constitutions of the society or particular agreements. The diocesan bishop has the right of pastoral visitation for churches, oratories, and other works of a society with the exception of schools for its own members (c. 683).

A diocesan bishop can prohibit a member of a society for a very serious reason from living in the diocese (c. 679). He is first to inform the major superior of the intended prohibition. If the major superior does not remove the member, the diocesan bishop refers the matter to the Holy See. The member can appeal the bishop's decision through the supreme moderator of the society.

Works entrusted to a society by a diocesan bishop are subject to the bishop (c. 681). This situation is different from the work of the society. The reader can refer to chapter eight on the apostolate for more information on how to proceed with works entrusted by the diocesan bishop.

A diocesan bishop may confer an ecclesiastical office upon a member of a society of apostolic life with at least the assent of the competent superior. The member can be removed from the office either at the discretion of the diocesan bishop or the superior, having notified the bishop. The law is applicable to pastors and parochial vicars according to canons 523; 538 §2; 547; and 552. Neither ordinary needs to consent to the removal (c. 682).

Common Life

Members of societies of apostolic life are obliged to live the common life in a legitimately constituted house or local community (c. 740). The constitutions determine what forms common life for the society. The proper law of the society determines lawful absences from the common life.

Temporal Goods

Societies, their parts, and their houses are made juridic persons by the law itself (c. 741). Therefore, each of these units is capable of acquiring, administering, and alienating temporal goods. Provinces and houses are not subsidiaries of the society or of one another. See chapter nine on temporal goods for further explanation about acquisition, administration, and alienation. Each society and each province is to have a finance officer distinct from the major superior (c. 636). Every house of the society is also to have a distinct finance officer to the extent possible. The finance officers and other administrators are to give accounts of their administration according to the norms of the proper law.

The proper law of the society determines acts of extraordinary administration that need approval of another agency and the procedures necessary for obtaining the permission (c. 638). Persons other than superiors may be designated for validly incurring expenses and performing juridic acts of ordinary administration. The designation should be in writing and include the powers and limits of the designee.

Individual members of societies of apostolic life are capable according to the constitutions of the society of acquiring, administering, and alienating temporal goods because they are not bound by a public vow of poverty. However, whatever comes to them on account of their membership in the society belongs to the society.

Departure and Dismissal

Departure of Members in Temporary Incorporation

Voluntary departures and dismissals of members not definitively incorporated are governed by the constitutions of the society (c. 742). The following section addresses members who are definitively incorporated.

Departure of Members Definitively Incorporated

Members definitively incorporated who wish to depart may obtain an indult of departure from the society from the supreme moderator with the consent of the council unless the constitutions reserve the indult to the Holy See (c. 743). When the indult has been obtained, the member no longer has the rights and obligations that come from incorporation. However, if the member is a presbyter or deacon, the indult is not granted until he has found a bishop who will incardinate him or at least receive him for five years with a view to incardination. In the latter case, he is incardinated after the five years have passed unless the bishop refused to incardinate him.

Transfer

Supreme moderators of societies of apostolic life can give a member permission with the consent of the council to transfer to another society of apostolic life (c. 744). Before the member is definitively transferred into the receiving society, the rights and obligations from membership in the society of origin are suspended for the member. The member has a right during this time to return to the original society.

If a member desires to enter an institute of consecrated life, he or she must receive permission from the Holy See. Likewise, if a member of an institute of consecrated life wishes to enter a society of apostolic life, the member must also receive permission from the Holy See.

Dismissal of Members Definitively Incorporated

Superiors seeking the dismissal of a definitively incorporated member follow the same procedures as for the dismissal of a member of an institute of consecrated life (c. 746). See chapter 7 herein for more information.

Living Outside the Society

Supreme moderators of societies of apostolic life can grant permission with the consent of the council for a member to live outside the society for a period up to three years and suspend the rights and obligations of the member not suitable to the new situation (c. 745). If the member is a presbyter or deacon, the local ordinary of the diocese in which he will live must also grant permission.

SAMPLE FORM FOR
ATTESTATION OF DEFINITIVE BOND

Attestation of Definitive Bond

I, ***Name of Member,*** a member of ***Name of Society*** born in ***Name of City or Town***, diocese of ***Name of Diocese***, on the ***Date*** day of the month of ***Month*** in the year ***Year***, son/daughter of ***Name of Father*** and of ***Name of Mother with Maiden Name***; received into the ***Name of Society and Province*** (if applicable) at ***Name of Place*** on the ***Date*** day of the month of ***Month*** in the year ***Year***, made definitive bond with the same Society according to its Constitutions, which I understand well, at ***Name of Place*** on the ***Date*** day of the month of ***Month*** in the year ***Year***, in the presence of ***Name of Superior or Witness to Bond***, who is a member of the same Society.

Signature of Member making Definitive Bond

Signature of Witness to Definitive Bond

INDEX

B

C

D

R

S

T

U

2021 Authors

Brian T. Austin, FSSP, is a priest of the North American Province of the Priestly Fraternity of St. Peter. He is an instructor in canon law at the University of St. Paul in Ottawa, Canada. He received a doctorate in canon law from the Katholieke Universiteit Leuven in Belgium.

Nancy Bauer, OSB, is a Sister of Saint Benedict of Saint Benedict's Monastery, St. Joseph, MN. She completed the doctorate in canon law at The Catholic University of America in Washington DC and is an associate professor of canon law in the university's School of Canon Law.

Phillip Brown, PSS, is a priest of the Society of Saint Sulpice. He is president and rector of St. Mary's Seminary and University in Baltimore, MD. He received his doctorate in canon law from the Gregorian University in Rome.

Sharon L. Holland, IHM, is a member of the Servants of the Immaculate Heart of Mary. Having completed many years of service at the Congregation for Institutes of Consecrated Life and Societies of Apostolic Life, she serves as a consultant to institutes of consecrated life regarding canonical matters. She received a doctorate in canon law from the Gregorian University in Rome.

Michael P. Joyce, CM, is a Vincentian priest of the Midwest Province. He serves as a canonical consultant for individuals and several institutes and as Promoter of Justice for the Diocese of Springfield-Cape Girardeau. He received a doctorate in canon law from the Catholic University of America in Washington, DC.

John Chrysostom Kozlowski, OP, is a Dominican priest of the Province of St. Joseph. He received the doctorate in canon law from The Catholic University of America in Washington, DC.

Rose McDermott, SSJ, is a member of the Sisters of St. Joseph. She is Delegate for Religious and Academic Dean of the Permanent Diaconate Formation Program in the Diocese of Trenton. She received a doctorate in canon law from the Catholic University of America in Washington, DC.

Rosemary Smith, SC, is a member of the Sisters of Charity of St. Elizabeth. She is the Cardinal's Delegate for Canonical Affairs in the Archdiocese of Newark. She received a doctorate in canon law from the Catholic University of America in Washington, DC.

Therese Guerin Sullivan, SP, is a member of the Sisters of Providence. Although she is retired from full time ministry, she continues to serve as canonical consultant to members of consecrated life. She received a licentiate in canon law from the University of St. Paul in Ottawa, Canada.

Victoria Vondenberger, RSM, is a member of the Sisters of Mercy of the Americas for over 50 years. She is the Tribunal Director, Promoter of Justice, and Defender of the Bond for the Archdiocese of Cincinnati. She was honored by the CLSA with the 2017 Role of Law Award and received a licentiate in canon law from the University of St. Paul in Ottawa, Canada.

Daniel Ward, OSB, is a Benedictine priest. He was Executive Director of the Resource Center for Religious Institutes for over a decade and has been a canonical consultant since 2014. He received a licentiate in canon law from the Catholic University of America in Washington, DC, and a juris doctorate degree from the University of Iowa.

2021 Editors

Donna Miller, JD, JCL, is the Executive Coordinator of the Canon Law Society of America. She received a licentiate in canon law from the University of St. Paul in Ottawa, Ontario, and a juris doctorate degree from the Catholic University of America.

Eileen C. Jaramillo, DMin., JCL, has degrees in ministry, education, theology, divinity, and canon law. She received her is licentiate in canon law from the University of St. Paul in Ottawa, Ontario, works extensively with religious institutes, and chaired the CLSA's Committee on Institutes of Consecrated Life and Societies of Apostolic Life for several years.

2001 Authors

The authors below contributed to the 2001 *Procedural Handbook* but did not take part in the 2021 revision.

Beverly K. Dunn, SP, is a member of the Sisters of Providence. In 2001 she was a canonical consultant for the Archdiocese of Seattle. She received a doctorate in canon law from the University of St. Paul in Ottawa, Canada.

David M. Hynous, OP, was a Dominican priest of the Saint Albert Province. He served as a judge on the Metropolitan Tribunal of the Archdiocese of Chicago. He received a doctorate in canon law from the Angelicum in Rome. (Died on March 24, 2016.)

Emmett J. Gavin, OCarm, is a Carmelite priest. In 2001 he was vice chancellor of the Archdiocese of Chicago. He received his licentiate in canon law from the Catholic University of America in Washington, DC.

Robert J. Kasyln, SJ, was a Jesuit priest of the New York Province. He received a doctorate in canon law from St. Paul University in Ottawa. (Died on March 13, 2019.)

2001 Contributors

The Committee on Consecrated Life in 2001 expressed gratitude to the following individuals who served as contributors to various authors of the original text:

Kathleen Ann Bierne, PBVM
Rita-Mae Bissonnette, RSR
M. Dominica Brennan, OP
Marianne Burkhard, OSB
James J. Conn, SJ
Jonathan P. Felice, OSB
Vincent B. Grogan, OFM
Joyce Hoben, SNDN
David M. Hynous, OP
Paulissa Jirik, SSND
Bernard M. Johnson, OSCO
Gary M. Luiz, CPPS
Margaret M. Modde, OSF
Francis G. Morrisey, OMI
David M. O'Connell, CM
Kevin D. O'Rourke, OP
Esther Redmann, OSU
Nancy Reynolds, SP
Elissa Rinere, CP
Kevin R. Seasoltz, OSB
Patrick T. Shea, OFM
Margaret A. Stallmeyer, CDP
Sally J. Tolles, DHS
Marlene C. Weisenbeck, FSPA
M. Madeline Welch, OSU
Richard B. Williams, OP

Made in United States
Orlando, FL
04 November 2026

90201332R00174